RECONTEXTUALIZING TEXTS

Narrative Performance in Modern Japanese Fiction

Harvard
East
Asian
Monographs
180

RECONTEXTUALIZING TEXTS

Narrative Performance in Modern Japanese Fiction

Atsuko Sakaki

Published by the Harvard University Asia Center
and distributed by Harvard University Press,
Cambridge, Massachusetts, and London
1999

Printed in the United States of America

The Harvard University Asia Center publishes a monograph series and, in coordination with the Fairbank Center for East Asian Research, the Korea Institute, the Reischauer Institute of Japanese Studies, and other faculties and institutes, administers research projects designed to further scholarly understanding of China, Japan, Vietnam, Korea, and other Asian countries. The Center also sponsors projects addressing multidisciplinary and regional issues in Asia.

Library of Congress Cataloging-in-Publication Data
Sakaki, Atsuko, 1963–
Recontextualizing texts : narrative performance in modern Japanese fiction / Atsuko Sakaki.
p. cm.
Includes bibliographical references and index.
ISBN 0-674-75094-2 (alk. paper)
1. Japanese fiction--1868– --History and criticism. 2. Narration (Rhetoric). I. Title.
PL747.55.S239 1999
895.6'3409--dc21 98-54779
CIP

Index by the author

Printed on acid-free paper

Last figure below indicates year of this printing
09 08 07 06 05 04 03 02 01 00 99

The epigraphs to Chapters 1–5 are translated from Kurahashi Yumiko, *Seishōjo* (1965).

Acknowledgments

My interest in the reasons why speakers, narrators, and writers in texts of fiction make statements in the way they do began with a term paper on Joseph Conrad's *Under Western Eyes* (1911) that I wrote for a survey course on English literature taught by Professor Namekata Akio, then at the University of Tokyo, in 1984. One of the many questions that intrigued me at the time (and have been haunting me in different guises since) is why some of the conversations that must take place in Russian are represented in English, and by whom?

I began theorizing such questions as I prepared for my Ph.D. qualifying examinations at the University of British Columbia. I am grateful to my examiner in the field of Japanese narratives and one of my mentors, Dr. Robert Kramer, who introduced me to *On Narrative,* a volume edited by W. J. T. Mitchell. In it, I found a most inspiring piece of critical work—Barbara Herrnstein Smith's essay, which I refer to in the Introduction to this book. Suddenly everything seemed to converge into a coherent picture. I also thank Dr. Lorraine Weir of the Department of English and the Comparative Literature Program at the University of British Columbia for further encouraging me to pursue speech act theory and its application to theories of the performative, and for calling my attention to works of Gerald Prince, a revisionist (and still revising) narratologist.

Although I was able to test some of the ideas inspired by such theorists in my dissertation on Kurahashi Yumiko and have reworked a portion of it in an article on her, I realized that the usefulness of the approach would become more evident if I were to deal with better-known narratives. I began teaching an annual graduate seminar entitled "Narrative Strategies in Modern Japanese Fiction" in the Department of East Asian Languages and Civilizations at Harvard University in Spring of 1994, which gave me an invaluable opportunity to probe in length and in depth narrative performances that take place in texts written by Natsume Sōseki, Mori Ōgai, Tanizaki Jun'ichirō, and Ibuse Masuji, among others. Every year brought about new discoveries, and I thank my students who shared my excitement: Charo D'Etcheverry, Emi Shimokawa, Hil Anderson, Hisaaki Wake, Javan Lee, John Frankl, Karen Thornber, Masako Sugihara, Matthew Fraleigh, Miho Nonaka, Samantha Kent, Ted Mack, Vyjayanthi Ratnam, and Wiebke Denecke.

I was also fortunate to have opportunities to make oral presentations of what would become sections in this book, and I thank the following institutions and organizations for providing venues to present my ideas: the Department of Comparative Literature and Culture at the University of Tokyo, and Professor Kawamoto Kōji, for inviting me, in July 1994; the Association for Asian Studies, and the chair of the panel, Professor Hosea Hirata, for the 1995 Annual Meeting in Washington, D.C.; the Department of Asian Languages at Stanford University, and especially, the host of the lecture, Professor Thomas Hare, for inviting me in March 1996; the Midwest Association for Japanese Literary Studies, especially the panel chair, Professor Komori Yōichi, who tolerated my discussion of his own work, the organizer, Professor Esperanza Ramirez-Christensen, and the proceedings editor, Professor Eiji Sekine, for the 1997 Annual Conference at the University of Michigan; the Edwin O. Reischauer Institute of Japanese Studies at Harvard University, Professor Jay Rubin as moderator and Dr. Galen Amstutz as organizer, for a Japan Forum lecture in December 1997; and the Department of East Asian Languages at the University of California, Berkeley, and Professor H. Mack Horton, for inviting me in February 1998. I wish I could mention all the people who responded to my papers, inspiring me with new possibilities and encouraging me to pursue the project, but in fear that I would miss some names, I simply state my gratitude to all of them.

I am very grateful to Professor Eve Zimmerman, who moderated a workshop organized by Professor Miryam Sas and funded by the Department of East Asian Languages and Civilizations, Harvard Univer-

Editorial Conventions

All Japanese names are given surname first, unless the person's work is in a European language. Quotations from translations reproduce the original punctuation and spellings, including the (occasional) omission of macrons. Several of the translations that I quote use suspension dots—i.e., . . . —to indicate a hesitation or a break in a character's discourse or thought. In order to distinguish these from my omissions in these texts, I place my ellipses within square brackets [. . .]. All translations from Japanese critical sources are mine unless otherwise noted.

RECONTEXTUALIZING TEXTS

Narrative Performance in Modern Japanese Fiction

INTRODUCTION

Reading Text Contextually

THE PRESENT STUDY IS the first systematic attempt in English, inspired by speech act theory and its applications to narrative studies, to read modern Japanese fictional narratives (*shōsetsu*) as performances. The attempt may need to be justified in regard to (1) the compatibility of speech act theory with prose fiction narratives in particular, if not with literature in general, and (2) the legitimacy of situating and discussing an ethnically distant content (*shōsetsu*) within the critical context of another culture (Euro-American). Or, to phrase the second issue in the form of a question, can we treat *shōsetsu* as the novel or *roman* has been treated?

This in turn leads to another question frequently asked in New Historicism: if we do not treat the *shōsetsu* as if it were equivalent to the novel or the *roman*, can we then treat it in the same way that the historically distant genre of *monogatari* has been treated? This question is relevant in the context of the present study, for works of *monogatari*—literally, "telling/recounting" of "things" or "thoughts"—seem more easily describable as speech acts. Whereas *shōsetsu* has its origins in both the novel/*roman* and the *monogatari*, its differences from either should be noted. Since *shōsetsu* are culturally distant from the novel or *roman*, examples of which have been studied as speech acts in Euro-American criticism for some twenty years, and historically distant from the *monogatari*, which are self-explanatorily acts of recounting, is it valid and meaningful to reread texts of *shōsetsu* as speech acts? To answer these questions and establish the grounds of this study, I first survey the development of speech act theory in the reformation of narrative studies "beyond narratology" (as Ian Reid puts it),[1] and then go on to suggest what might be accomplished by viewing texts of *shōsetsu* as speech acts.

The genre of the novel has been studied in many different ways: for example, as a medium of a given author's self-expression; as a story told in a particular discourse, or vice versa (i.e., a form used for the telling of a particular content); or, as a product of certain socioeconomic-historical conditions. The first approach is typical of Romanticist, author-oriented criticism, which attempts to re-create the author's life and to interpret his or her work as a reflection of that life. The second eliminates the author and dissolves the text into two layers—content and form, or story and discourse—and is valid in a formalist/structuralist framework. The third approach produces the type of political readings that dominate "cultural studies." Reading narratives as speech acts is a method that, although not contradicting the first method, has little to do with it; a method that, having sprung from a critical review of the second method, both is constrained by and strives to go beyond it; and a method that shares concerns about perspectives with the third approach while operating inside language rather than around it.

J. L. Austin's *How to Do Things with Words* (1962) casts doubt on the comprehensiveness of the schema of signifier and signified in Saussurean linguistics by calling attention to a function of language independent of signification—its performative dimension. Austin first defined "performative utterances" as those that "do not 'describe' or 'report' or constate anything at all; are not 'true or false,'" because "the issuing of the utterance is the performing of an action"; and thus "would not normally be described as, or as 'just', saying something."[2] In later lectures, he revised his thesis to suggest that every utterance is performative. An aspect of Austin's hypothesis that is particularly important for this study is that whereas Saussurean linguistics confines the function of utterances to "describing" or "reporting"—or "'just' saying something," speech act theory looks at a given utterance not in terms of its meaning but in terms of its effects—either those intended by the speaker or those perceived by the listener. The issue here is no longer "true or false" but effective or not *or* convincing or not.

Since Austin, speech act theory has been developed by John Searle and others and questioned by philosophers and critics such as Jacques Derrida.[3] The first systematic application of the theory to specifically literary problems appeared in Mary Louise Pratt's *Toward a Speech Act Theory of Literary Discourse* (1977). Pratt challenged the conventional distinctions between literary and nonliterary discourses and, enumerating the factors that define a given speech act as literary or nonliterary, demonstrated how speech act rubrics may be applied to "literary" texts. Especially relevant to the present context are her explorations of narrator-audience relationships in written and printed texts, as opposed to those in oral narration (conversation or speech). Having termed the audience that voluntarily agreed to listen to the speech the "Audience" and having examined its relationship with the speaker in oral narration, Pratt characterized the parallel relationship in literary texts:

> Our role in the literary speech situation has the main formal characteristic I have been using to define an Audience: we knowingly and willingly enter a speech situation in which another speaker has unique access to the floor. [. . .] Titles, subtitles, chapter headings, and summaries, for example, perform the "request for the floor" role of Labov's abstracts and similarly correspond in function to the public speaking conventions just discussed. Readers of literary works usually feel that the writer is under obligation to make their attention worthwhile, and that they have the right to judge what he has done. [. . .] Nor are most writers unaware of their indebtedness to the Audience. The "dear reader" remarks common to eighteenth- and nineteenth-century novels, like the "my fellow X's" address of the orator, are readily interpreted as acknowledgments of the peer relation which holds between author and reader, of the sense of obligation the author feels as a result of that relation, and of his awareness of being in jeopardy.[4]

Although Pratt's analysis seems to focus on "real" authors and readers, it is in fact the relationship between "narrator" and "narratee" or between "implied author" and "implied reader" to which the text itself gives us access.[5] The expectations of the narratee and a sense of responsibility on the part of the narrator give the narrative the form it has. There are some specific factors pertaining only to the written text; yet, just like oral narratives, "literary" narratives are not static but are constructed out of the dynamics of the narrator-narratee situation, or of the encoded author-reader interaction.

Critical of Saussurean-derived narratology, Barbara Herrnstein Smith, in her short essay "Narrative Versions, Narrative Theories" (1980), suggested possibilities for applying speech act theory to literary criticism and proposed a new view of narrative not as structure but as performance.

> An alternative conception of language views utterances not as strings of discrete signifiers that represent corresponding sets of discrete signifieds but as verbal responses—that is, as acts —which, like any acts, are all those circumstantial and psychological variables of which every utterance is a function. Although *some* of these conditions are conventionally implied by and are, accordingly, inferable from the linguistic form of an utterance, they are not confined to and cannot be reduced to specific "referents" or "signifieds." In accord with this alternative view of language, individual narratives would be described not as sets of surface-discourse-signifiers that represent (actualize, manifest, map, or express) sets of underlying-story-signifieds but as the verbal acts of particular narrators performed in response to—and thus shaped and constrained by—sets of multiple interacting conditions. For any narrative, these conditions would consist of (1) such circumstantial variables as the particular context and material setting (cultural and social, as well as strictly "physical") in which the tale is told, the particular listeners or readers addressed, and the nature of the narrator's relationship to them, and (2) such psychological variables as the narrator's motives for telling the tale and all the particular interests, desires, expectations, memories, knowledge, and prior experiences (including his knowledge of various events, of course, but also of other narratives and of various conventions and traditions of storytelling) that elicited his telling it on that occasion, to that audience, and that shaped the particular way he told it.[6]

Originally presented at a conference as a critical response to Seymour Chatman's paper "What Novels Can Do That Films Can't (and Vice Versa)," Smith's paper, though short, succinctly outlines the limitations and contradictions of narratology and proposes conditions that a new approach to narrative should satisfy: an awareness of the contextuality, as opposed to the autonomy, of narratives; dynamism as opposed to mechanism; and a responsiveness to the complex web of factors that shape the particular narrative, as opposed to the supposedly sustaining and universal binary opposition between signified (story) and signifier (discourse).

Since these groundbreaking efforts by Pratt and Smith, many have attempted actual applications of speech act theory to the reading of prose narratives: Shoshana Felman's *The Literary Speech Act: Don Juan with J. L. Austin, or Seduction in Two Languages* (1980; trans. 1983); Susan Sniader Lanser's *The Narrative Act: Point of View in Fiction* (1981), whose title echoes Gérard Genette's *Narrative Discourse: An Essay in Method* (1972; trans. 1980); Ross Chambers's *Story and Situation: Narrative Seduction and the Power of Fiction* (1984), which is, as the author's explanation of his title makes clear, intended as a challenge to Chatman's *Story and Discourse: Narrative Structure in Fiction and Film* (1978)—a pinnacle of structuralist studies of narrative in the United States, rivaling the work of Genette in France.

Chambers's comments in his introduction are of particular relevance to the present study, and accordingly I quote them at length:

> Meaning is precisely the *perception of a relationship* between discourse and its context. As far as narrative goes, common language has always recognized the contextual nature of meaning through the concept of "point": the "same" story can have a quite different point when it is told in different situations. [. . .] The significance of the story is determined less by its actual content than by the point of its being told, that is, the relationships mediated by the act of narration. That is why, when one looks hard at stories, it becomes extremely difficult to distinguish them from their *telling*, so true is it that people "do things with narrative," just as they do with words. A story is always, as Barbara Herrnstein Smith reminds us, someone telling someone else that something happened (be it fictionally or otherwise), and this narrative act is always available as a vehicle whereby people may "do things"—that is (and the double meaning is itself significant), *relate*.
>
> In light of such everyday observations, it seems strange that literary criticism and theory have paid so little attention to the performative function of storytelling, preferring to limit themselves arbitrarily to the study of narrative structure and the discourse of narration conceived in each case as a set of relationships internal to a context-free text. As a consequence, we possess a fine "grammar" of stories, deriving from the work of [Vladimir] Propp, [A. J.] Greimas, [Claude] Bremond, [Tzvetan] Todorov, [Gerald] Prince, and others. We possess, too, a useful "rhetoric" of narration, elaborated by Booth and especially by Genette, as a grammar of possible relationships between text as narration ("discourse") and text as narrated ("story"). All this work has been summated, added to, and worked into a synthesis by Seymour Chatman in a handbook entitled,

precisely, *Story and Discourse*. But what is lacking is recognition of this significance of situational phenomena—of the social fact that narrative mediates human relationships and derives its "meaning" from them; that, consequently, it depends on social agreements, implicit pacts or contracts, in order to produce exchanges that themselves are a function of desires, purposes, and constraints. We owe it to the *Rezeptionsästhetik* movement in Germany that there is now some perception of the act of reading as based on a relational "contract" with a text (cf. the work of W. Iser) and as a historical, that is, historically determined and determining, process (cf. the work of H. Jauss), and Philippe Lejeune has elaborated a contractual definition for the genre of autobiography. But the implications of the contextual nature of meaning for the analysis of narrative texts themselves remain to be explored; and the main title of this book, echoing Chatman's, is meant to focus attention onto the need, not simply to read texts in situation (which is inevitable) but also to read, in the texts, the situation that they *produce* as giving them their "point."[7]

The last sentence helps me draw the line between what I am and what I am not going to do in this book; this is *not* a study of contexts—historical, political, or economic—that surround texts; rather, this is a study of contextuality *within* texts. The title *Recontextualizing Texts* should be understood accordingly: I am not situating texts in historical, cultural, or economic contexts but re-viewing texts themselves as intrinsically context-bound.

This, of course, should not be taken as an attempt to suggest that studies of contextuality within the text should be prioritized over, or replace, that of contextuality in the material production of texts. On the contrary, this approach is based on the understanding that language, thought by classical structuralists as either "merely" a transparent tool or a control over "what is happening" outside the text "here and now," is just as context-bound as any other activity that either involves or ignores the text in question. The use of language, of speech or inscription (the distinction between the two is discussed below), of listening or reading (also discussed below), is an act, just as are the printing, selling, and buying of books, or any other act of production, consumption, conciliation, or violation. The use of language, as is any other act, is formed and confined in a context; thus, it also produces effects. Language is not transcendental, universal, or static; it is activated by a specific agent, for specific purposes, under specific circumstances.

My work thus is not an attempt to disclaim the significance of political readings, which focus on contexts exterior to the texts, or of works concerned with the structure of a given text. The present work tries to look at what seems to have been left unexplored, forgotten in the flow of scholarly tradition: contextuality *within* texts, as distinct from the *textuality* of texts or the contextuality *around* texts.

Drawing on the work of Smith and Chambers, in the subsequent chapters I read a number of works of modern Japanese fiction with certain sets of questions in mind regarding the players in the narrative performance: narrator, narratee, writer, and reader (see below). Although many of these questions may appear to be the same as those asked by later structuralist-narratologists (such as Gerald Prince, as will be discussed shortly), they are asked from the distinct consciousness that they *control*, rather than supplement, more classic structuralist questions of the voice, perspective, and mode. As will become evident, the positionality of each agent (of speaking, listening, writing, and reading) in a given text is not neutralized but substantiated and highlighted, with attention to his or her specific background, personality, motivation, intention, expectation, and desire. Each agent's position is not a blank space of presumed neutrality, but is shaded by, and fleshed out by, marks of specific characteristics (such as gender, as I discuss later in the Introduction). Each verbal act is prompted not only by the positionality of the agent, but, and more important, by the kind of relationships he or she has had and develops with others involved in the narrative circumstance. No agent acts alone; even if he or she is alienated, or alone in the narrative performance, his or her narrative act is colored by the absence of actual company (as well as by the hypothetical audience that is theoretically present in any utterance), rather than remaining autonomous of the context.

The first set of questions centers around, but is not confined to, the narrator: What makes the narrator tell the story? Is there a request, either from an audience or from someone directly involved in the incidents in question, that the narration take place? Or is the narrator, rather, tempted to reveal a secret? Does the narrator feel compelled to tell someone about something he or she has been pondering alone, to make himself or herself feel better? Or is the intent to entertain? Also, how far is the narrator aware of his or her mission? Is the narrator aware of what may be accomplished by telling the story? Is the narrator aware of the impact the telling might have on the audience? Next, what medium is used for the telling? Further, how does the narrator seize the occasion for the narration? Does the narrator tell the story retrospectively or concurrently with the narrated incidents? Is the story told in one sitting from beginning to end, or in installments? Was the narration planned, or did the occasion occur by accident? Is the narrator a skilled storyteller? How honest does the narrator intend to be with the audience, or with those involved in the narration?

The second set of questions concerns the narratee. Since Gerald Prince modified structuralist studies of narrative by suggesting a shift of focus from the narrator to the narratee, a role till then neglected as merely passive,[8] there have been many studies of the narratee in British, American, French, and other literary studies.[9] Following such predecessors' footsteps, I will ask, in the hope of radically substantiating the agent who plays this role with so much circumstantial information: Why does the narratee end up listening to the narration? Is the act of listening voluntary, or does it derive from a sense of duty, or come at the request of another, or even by force? Is the narratee happy with the fact that he or she is to listen? How carefully is the narratee listening? Is he or she a good listener? The most desired listener for the narrator? On good terms with the narrator? Superior or inferior to the narrator? Is he or she disinterested or involved in the events of the narration? Is the narratee aware of the effect the narrator expects the narration to produce? How does he or she react to the narration?

Prince briefly distinguished the different media that the narratee utilizes in receiving narration—listening and writing: "The narratee can be a listener [. . .] or a reader. [. . .] Obviously, a text may not necessarily say whether the narratee is a reader or a listener. In such cases, it could be said that the narratee is a reader when the narration is written. [. . .] And a listener when the narration is oral."[10] In the narratives I have chosen for the present study, it is made clear in *Kokoro, Gan,* and *Manji* that the narration is inscribed; each narrator mentions his act of jotting down the narration. This is not made clear in *Kuroi ame* and *Kusamakura*; although their styles are typical of written discourse, the process of textualization is not textualized itself. In either case, the distinctions between written and oral narrating, like those between reading and listening, deserve more radical attention. Although technical terms such as "implied author/reader" (Wayne Booth, Wolfgang Iser, among others) or "virtual (writer)/reader" (Gerald Prince) have been applied to someone who is writing or reading within the text and seems responsible for, or conscious of, the formation of the *entire* text,[11] neither pair of terms is quite the same as the textualized author/reader that I am focusing on. "Implied author/reader" suggests an idealized and impersonal role, each aspect of which is in absolute agreement with the other, without traces of specific personality, whereas the textualized author/reader is no less constrained by his or her positionality. The "virtual (writer)/reader" responds intrinsically to the real author/reader's image of the other, which is not the case with the textualized author/reader. What Susan Suleiman calls the "encoded author/reader" is perhaps closest to the author/reader specified in the text:

> Clearly, a first-level narratee (one who receives the whole narrative, not just a part) may be considered the inscribed or encoded reader of the work. How, then, does the notion of inscribed reader differ from Booth's notion of the implied reader? The difference is that the latter functions as an "ideal" interpreter of the text, whereas the former's place must be located somewhere this side of interpretation. An interpretation of the work necessarily takes account of the inscribed reader, as well as of narratees that may be present in the work on other levels, but it treats the inscribed reader as simply one element among other meaning-producing elements in the text (e.g., temporal organization, variations in point of view, system of characters, thematic structures). The inscribed reader thus has no privileged status as far as interpretation is concerned; a description of the inscribed reader in a work allows a variety of interpretations, or even the possibility of hazarding no global interpretation of the work at all. Booth's notion of implied reader, on the other hand, is indissociable from a global interpretation, for as we saw earlier, the implied reader is called

upon to "agree" with the values of the implied author, values that ultimately determine the meaning of the work as a whole.[12]

Although Suleiman's discussion is focused on the audience, I would extend the epithet "encoded" to the textualized author as well as the textualized reader. I use these terms in this work to refer to someone who says, or of whom it is said, that he or she is writing/reading the narration: *watakushi* in *Kokoro*, *boku* in *Gan*, and *sakusha* in *Manji* are thus encoded authors. Having defined the territories of the author and reader of the *entire* text and yet still *inside* the text, I will ask: How does the textualization of the narration come about? How has the text been made available to the reader? In what capacity should the reader read the text?

In asking these sets of questions, I will introduce gender as a factor that shades each occurrence of narrative act a distinct color. As Kathy Mezei notes in her editor's introduction to an anthology of feminist narratological works, however, most feminist-narratologists are concerned with asking if female authors' gender had informed their narratives with narrative features distinct from those of male authors. Some also problematize the male-centered-ness of the canonization of some (often male-authored, or otherwise acceptable to males) narratives, and of narrative theories that till recently had claimed universal validity. Examples of such feminist-narratologists include Susan Lanser, mentioned above as a speech act theorist in narrative studies. She later wrote a frequently quoted essay, "Toward a Feminist Narratology," in which she modified Genette's taxonomy by introducing yet another axis of "public versus private," a key issue for women's writing.[13] Her practice of this theory culminated in *Fictions of Authority* (1992), a book on women's fiction. Robyn Warhol is another example; she suggested in *Gendered Intervention* (1989) that female authors tend to create distinctly different narrator-narratee relationships, in which the narrator speaks directly to the actual audience, one that Warhol perceives as a trait typical of female authors.[14] Such works, despite their unique and valued contribution to scholarship, have less to do with the present study than does Sally Robinson's argument: "I am concerned with how gender is produced *through* narrative processes."[15] This corresponds to the territory defined by Chambers; his declaration of methods, which focuses on textually evidenced contextuality, has inspired my work. Specifically, I will examine how female spectatorship, spectacle, narratorship, listenership, authorship, and readership are represented, and how the ways they are represented in the texts affect the other parties' reactions to their performance.

I now turn to the question of the validity and significance of looking at Japanese narratives as speech acts. In general terms, I share Pratt's belief that insofar as literary texts are written in languages, any linguistic theory should be relevant to literary texts as well as to "extra-literary" texts. Since Japanese is a language, Japanese literature should not be unsuited to linguistic study. This is not to suggest that Japanese literature should surrender to the control of speech act theory, which has largely been developed from examinations of European languages, but to suggest that, with cultural specificities in mind, Japanese literature, like any other ethnic literature, should be open to linguistic theoretical approaches.

As a means of reflecting on the dynamics of the ethnocentric refusal of "acculturalization" by alien theoretical systems, it may be useful to review studies of another "indigenous" Japanese fictional genre: the *monogatari* of the Heian period. As will become evident shortly, this is not to suggest that one should discuss the genres of *shōsetsu* and *monogatari* ahistorically. Rather, an archaeological study of prose fiction genres from different periods should show both how contingent the format of each genre is upon linguistic and other conventions of the time and how "naturalized" and forgotten some of the aspects of the genre are; these would be illuminated by comparing the genre with another genre of a similar kind. Also, the fact that I do not compare *shōsetsu* with any other prose fiction genre of Japan should not be taken to suggest that Heian prose literature is the immediate and exclusive origin of modern Japanese fiction. It is simply not my purpose here to survey the history of prose in Japan. My goal is to explain contextuality in *shōsetsu*, something that has simply been forgotten in studies of the modern genre. To achieve that goal, the extensively studied genre of *monogatari* is strategically the most convenient for comparisons.

The genre of *monogatari* was a major focus of Japanese literary criticism in the 1970s and 1980s, both by itself and in contrast with the genre of *shōsetsu*. Members of Monogatari kenkyūkai (*Monogatari* study group), such as Fujii Sadakazu, Takahashi Tōru, and Mitani Kuniaki, reexamined and foregrounded the contextuality of *monogatari* narrative, discussing gaze and voice, not only in terms of honorifics and other linguistic features that had already been carefully studied but also in the light of theories of narratology and gender studies.

Perhaps inspired by such theoretically informed classicists, literary critics specializing in modern literature began to look at *shōsetsu* as *monogatari*. Saeki Shōichi, originally a scholar of American literature in Japan and a visiting professor of Japanese literature in North America, published *Monogatari geijutsu ron* (On *monogatari* as an art; 1979; written originally for a serialization in 1974–77, and revised), which ardently praised the traditional genre of *monogatari* and defended certain *shōsetsu* as the successors of *monogatari*. On the opposite pole are the works of Hasumi Shigehiko, a scholar of French philosophy and film studies and an acquaintance of Roland Barthes and Michel Foucault. His *Shōsetsu-ron = Hihyōron* (On *shōsetsu* = on criticism; 1982), *Monogatari hihan josetsu* (Introduction to criticism of *monogatari*; 1985), and *Shōsetsu kara tōku hanarete* (Far and away from *shōsetsu*; 1989) relentlessly highlighted the dependency of *shōsetsu* on what Hasumi conceived as the conventional plot patterns of *monogatari*. Although Saeki views the correspondences in a positive light, celebrating the artistic mastery of each author-genius, and Hasumi sees them in a negative light, frowning upon what he perceives as the absence of modernity and timeless reproduction of old patterns, both critics suggested that *monogatari*-like qualities are inherent in *shōsetsu*.

I am opposed to the heuristic identification of *shōsetsu* with *monogatari*, because it implies a complete disregard of the utter gap in social conditions that formed distinct narrative contexts both within and around texts in the two genres. Any attempt at re-reading *shōsetsu* as *monogatari* should first provide a defense of such ahistoricity. On the other hand, rather than simply rejecting any association with studies of *monogatari*, I find it useful to reflect on the different degrees of attention to narrative context observable in the texts and readers of the two traditions. In *monogatari*, the context of narration is often explicitly specified (as, for example, in *Ōkagami*, ca. 1077?; trans., *Ōkagami, The Great Mirror*, 1981) and at other times only vaguely implied (as in *Genji monogatari*). In any case, the presence of the particular circumstance under which the narration took place, if not the circumstance itself, is made explicit at least by the use of the auxiliary verb *keri* to label hearsay about past events or by sentence-ending phrases such as *to zo hon ni* (lit., "such as the above is in a book") to suggest the secondhand nature of the narration. In *shōsetsu*, on the other hand, we often do not know why and how the narration has come about.

Critics have suggested three ways of accounting for the loss of context-markers in *shōsetsu*. First, the extra-textual context of production of *shōsetsu* is considerably different from that surrounding the production of *monogatari*. Texts in the earlier genre were commissioned by the authors' patrons and written for readings by, and recitations for, the commissioner and a limited number of acquaintances who more or less were expected to share the same knowledge of pre-existing literature. *Monogatari* texts circulated in handwritten copies in very limited numbers, which introduced an element of the copyist's personality, through the handwriting style if not through textual errors or outright editorial changes on the copyist's part. In contrast, *shōsetsu* texts were inscribed in isolation and mostly in silence and were reviewed for possible publication by editors who might not necessarily know the author in person. Once accepted, the texts were printed mechanically, produced and marketed for a mass audience; received by just about anyone who could afford to buy (or borrow) a copy and was able and willing to read the text; and reviewed in public media rather than in personal correspondence. At each of these steps, forces work toward the erasure of the author's positionality, as well as the relationality of the author to the audience. The lifeless text is transmitted from the speechless author to the faceless reader. Has the extra-textual context surrounding *shōsetsu* texts affected the intra-textual context of narration within them? Perhaps. Any author who would rather not contextualize acts of narration within *shōsetsu* can easily do so, and any reader can as easily overlook the omission.

Second, the argument had been made along the lines of Roland Barthes's discussion of *roman* in *Writing Degree Zero* (1953; trans. 1967) that it is the different language employed for most of the *shōsetsu* texts—the *genbun itchi* style—that has enabled them to dispense with open mention of their context-boundedness.[16] This style, typified by the use of the *-ta* ending for the past tense, and the *-de aru* ending for affirmation of facts,[17] and by the presence of the omniscient narrator, was invented to match an imagined modernity. To a considerable extent, the style neutralized markers of class, gender, and social status of the narrator and created the illusion that he or she is omniscient and omnipresent, free of any position and relation to others.

Third, humanism and democracy as icons (dogmatic ideologies) of modernity helped create the illusion of a non-hierarchical relation between narrator and narratee and of a communicative act in which the narratee is interested in, and capable of, understanding all that the narrator has to say. This illusion is perceived as problematic for two reasons. First, according to Hasumi, "if one writes [about something], one can write, and if one reads it, one can read it."[18] One writes not "intransitively," to translate the passage into Barthesian language, but "transitively,"[19] or *about* something, and one reads to receive the "something." The exchange of the content of *shōsetsu* is made possible in part, in my own view, by the perceived nature of modern Japanese—a transparent medium by which to convey messages in such a way that everyone can decode the messages. That is to say, communication is perceived not as performance but as medium. Second, as Suga Hidemi and Watanabe Naomi argue: "One would not have been able to become a literary man/woman until [the institution of] *genbun itchi* if one could not write in *kanbun* or read *The Tale of Genji*. The destiny of modern literature is to have enabled everyone to write and read it."[20] Access to literature was no longer a privilege of a select group of the elite or literati who had acquired a particular type of knowledge and skills, but a human right everyone shared by birth.

Thus, the institutional, abstract, and universal nature of *shōsetsu* was confirmed by its mode of production, language, and ideology, at the expense of the spontaneous, concrete, and context-bound nature of *monogatari*. There are, however, a few significant exceptions. Some writers, such as those whose works I discuss in this study, resist such a renunciation of narrativity and persistently remind us that narrative performance is in motion.

There are a few, significant critical works in English that have systematically asked questions about agency, subjectivity, and communality in *shōsetsu*, such as Irmela Hijiya-Kirschnereit's *Rituals of Self-Revelation: Shishōsetsu as Literary Genre and Socio-Cultural Phenomenon* (1981; trans. 1996), Edward Fowler's *Rhetoric of Confession: Shishōsetsu in Early Twentieth-Century Japanese Fiction* (1988), and Tomi Suzuki's *Narrating the Self: Fictions of Japanese Modernity* (1996). All these works deal with the *shishōsetsu*, or *watakushi-shōsetsu*, as a concept, genre, or paradigm, and thus inevitably question the identity of the author or of readers, and their relationship with the intra-diegetic narrator and/or protagonist. Thus, these three works are necessarily concerned primarily with extra-textual matters and accordingly differ in their fundamental orientation, as well as their choice of texts to be examined, from the present work.

As noted above, this project, in agreement with Chambers, proposes to read the texts themselves contextually—to search, that is, for the contextuality implicit in the texts. All the prose narratives discussed in the following chapters reveal a sharp awareness of why and how the act of narration is taking place. The encoded author, narrator(s), and/or speaker(s) self-reflexively mention the motivations and processes underlying their acts of inscription, narration, or enunciation. Such an awareness of narrative as act highlights the contextuality of narration; this contrasts with the situation in other works, such as Shiga Naoya's *An'ya kōro* (1921–37; trans. *A Dark Night's Passing*, 1976), in which the agents of writing, narrating, or speaking do not reflect on the fact that they are *doing* things through speech acts, rather than simply *describing* something in words.

Would it be valid to define the distinction between works such as those examined in this study and those like *An'ya kōro*, which are actively excluded, as that between "anti-*shi-shōsetsu*" and *shi-shōsetsu*? As Suzuki rightly argues, it seems futile and tautological to label one set of texts *shi-shōsetsu* and another set "not *shi-shōsetsu*." As Suzuki points out, *shi-shōsetsu* should be understood as a "reading and interpretive paradigm" that allows a certain way of reading rather than an "intrinsic" quality found in some texts and not in others (though this is the general condition of generic designations and not the sole province of any species).[21] It is also true, however, that some texts have more persistently been read as *shi-shōsetsu* than others. What, then, has encouraged a majority of readers to choose this specific mode of reading—to identify the protagonist and/or the narrator with the author—in the case of such texts? Are there features of these texts that lure readers into the illusion that they are *shi-shōsetsu*? And why have other texts, such as the ones I chose for this study, been viewed much less often, if at all, as *shi-shōsetsu*?

I suggest that texts commonly received as *shi-shōsetsu* are comparable to what Austin termed "constative" utterances—utterances that simply describe or state something—whereas these other texts are akin more to "performative" utterances. Although any narrative should, in theory, be performative, some examples are less explicit about their performativity. *Shi-shōsetsu* texts tend to imply that they are transparent narrations through the absence of references to the contextual formation of the narrative, thus allowing the reader to believe that the "story" is objectively true, independent of the context of narration. The texts I have chosen for this study, in contrast, refer explicitly to their own context-boundedness. Rather than focusing on the "truth" of their stories, they instead display performativity by depicting narrations as being deployed in this way or that, and suggesting the reasons why. All the primary narratives dealt with here are thus, in a sense, narratives about narratives—or what Linda Hutcheon calls "narcissistic narratives."[22] This self-reflexivity in fact is displayed partially as a means of flirting with *shi-shōsetsu*—that is to say, some texts in this category actively pretend to be *shi-shōsetsu*, which might mislead less competent readers to identify the historical author with the encoded author or the narrator. Such active obscuring of the boundaries between the text and the surrounding context (which should be distinguished from the absence of drawing of the boundaries pointed out above as a feature of *shi-shōsetsu*) is commonly found in meta-fiction. The historical author, or, to be more precise, a figure who bears the same name as the historical author, or shares identical characteristics with him or her, makes an appearance within the text in order to question the closure of the text and to remind the reader of the context in which the particular narration is taking place. We need only be reminded of Cervantes' *Don Quixote* (1605, 1615), or Italo Calvino's *If on a Winter's Night a Traveler* (1979; trans. 1981), for an example of such flirtation with the I-novel and parody of the Author-oriented criticism. Although none of the narratives I use here articulates the meta-fictional paradox, I will briefly refer to some parts of the texts that have been interpreted as traces of the historical authors. I do so, however, not to explore the historical, extra-textual circumstances in which they wrote, but first to overview what has been studied and what has been left unanalyzed, and second to delineate the territory of my study and define it as one that is not reading works as *shi-shōsetsu*.

To repeat myself, this is not to challenge or criticize studies of the historical circumstances surrounding the texts but to complement such studies, which seem to have been established as a subfield of literary studies. I share Chambers's urge to fill the gap left unexplored. It has long been pointed out that the history of Japanese literary studies in the United States has a lacuna of exposure to intra-textual studies—the field shifted from a concentration on translation and studies of authors' lives to a concentration on studies of the ideological, political, and economic frameworks in which literary production and consumption occurred. This study is an attempt at offering the "middle ground," without suggesting that either "traditional" or "progressive" scholarship is invalid.

The narratives treated in the following chapters are works of prose fiction by male writers that are well known in Japan and available in English translations. To be more precise, each of the narratives fulfills the following conditions: its author has enjoyed the privilege of having more than one *zenshū* ["complete" works] published; it is available not only in a volume in such a series but also in *bunko-bon*, or paperback edition(s); it is usually, if not always, studied in critical studies of its author's work; an English translation is available in a paperback edition; critical work has been written on it in English. In other words, prospective readers of the present work must already have built an image of the work, either as the author's (signature) piece, as a text that offers the pleasure of reading, or as a subject of research. The uniqueness of my reading, or the paradigm in which I read, will thus, I hope, be more evident, since the material is familiar and my expected audience will already have read it in other ways. Although many works reflect on their performativity, I have chosen the following for the strategic reason of demonstration rather than information.

The choice may give some readers the impression that I am merely restoring the "glory" of "aesthetic" or "aestheticized" novels, which have been for that very reason treated, perhaps without rigorously theoretical justification, as canonical. It is true that my stated conditions, which may be summarized as a wide range of circulation and a high degree of accessibility, have played important roles in the process of canonization. I also do not deny that I, as an actual reader, did enjoy reading these narratives in the past. These conditions alone, however, should not justify the choice of these works for "scholarly" studies such as this. My mission here is to articulate, in terms of linguistics-inspired literary theories, what has previously been conceived, in vague terms, as the masterful art of storytelling with which talented authors have entertained readers.

In addition, I believe that my selection provides an extensive, though not complete, variety of samples of narrative performance: first-person, third-person, and combinations thereof; intra-diegetic and extra-diegetic narrators; homodiegetic and heterodiegetic narratives; presence or absence of the "encoded author" in the text; and presentation of gendered voice and inscription. With the range of types of performance showcased here, it should be easier to examine narrative performance in other texts. I think the principle of "more is more" holds here. This is not to suggest that the texts I have chosen are "privileged" because they are performative and for that reason alone worth studying. Theoretically, any text is performative. If Fowler tried to disinter performativity—or, in his terminology, rhetoricity—in what had appeared to be texts without rhetoricity, then I am trying to highlight the optimally performative narrative circumstances. The texts show a wide array of possible formats and patterns of communication, some of which should be visible in other texts in different combinations.

The first chapter, on Natsume Sōseki's *Kokoro*, involves both textual interpretation and reflections on critical methodology, and for that reason it may be advantageous to postpone discussion of it until the topics of the other chapters have been introduced. My analyses of the remaining four narratives are arranged by the degree of apparent suppression of the female subjects of observation, speech, and inscription, which coincides with the degree to which each narrative refers to the context of its making—in other words, the degree of self-referentiality.

The second chapter is entitled "Obsessed with Inscription: Ibuse Masuji's *Kuroi ame*, or (Re)Writing Memories." *Kuroi ame* (1966; trans. *Black Rain*, 1969), while known primarily for its overwhelming themes of the atomic bomb and its aftermath, is marked by multivalence and a voracious desire to inscribe the past. A third-person narrative with an omniscient narrator, *Kuroi ame* is nonetheless polyphonic—the protagonist Shigematsu, his wife Shigeko, their niece Yasuko, and other marginal characters all write memoirs, and citations and paraphrases from their memoirs make up most of the text. The diversity of style evident in these quotations is significant in that it suggests that narratives are always versions, rather than representations, of the truth. Furthermore, the retelling of a narrative—by paraphrase, annotation, excerpt, or reading—itself creates another narrative, for the retelling occurs in another context.

Unlike the situation in Mori Ōgai's *Gan*, discussed in Chapter 4, the embedded narratives in *Kuroi ame* are for the most part documents rather than interior monologues or orally narrated tales. A mistrust of orality becomes evident when Shigematsu notes how wrong hearsay and rumors have proved after the fact. By contrast, he places his trust in documents and tries to copy and edit his memoir so that the local library will have a reliable source of "what really happened."

Whereas the inscriber in Tanizaki Jun'ichirō's *Manji* (the subject of Chapter 5) remains invisible, this text persistently describes the context in which each document is inscribed: when (that is, concurrent with the incidents related or in retrospect), by whom, for whom, and for what purpose. This awareness of the contextuality of the narrative is exemplified in the frequent descriptions of writing implements, paper, desks (or a substitute surface), and handwriting, as well as writing styles. The insistent attention to such "marginal" factors seems calculated to demonstrate how the narrative is inevitably context-bound; even the texture of the paper on which a narrative is written reflects the author's motives in writing, the desire to appear in a certain way, and the compromises made to suit the circumstances.

In the foregrounded acts of (re)writing and (re)reading, "story time" and "discourse time" (to borrow Genette's distinction) overlap, blurring the distinction between past and present. The dialogue between the two suggests that the past exists only in its retelling in the present, and the present exists only as the context for remembering the past. Thus in a sense history, reality, and truth occur simultaneously with narrative.

Chapter 3, "Unmaking the Tableau: Natsume Sōseki's *Kusamakura* and Gender/Genre Politics," explores narrative strategies in *Kusamakura* (1906; trans. *The Three-Cornered World*, 1965), in relation to the contrasts it makes between prose and poetry, literary/imported and colloquial/native languages, and male and female voices. These aspects of the narrative have suffered from relative neglect, in comparison with thematic contrasts such as East versus West, antiquity versus modernity, idealism versus pragmatism, and so on.

Karatani Kōjin has argued that Sōseki intended to write *bun* ("high literature") rather than *shōsetsu*, and he refers to *Kusamakura* as evidence of this intention.[23] Rather than discussing authorial intent here, however, I focus on the role of the first-person narrator—the ways in which he claims narrative authority, the different registers in which he thinks to himself and speaks with others, and his gaze upon "woman, native, other"—to borrow Trinh T. Minh-ha's triad. While manifestly privileging poetry over prose and crystallized images over an evolving story centered on characters, the first-person narrator ends up ethnographizing a local woman called Nami by interviewing native residents of the town he is visiting. In this role, the narrator-protagonist becomes overtly interested in "what happened next" (the story) and "why" (the plot)[24] of

Nami's life to date—the very features of prose narratives that he disdains when he speaks to an unspecified and yet presumably intellectual audience in heavily Chinese-imbued formal/literary discourse. However, whereas the first-person narrator mythicizes the Other (Nami), she subverts the power hierarchy between herself and him by parodying his poems about her, performing roles that he dreams of assigning to her (e.g., Ophelia), and catching him red-handed at voyeurism when she meets with her ex-husband. Thus, the object of observation objectifies the observer in turn, presenting a meta-fictional paradox in the narrative. Further, Nami disrupts the colonizing narration that the narrator imposes on her by creating a dialogic mode of speech and a dynamic narrative flow.

Chapter 4—"Thinking Beauty, Unseeing Scholar: Displaced Narrative Authority in Mori Ōgai's *Gan*"—focuses upon the anti-patriarchal presentation of gender relationships in *Gan* (1911–13, 1915; trans. *The Wild Geese*, 1959; *The Wild Goose*, 1995), which has usually been read as the story of an unfulfilled love affair between a student at the elite Tokyo Imperial University and the concubine of a moneylender. I will underscore the gender politics in the text, which have largely been overlooked beneath the novel's seemingly conventional settings.

A polyphonic narrative in which the primary narrator also appears as a character in the story, *Gan* seems to suggest that there can be no ultimate "truth," that there are, rather, as many narratives as there are narrators. The reader is occasionally reminded that the first-person narrator is telling the story as he chooses, that he does not know everything, and that he will not tell us all that he knows. Thus, neither the narrator nor Okada, whom the narrator designates as the protagonist, assumes narrative authority. Rather, Otama, the docile and quiet heroine, narrates part of the text in the first person as an interior monologue, as do other characters who are peripheral from Okada's standpoint in terms of their social status. In short, those whom the narrator or protagonist (the center) would consider the Other are given voices of their own.

The text of *Gan* not only dissolves narrative authority but also destabilizes relationships between viewer and viewed, and between the desirer and the desired. Although literary conventions may have privileged the pattern in which Woman is viewed and desired by Man rather than the other way around, this text presents Otama's gaze upon and desire for Okada in much more detail than Okada's on and for her. Another example of such subversion of gender hierarchy occurs when Otama's insight into herself surpasses that of her patron Suezō, and she begins to manipulate him without his being aware of it. Thus *Gan* "objectifies" male gaze, desire, and narration, while giving the Other a viewpoint and a voice.

Manji (1928–30, 1931; trans. *The Quicksand*, 1993), the topic of Chapter 5 ("Doing Things with Words: Acts and Effects in Tanizaki Jun'ichirō's *Manji*"), presents a female narrator and male narratee, who is also the encoded author of the text. The dialogue between the two is markedly unbalanced, as opposing responsibilities are distributed between them. The woman's confessions manifest orality in their use of "dialect" (although this is fictionally constructed to further aestheticize the traditional Japanese ambience), repetitions, ellipses, and anachronism. Her explicit admission of the illogicality of her own narrative and the interviewer's annotation of her text seem to suggest a surrender to logocentricism and to define her feminine/oral discourse as inferior to masculine/literary discourse. The man's annotations on the woman's narration are bracketed in parentheses and marked "author's note," a mark of distinction from, if not control over, the woman's account. This secondary narrative manifests literacy by its use of "standardized" language and formal discourse, by self-reference as "the author," and by foreshadowings of content to be narrated later.

Feminine/oral discourse occupies most of the text, however, and thus appears either privileged or objectified, whereas the masculine/literary discourse is largely submerged or naturalized. Although the female voice heard by the male ear and her body observed by the male eye are inscribed by the male hand, the male narratee/encoded author remains always invisible and inaudible. The questions he has asked the narrator, which we must infer in order to account for the form the narrative has taken, have been erased from the text of the interview—although they leave traces. Beneath the apparent privileging of orality is concealed the familiar binary opposition between the female as body and the male as mind.

This neat gender distinction breaks down, however, inside the primary narrative. The theme of lesbianism features a female spectacle and a female spectator (the primary narrator), presenting a female gaze upon another female. Furthermore, the sadomasochistic performance of confession, forgery, and concealment in which the characters are entangled effectively destabilizes the one-sidedness of gaze, desire, and narration, calling into question any definite hierarchy between the subject and object. Also, the persistent protestations of transparency or "truthfulness" and their equally persistent debunking suggest a conception of narrative as essentially a performance rather than as revelation of an objective truth.

It might be worthwhile to add a note here on the making of this book, as well as the unmaking of my own book on much the same subject, written and published earlier in Japanese—*Kōi to shite no shōsetsu: naratorojii o koete* (*Shōsetsu* as an act: beyond narratology, 1996). Each book is itself a narrative and, as such, is presented in a certain mode, for a certain kind of audience, and at a certain time. All these factors have contributed to making this book different from the earlier Japanese version. Since narrative is not "a form which expresses a particular content" but rather a performance enacted in a particular context, this book is, like its predecessor, "about" modern Japanese fiction as speech act, while it is also a performance made at a later date, in English, and for an English-speaking and primarily academic audience. Let me describe the differences more specifically, beginning with the obvious. The Japanese book was written intermittently, from August 1994 to December 1995, based on my notes for a graduate seminar on the subject, taught from Spring 1993 through Fall 1995. Since publication, I have come across many new findings, as well as weaknesses in the Japanese version, both from my own rereadings and from reviews of the Japanese work. I incorporated such reflections into Chapters 2 to 5 in this version. Chapter 2, on *Kuroi ame*, in particular, is significantly different from the corresponding chapter in the Japanese version.

One of the sources of my new discoveries has been the English translations of the Japanese texts, which have made me more aware of certain linguistic features of the originals. And although I feel privileged to have been able to approach modern Japanese fiction both in Japanese and in English, I decided to forgo, in this volume, discussion of two untranslated narratives—Kanai Mieko's 1995 *Kishibe no nai umi* (The ocean without a shore), and 1985 *Bunshō kyōshitsu* (Creative writing class)—which I used in the Japanese version as a conclusion, as reflections of a postmodern consciousness of narrative contextuality.

I might add that the translations I cite here—Edwin McClellan's *Kokoro,* Alan Turney's *Three-Cornered World,* Ochiai Kingo and Sanford Goldstein's *Wild Geese* and Burton Watson's *Wild Goose,* Howard Hibbett's *Quicksand,* and John Bester's *Black Rain*—are all first-rate accomplishments. I do occasionally depart from specific portions of the English texts to discuss expressions in the originals, but this should not be taken as implying any lack of respect for them. The problem, rather, is simply that translation and critical analysis require different types of reading and rewriting of the primary text. As a translator myself, I understand how many implications, associations, and literary connotations translators are compelled to sacrifice for the sake of readability. In a sense, my analysis here works in the opposite direction—collecting the eliminated pieces and reconstructing the text in "un-readable" form. I have tried to show how complicated, rugged, and confusing a given text is—focusing on the "shagginess" of the text, rather than smoothing it out for presentation. In the process, I have at times had to unravel the beautifully woven texts of these excellent translators.

Furthermore, I have, in the present version, included references to a range of scholarly writings, both in Japanese and in English; in the earlier version, which was not necessarily intended for students in literary studies or Japanese literature, I kept secondary references to a minimum. This will be obvious from a glance at the bibliographies of the two versions. My motivation for including the English-language materials should be obvious—I needed to situate my work in the North American critical context, and for an English-speaking audience. In including Japanese critical materials, I had two things in mind: first, simply to introduce what may be new information; and second, and more important, to present an aspect of Japanese academic discourse, and to show how that discourse asks and answers different sets of questions and sets itself different goals. Although many of the Japanese sources may be intended less for professional scholars in Japanese literature and more for college and graduate students, literary critics, and literary-minded readers in general, those I have selected speak to issues discussed in American academism.

It was with a similar purpose in mind that I wrote the Chapter 1 of this version on the debates on *Kokoro*. This chapter was not included in the Japanese version, since the Japanese audience was already familiar with these debates and with the issues involved. What I hope to achieve in this chapter is not so much to provide a synopsis of these disputes as to de-naturalize the Japanese critical context in which the various approaches involved—the Romanticist author-oriented approach, the New Critical or formalist reading of text as an autonomous artifact, and the post-structuralist concerns with socio-political-economic contexts—clashed here. *Kokoro*, by virtue of having been explored within many more critical frameworks than any other text I deal with here, seemed the best choice for the purpose of illustrating the range of literary studies in present-day Japan.

Throughout Chapters 2–5, I remain devoted to examination of textualized contextuality. As I have noted several times in this Introduction, I am aware of possible criticism of such a "confined" approach as formalistic (rather than formalist) and thus apparently retrograde. Prevailing approaches to literature privilege the problematization of the textual boundaries and the actual relationships between readers and texts. Intratextual contextuality, as I noted earlier, has been relatively, if not entirely, neglected by the majority of contemporary literary studies. Some readers, especially those who practice political readings of literature, may be disappointed at the lack of references to extra-textual contextuality and may conclude that I am unaware of the limitations and contingency of the framework of my own work. I hope that I have successfully delineated the boundaries of the present study and, in so doing, have suggested both its range of validity and its limitations. In the Conclusion, I attempt, however briefly, to place my own work in perspective by musing on my own readership and by taking a brief look at several other works of a similar kind. The final pages of my text will show myself gazing both back at what I have accomplished and toward what we could do beyond it.

CHAPTER I

The Debates on 'Kokoro': A Cornerstone

"I mailed something to you this morning—my memoir. I'd like you to read it. I can't make sense of it; it appears the Miki who died of the accident wrote it. I'd like you to help me decipher the text, which is like a mysterious inscription in hieroglyphs, unearthed from a ruin in the desert."

I felt as though confronted with a sharp knifelike anxiety. To be frank, I thought that the memoir would be a testament which had a certain decisive meaning, and that once the pages were opened, the relationship between me and Miki would be clarified. For example, I thought, the Miki of the past might have expressed a certain will toward me—I shall call it "love," according to my obsession. I also thought at the same time that reading the memoir would annihilate this obsession relentlessly.

The notebook arrived on my doorstep by express mail around 9 o'clock the following night. As I read, I fell into confusion, as though floating in a zone of no gravity.

What Is the 'Kokoro ronsō'?

No case study could better serve as a cornerstone for an exploration of modern Japanese fictional narratives and of narrative studies in modern Japanese academe than a survey of the so-called *Kokoro ronsō* (debates on *Kokoro*), which began when Komori Yōichi published "'Kokoro' o seisei suru 'hāto'" (The "heart" that generates *Kokoro*) in March 1985.[1] The polemical nature of this essay stimulated new interest in this topical novel by Natsume Sōseki and provoked many impassioned reactions either supporting or attacking Komori's thesis, both in print and in oral presentations. Komori himself issued a series of defenses, as well as criticisms, of his initial thesis up to 1994, when he announced that he would quit the debate, because his attempts to decanonize the novel had perversely ended in strengthening its position in the history of modern Japanese literature.

This explanation suggests that one of the motivations behind Komori's analysis was to question or undermine the centrality of *Kokoro* in studies of modern Japanese fiction. Given Komori's ideological polemic—that *Kokoro* had been canonized in the context of imperialism and the ethical code it validated, as James Fujii among others has also claimed[2]—it is understandable that he realized the paradox of decanonization: that one might rewrite and reinforce the canon in attempting to erase it.

But Komori's contributions to the study of this novel are not limited to setting it within the political context of modern Japan. What was unprecedented in his study was his conscious and explicit application of structuralist/narratological approaches to modern Japanese prose fiction.[3] By applying this "new" framework, Komori challenged the authority of the *kindai kokubungaku* methodologies that prevailed at that time—that is, Romanticist studies of the author-genius and the work-masterpiece. Earthshaking as his argument might have been in 1985, in the years since it appeared, Komori's views have been subjected to severe criticism from post-structuralists such as Nakamura Miharu,[4] as well as Komori himself.

This does not mean, however, that his structuralist reading is no longer valid, or that it is not worthwhile to retrace the steps of the *Kokoro ronsō*. The issues in dispute foregrounded fundamental discrepancies among the frameworks of the participants. Rather than disagreeing with one another over a particular issue, or reaching a conclusion about it, they often focused on completely different issues, seemingly unaware that they were in fact addressing different questions. The disputes are, in fact, more about the values that privilege one set of questions over another than about the specific questions themselves.

It is for this reason that an examination of these disputes is relevant to this volume. In the following overview of the debates, it will become evident which questions I am and am not asking. The participants in the debate on *Kokoro* have approached the novel from three different orientations: one centers around the historical author and his historical context; another focuses on the structure of the text; and a third emphasizes the dialogue (or the lack and/or the refusal of it) between narrator and narratee. My focus on intra-textual narrative contexts means that I work primarily within the third orientation. Although I occasionally refer to historical contexts, and perhaps more frequently examine how a given narrative is arranged to constitute a structure, such ventures are meant to complement the main flow of my argument and to put it in perspective in order to see both its potentials and its limitations. It is thus meaningful to examine how such attempts at studying the intra-textual contexts of narration have been received in Japan and elsewhere, since this will show how the validity of certain approaches has been tested and help define the area that the present study intends to cover.

A Structuralist Reading of 'Kokoro' and Its 'Naturalness' in the North American Critical Context

Like many Japanese, Komori first read *Kokoro* as an assignment in high school. As is typical in *kokugo kyōiku* (national language education) classes, his teacher emphasized the ethical aspects of the novel to the exclusion of any other approach to the work. Indeed, had structural aspects been treated at all, they would have been presented as matters of secondary importance. Several structuralist questions, however, occurred to Komori at that time: What happened to the primary narrator, *watakushi* ("I"), between the time he finished reading the testament of the secondary narrator, Sensei, and the time he began to write his own narrative? What impelled him to write? For whom is he writing? More specifically, does Sensei's widow—Okusan as *watakushi* calls her—know that *watakushi* is writing about her deceased husband? Sensei had entreated *watakushi* not to let her know of his past—has *watakushi* honored this request? Or is *watakushi* ignoring it by breaking silence and narrating Sensei's story in such a way that Okusan herself might read it?

Komori, in other words, was interested more in the first-person narrator of Part I, "Sensei and I," and Part II, "My Parents and I" than in Sensei, the first-person narrator of Part III, who had up to that time been the focus of scholarly and educational interest. As Komori pointed out, *Kokoro* had been one of the most frequently quoted works of modern Japanese fiction in high school *kokugo* textbooks, but it had been always Part III—"Sensei's Testament"—from which passages were excerpted.[5] Moreover, the questions attached to the excerpt tended to focus on Sensei's moral sense: the dilemma between his friendship with the late K and Sensei's affection for his wife, whom K had loved, and whose betrothal to Sensei drove K to kill himself. Komori claimed that this reading of *Kokoro* functioned to reinforce emperor worship and imperialism.[6]

Another element in Komori's comments on his high school teacher is relevant to my aims in this volume. That teacher had suggested to

Komori that he disregard anything not explicitly written in the text. But is this a valid methodological principle? Komori does not think so, and I agree with him. What is not inside the text is not simply nonexistent but may exist as an absence, a rupture, or a space intentionally left blank. Komori thinks that what one can recognize as *not* written conveys meaning because of the conception of the text. The text is the product of an intention to tell some things and not to tell others.

Kokoro closes as the end of Sensei's testament, which the narrator of the first two parts has been reading on a train bound for Tokyo, appears to be approaching. The novel begins with this same narrator explaining how he has come to write about Sensei; among other things, this explanation makes clear to the reader that, in the narrative present of the novel, Sensei is already dead. Thus, the chronological order of events is easily reconstructed: *watakushi* read Sensei's narrative and then decided to write his own narrative on Sensei. However, what happened to *watakushi* between the two points, in terms of his writing and also of his relationships with the other characters in *Kokoro*, remains untold.

Komori tries to fill the gap between the end of Part III and the beginning of Part I with suggestions of how the human relationships described in Parts I and II may have developed in the interim. In Komori's opinion, during the textual rupture, (1) the narrator has come to differentiate his relationship with Sensei, which was human and warmhearted, from Sensei's relationship with K, which was distant and cold; (2) by the time the narrator begins to narrate the story, he has established a fulfilling relationship with Sensei's widow, based upon physical consummation and the fathering of a child, which Sensei could not do; (3) in the narrative present, the narrator is telling Okusan the truth of Sensei's agony over his betrayal of K, despite Sensei's previous request that the narrator not tell her. As we will see, many found these interpretations unacceptable. The second point in particular provoked a torrent of antagonism, which Komori saw as reflecting a tabloid-like interest in sexual relationships among characters, as well as an absorption in the myths of male bonding, female chastity, and the institution of marriage.

Scandalous as it may have sounded to many scholars in Japan, Komori's argument is not in itself absurd and in fact found parallels in criticism outside Japan. A similar inquiry into the unspecified link between the ending of Part III and the beginning of Part I was made in 1988 by Patricia Merivale, who had read *Kokoro* not in Japanese but in Edwin McClellan's English translation.[7] Although Merivale had no access either to the original text or to the many scholarly works on the text available to Komori, she was similarly concerned with structural details—including the missing conclusion to the story. Let us first examine her interpretation, which came out of nowhere from the perspective of Japanese scholarship, to see how far removed Komori's stance might be from it and to consider whether his basic argument might have had a certain universal plausibility.

Merivale begins with questions about the disproportionate size of Part III and the failure of the narrator to reappear at the close of the novel:

> The book we read is made up of the narrator's retrospective story of his acquaintance with Sensei, to which is added Sensei's long account (exactly half the book) of events which considerably precede those of the main narrative and even his first meeting with the narrator. We never return to the perspective or to the present time of the narrator. [. . .] "Why is there no epilogue?" What impact does learning about Sensei's earlier life have on him? And what is the effect upon us of the abrupt juxtaposition of these two narratives?[8]

As we have seen, the abrupt ending and the absence of any return to the "perspective or to the present time of the narrator" also stirred Komori's curiosity. Merivale goes on to describe what seems to her the natural response to these structural enigmas: "We would then *want* the focus to be shifted from Sensei to the narrator; we would be puzzled and irritated at being left up in the air with Sensei's last words; we would try to figure out what happens to the narrator insofar as it can be extrapolated from the text."[9]

To justify such responses on the part of readers of *Kokoro*, she compares the structure of *Kokoro* with that of *Heart of Darkness* by Joseph Conrad and what she calls "elegiac romances" in Canadian literature—

"first-person narratives in which the autobiography of the narrator masquerades as the biography of a dead hero."[10] Indeed, *Kokoro* is a first-person narrative, which to many has seemed to be the biography of a hero by the name of Sensei, and which some, like Komori, propose to read, rather, as the autobiography of the narrator, "I." However, Merivale points out the uniqueness of *Kokoro*'s suspended ending:

> The (hypothetical) Kokoro epilogue ought, by analogy, to show the consequences for the narrator both of Sensei's death itself and of its corollary, his discovery of the secret of Sensei's life from beyond the grave. The reader is left to extrapolate this epilogue from the text to discover the narrator's response to those things. This is the only way to fill in the gap between what "happened" in the narrative and the (present) time in which the narrator tells his story. The reader can do this by considering as predictions the numerous statements of possibility or anticipation given in the narrator's part (section I and II). [. . .] It can also be done by completing the syllogisms suggested by many partial analogies between the narrator's part and Sensei's (section III).[11]

Regarding the possibility of an involvement between *watakushi* and Sensei's widow, Merivale writes (the page references are to McClellan's translation):

> "I tried, as far as I was able, to comfort Sensei's wife" (42, emphasis mine). Although the narrator is still in the dark about Sensei's secret, he senses her loneliness; he has been impressed from the beginning by her beauty and courtesy (16ff). And touched by her "sympathy and understanding" (37), "she had begun to move my heart" (40). Her quasi-maternal relationship to him (most clearly evident in the scene of her sewing his clothes) is not stressed in the way that Sensei's quasi-paternal relationship is.
>
> Yet would he be free, either psychologically or culturally, to "inherit" her in an erotic or marital context [. . .] after Sensei's death?[12]

Merivale continues her inquiry by speculating about the ages of the three characters, just as we will see Hata Kōhei do in the next section. Evidently, she sees the possibility of an erotic connection between Sensei's wife and *watakushi*, both in textual details in Part I that suggest that the latter feels an attraction and in the nature of the genre, which seems to predispose narratives to a certain kind of development. Although

Merivale does not seem prepared to give a positive answer to the question: Will *watakushi* marry Sensei's widow? She, like Komori, does point out that we would expect *watakushi* to emerge from Sensei's shadow if he is to have any productive relationship with the widow:

> The final lines of the book are extraordinarily emphatic in implication, because they conclude the book without, in the usual novelistic sense, "ending" it: "So long as my wife is alive, I want you to keep everything I have told you a secret—even after I myself am dead" (248). The logical or emotional ending the reader is left to supply. We are forced to go on thinking of the consequences of this dead hand laid upon the narrator. He can comfort Ojosan [i.e., Okusan], as he has done in earlier conversations, by talking about Sensei and Sensei's relationship with her, but it will be an empty and useless comfort; having by this time discovered what might really succeed in comforting her, he is expressly forbidden to reveal it, and so the murderous silence is passed on from "father" to "son." [. . .] The narrator must continue, for however long Ojosan survives (we remember, however, that Sensei's mother did not long outlive his father), the same deadly reticence that turned first K and then Sensei into men so lonely that, despite the presence of a friend, their only escape lay in suicide. There are several reasons why each man in turn keeps the secret of someone's love for Ojosan from her. One is that their deeper loyalty is to each other. Ironically, only by revealing that secret can their solitude, or for that matter (though it is less central to the fiction) hers, be remedied. Lines like "she was not free to tell me all she knew" (42) and "it was too late [for me] to tell the truth" (112) could easily be transposed into the epilogue.[13]

Even though Merivale seems skeptical about the possibility that *watakushi* might tell Okusan the truth and go on to live with her—this is at least partly due to a discrepancy between the original and the English version that she read—she feels, as Komori does, that it would be awkward if *watakushi* were to keep Sensei's secret. Thus, Merivale's analysis suggests we question the "naturalness" of the conspiracy of silence between Sensei and *watakushi* at the expense of the wife. There is no reason to accept traditional interpretations that have assumed *watakushi* honored his mentor's request and that he would never think of his mentor's wife (or widow) in romantic or sexual terms.[14]

The Place of the 'Author': The Reception of Komori's Article in Japan

Komori's thesis—that *Kokoro* should be read from the perspective of the narrator's involvement in the story beyond his purely passive role as the reader of Sensei's testament—was first received enthusiastically. One of the earliest responses to Komori, by Ōoka Shōhei, the author of many stories in the genre of "war literature" and a well-known critic of modern Japanese literature, appeared in October 1985.[15] In a diary-style essay serialized over a long period in the *Bungakukai*, an established literary journal, Ōoka related that he had been studying Sōseki since 1972 and had come across a review of Komori's article by Yoshida Hiroo in the August issue of *Kaien*, a much newer and more experimentalist literary journal. Although he had not intended to collect every article on Sōseki for his work, Ōoka went out of his way to obtain a copy of the first issue of *Seijō kokubungaku*, in which Komori's article appeared. Ōoka summed up his impression of Komori's article, as well as one by Ishihara Chiaki in the same journal:

> Both take note of the fact that *Kokoro* consists only of the first-person narratives of *watakushi* and Sensei and lacks any objective description. I had understood that much myself, but [what was new to me is that] the authors of the articles problematize the fact that although Sensei forbids him to tell his wife that his death was due to suicide, *watakushi* "narrates" the truth in *Kokoro*.
>
> [. . .] Mr. Komori thinks that the marriage of Sensei and his wife, brought about by K's suicide, has not been physically consummated, and that *watakushi* goes to Tokyo to protect Sensei's wife. I was astonished by Mr. Komori's miraculous interpretation that *watakushi* has married her, produced a child—in other words, done everything that Sensei couldn't—and then begun to narrate. I think that this is the most courageous and distinguished of the interpretations of the theme of the "narrative" without objective description.[16]

As we can see, Ōoka was partly in error (Sensei requests *watakushi* not to tell his wife that he had been tormented by his relationship with her and with K rather than to hide the fact that he committed suicide) and may not have grasped the theoretical framework in which Komori worked. Ōoka spoke from the perspective of author-centered criticism in claiming that the reader should "decipher the sign that Sōseki has issued."[17] Still, Ōoka was persuaded by Komori's reading and welcomed his shift of focus from Sensei to *watakushi*. This positive "review" by an established writer appearing in a journal like *Bungakukai* must have drawn more attention to Komori's article than did its primary vehicle, the first issue of *Seijō kokubungaku*, of which Komori himself was a co-editor and whose reputation had yet to be established.

Ōoka's positive comments did not guarantee, however, wholesale acceptance of Komori's interpretation. Outspokenly negative reactions to Komori's thesis were to follow, as we can see in the survey compiled by Oshino Takeshi.[18] As Oshino observes, regardless of whether they agree with Komori, the comments of many, if not most, of the critics who participated in the *Kokoro ronsō* reveal the contradictions between the so-called author-oriented criticism (*sakusha ron*) and text-centered criticism (*tekusuto ron*). Oshino notes, for example, that Ōkawa Kōichi, speaking from the perspective of the "author-as-origin," criticizes Komori for treating the narrative as a text produced by *watakushi* rather than by "a man called Natsume Sōseki."[19] Oshino also puts Tanaka Minoru in a negative light by noting that Tanaka "similarly criticized [Komori] for the possibility [he suggests] of *watakushi* living with Okusan, as 'a digression from interpretation of the work.'"[20] Oshino's comments are correct as far as they go, but other aspects of Ōkawa's and Tanaka's positions deserve attention.

Tanaka Minoru raises one point that is hard to sidestep, although, *pace* Tanaka, it does not necessarily contradict Komori's reading of *Kokoro*. (Komori refers to the problem as "a logical contradiction."[21] In fact Tanaka is following Komori even as he claims to criticize him. I paraphrase Tanaka's argument here simply because he treats the point at greater length than Komori.) Tanaka points out that Sensei's testament has been edited by its primary reader, *watakushi*, in the act of copying it. This claim is corroborated by the fact that the following quotation from Sensei's testament that *watakushi* gives in Part II cannot be found anywhere in Part III, which is presented as if it were a complete transcription of the testament. *Watakushi* receives the letter from Sensei while visiting his parents in the countryside. Since his father's condition is critical, he does not have the time or the peace of mind to read the letter carefully when it arrives:

In this unsettled state, I read the first page.

"You asked me once to tell you of my past. I did not have the courage then to do so. But now, I believe I am free of the bonds that prevented me from telling you the truth about myself. The freedom that I now have, however, is no more than an earthly, physical kind of freedom, which will not last forever. Unless I take advantage of it while I can, I shall never again have the opportunity of passing on to you what I have learned from my own experience, and my promise to you will have been broken. Circumstances having prevented me from telling you my story in person, I have decided to write it out for you."[22]

As Tanaka suggests, the passage within quotation marks should appear before the first paragraph of Part III. This apparent omission, combined with the fact that no greeting is given at the end, suggest that we are not given the full text of the testament.[23] Tanaka further suggests that the names of addresser (Sensei) and addressee (*watakushi*) must have been omitted from the "original" testament. Tanaka concludes that although the contexts in which "Sensei's testament" was initially written and that in which the rest of the narrative is written would seem to have been different, the "two contexts" consistently comply with the editorial intent of *watakushi*. Tanaka stops here, but I would further claim that this suggests that "I" exerts narrative authority over Sensei, and that the narratives related by *watakushi* and by Sensei are thus asymmetrical. This brings us somewhat closer to a later deconstructionist article by Komori, to which I will return below.

Who Is the 'Reader' in Reader Response Criticism?

The *Kokoro ronsō* entered its next phase when an even mightier voice than Ōoka's responded to Komori: Miyoshi Yukio, then professor emeritus of *kokubungaku* at the University of Tokyo and an authority in Sōseki studies. The first engagement between the two, as far as *Kokoro* is concerned, occurred in Miyoshi's survey of national literature studies in 1986.[24] In this short survey, Miyoshi refers to only two articles and three oral presentations from the year; Komori's is one of them. "A good essay, attractive because of the sharp textual analysis and distinguished rhetoric for which Mr. Komori is famous,"[25] Miyoshi begins. But Miyoshi goes on to question the possibility of *watakushi*'s living with Sensei's widow and having a child by her, by pointing to her ignorance of the true reason for Sensei's agony. Miyoshi persuasively suggests: "If *watakushi* had begun to live with Okusan without telling her of the tragedy involving Sensei, then it would be the case that he rather radically followed Sensei's mode of living."[26] Later, the site of their dispute moved to the eminent literary journal *Bungaku*, published by Iwanami, one of the most prestigious publishers in Japan.

Another factor that affected the course of the *Kokoro ronsō*, despite the fact that Komori himself had not initiated it, was the dispute between Hata Kōhei and Miyoshi. Known primarily as a playwright, Hata has frequently stirred up scholarly controversy by his stage adaptations of modern Japanese stories. Perhaps for the sake of dramatic effect, he needs denouements, which, as many have pointed out, are often missing from *shōsetsu*. He needed, for example, to have *watakushi*, the observer/narrator, propose to Okusan, his mentor's widow, in the last scene of his scenario:

Shizu [i.e., Okusan]: It should not be just the testament that he entrusted you with.
I: . . .
Shizu: Sensei trusted you, so his precious . . . his most precious thing . . . me
I: Madame, you . . .
Shizu: . . .
I: Madame, . . . Madame, . . . we. . .
Shizu: Yes.
I: We shall get married.
Shizu: Yes.[27]

Hata's scenario was published in its entirety, with his own annotations, as *"Kokoro" no kodoku to ai* (The solitude and love of *Kokoro*) in *Umi no hon* 2 (September 1986), a "journal" he edits and circulates personally. It might never have been discussed in academia until the October 1987 stage production by Haiyū-za of Hata's version with some modifications as *Kokoro: Waga ai*, had Miyoshi not responded in November 1986 with "<Sensei> wa kokyu ka" (Is "Sensei" a cuckold?) in *Kaien*.

The ending of Hata's scenario was equated with Komori's suggestion that *watakushi* might "live—with—Okusan"[28] and generated some excitement about the potential of a love triangle involving Sensei, his wife, and *watakushi*. Despite a surface resemblance between Hata's script and Komori's thesis, which Miyoshi takes up and Komori mentions in order to refute,[29] Hata does not mention Komori in his response to Miyoshi—which was in fact written in anticipation of Miyoshi's review rather than in reply to it—entitled "'Sensei' wa kokyu de wa nai" ("Sensei" is not a cuckold). Meanwhile, Miyoshi's comments on Komori's article in *Kokugo nenkan* in December 1986 invited Komori's counter-response, "*Kokoro* no yukue," and his then-colleague Ishihara Chiaki's "Seido to shite no 'kenkyū buntai'" (The institution of "academic discourse"). As a response to all three articles, Miyoshi wrote "Watoson wa haishinsha ka: *Kokoro* saisetsu" (Is Watson a traitor?: *Kokoro* revisited) published in *Bungaku* in May 1988. The title suggests a similarity between *watakushi* and Watson in the Sherlock Holmes stories—both narrators tell their stories in retrospect, and they thus know more than the reader at any point in the narrative. Although both are willing to share their information with the reader, their willingness was problematized by Komori in the case of *watakushi*, since he is, unlike Watson, forbidden to tell his story to Okusan. Miyoshi, in contrast, tries to deny the possibility of betrayal on the part of *watakushi* by claiming that Okusan will not hear him narrate the story.

A useful entrance into the Komori-Miyoshi debates is a contentious point Komori makes in his first article:

> *Kokoro* for me seems to exist as a text in which the act of reading—the movement to weave the text, in linearity and in two dimensions, or the act of both passing behind the "present" to meet each word and maintaining the memory of each word of the text—could not cease unless one dissects the text and returns to the "beginning." Even after I stop the act of reading, the accumulated

words that I have come across do not stop the movement by which they respond to one another.[30]

Then Komori quotes the first paragraph of *Kokoro*, since it contains an important "memory" of "words" that "respond" to other "words" in the text. Let me quote the paragraph in its entirety, both in Japanese and in McClellan's English translation:

Watakushi wa sono hito o tsuneni sensei to yonde ita. Dakara koko de mo tada sensei to kaku dake de honmyō wa uchiakenai. Kore wa seken o habakaru enryo to iu yori mo, sono hō ga watakushi ni totte shizen dakara de aru. Watakushi wa sono hito no kioku o yobiokosu goto ni, sugu 'Sensei' to iitaku naru. Fude o totte mo kokoromochi wa onaji koto de aru. *Yosoyososhii kashira-moji nado wa totemo tsukau ki ni naranai.* (Emphasis added)[31]

I always called him "Sensei." I shall therefore refer to him simply as "Sensei," and not by his real name. It is not because I consider it more discreet, but it is because I find it more natural that I do so. Whenever the memory of him comes back to me now, I find that I think of him as "Sensei" still. And with pen in hand, I cannot bring myself to write of him in any other way.[32]

The last sentence in this paragraph is missing from the English text, but it translates: "I do not at all feel like applying indifferent-looking initials to him."

Since McClellan is an acclaimed, first-rate translator, we may assume that the omission was not simply an oversight. He must have felt, along with many Japanese scholars, that the sentence did not carry much significance. But Komori thinks otherwise:

Despite the brevity, the few lines in effect differentiate the whole structure of Sensei's testament. Sensei begins to write his most crucial confession with the sentence, "I shall here call my friend 'K'" [Natsume 3; McClellan 163]. Indeed, Sensei inscribed an "indifferent-looking initial" of "K" for the close friend who had left a crucial trace in his mind. [. . .] *Watakushi* begins to utter his own words in such a way as to distance himself from a mode of writing or a usage of words. This act implies that Sensei's relationship with (or his memory of) K was "indifferent" and makes manifest that the relationship (or memory) between *watakushi* and Sensei is entirely different from that between Sensei and K.[33]

Komori further defines the difference between the two relationships, or the two ways that memories of the dead are presented, as one between "second-person interaction" and "third-person interaction":

> The existence of "him," referred to in the sentence "Whenever the memory of him comes back to me now, I find that I think of him as 'Sensei' still," is not confined in a past separated from the present, but coexists as a mutually communicating existence and generates a new interaction [with *watakushi*] in the second-person relationship of "coexisting with you now." . . .
>
> The language of "Part III: Sensei's Testament," in which Sensei represents his close friend by "K"—an "indifferent-looking initial"—suggests the third-person relationship that would objectify the existence of the Other, in other words, that makes the Other into a sign, a homogeneous meaning.[34]

Komori's structuralist reading—connecting separate instances and contrasting them with each other—as well as his "discovery" of the message that he suggests is implied by the contrast, had not gone unchallenged. As early as March 1986, Ōkawa Kōichi picked up on Komori's interpretation of the "indifferent-looking initials":

> Mr. Komori [. . .] explains the difference between the *watakushi*-Sensei relationship and Sensei-K relationship as "second person" and "third person," which seems to me a little far-fetched. The two relationships are too different from each other in many ways, such as the age difference [to be compared only in this term of degree of intimacy/distance]. The reason that Sensei calls his friend "K" without further fuss is nothing other than that he is a "close friend who had left a crucial trace in his mind"—how else could Sensei refer to the friend whom he thinks he forced to commit suicide, than by "writing of him by an 'indifferent-looking initial' "?[35]

It is not because Sensei feels "indifferent" to his deceased best friend that he refers to him in the third person or by an "indifferent-looking initial." Rather, it is because it would pain Sensei to call him by his real name or by the nickname he once used to address "K"—the real name must seem inseparable from the intimacy they enjoyed. For Sensei, the real name must evoke a friendship that he believes he marred, and it is only natural that this haunting quality is missing from the term of address "Sensei" that *watakushi* employs to refer when his mentor is alive as well as after his death. Sensei's death is not *watakushi*'s fault, and there is no reason for *watakushi* to feel any qualm about referring to Sensei as he always has.[36] Thus, the message conveyed by the mention of the use of "initials" in the text—if indeed there is such a message—seems different from that suggested by Komori. For better or worse, Sensei and K were much more closely involved with each other than *watakushi* and Sensei, and this is why the first pair needed to be intentionally distanced by the use of an "indifferent-looking initial."

Although I am ready to accept this particular argument of Ōkawa's, I must say that *watakushi* does not seem to share Ōkawa's view when he writes the sentence. The word *yosoyososhii* does not convey an effort to distance the other. It simply suggests a lack of interest in the other. Sensei's decision to use the initial "K" to detach himself from a complex emotional entanglement does not mean that *watakushi*, the reader of Sensei's testament, understood this reason. The use of *yosoyososhii* seems, rather, to suggest, as Komori claims, a determination to be different from Sensei in terms of how one treats a close friend.

Miyoshi's refutation of Komori has the potential for developing a more general and more theoretical problem than Ōkawa's, although I disagree with him on the particular point he addresses here:

> Let me begin with the obvious. *Kokoro* was serialized in a newspaper. The first reader (the first that we must expect Sōseki to have been conscious of) would come to read the story day by day as the newspaper was issued. The author's (or the narrator's) intention is responsible for where one begins the narration. The reader was forced to read as the author (the narrator) intended. [. . .] The time from the first encounter of *watakushi* with Sensei on the Kamakura seashore until the present—"the fictional time"—matches the time during which the novel was serialized in the *Asahi shinbun*—the time during which the original form of the text was taking shape ("the textual time"). The first reader necessarily read the story within this textual time. When *watakushi* began to narrate the story, claiming that he would not like to refer to Sensei in "indifferent-sounding initials," the reader may perhaps expect how the story would unfold to some extent from the subtitle "Sensei's testament," but they should in no way be able to know in advance that Sensei would refer to his friend with his initial "K" in the testament. It is out of the question that he should be able to discern

> this differentiation of Sensei by *watakushi*. For the referent "Sensei" to have the significance Mr. Komori suggests, the reader must have known of the initial "K" as the reader now, who has been given the whole text at once, does. The first reader was not affected by the word "indifferent-sounding" as it occurred in the original form of the text. Sōseki would not have been able to expect this reader to be aware to that extent.[37]

Miyoshi's argument is based upon the fact that *Kokoro* was serialized. Readers at that time, who read it daily, could not have known how a piece of information in a given section might be interpreted in light of what was to happen later. This much seems "obvious." What is questionable in Miyoshi's argument, however, is the view that since the reader would not have known what was meant by *watakushi*'s refusal to refer to Sensei by initials, the author could not have intended to convey the message that *watakushi* was implicitly criticizing Sensei.

One can refute Miyoshi's point, without stepping out of his own paradigm, which is based on the shared contemporaneity of the author and this newspaper reader. Although it is true that such a reader might not recognize the significance of the statement—since the reader cannot know that Sensei will eventually refer to his "best friend" as K—the text does make it possible for the reader to connect the two textual instances and conclude that *watakushi*, as the primary narrator of "Sensei and I" in *Kokoro*, intended the analogy. This is because the time when *watakushi* reads Sensei's reference to K ("I shall here call my friend 'K.'") precedes the time when he writes "I do not at all feel like applying indifferent-looking initials." If we pay attention not to the range of knowledge of the "reader" but to that of the first-person narrator, then it is easy to conclude that *watakushi* knows what he means by his mention of "use of initials." Furthermore, it is quite possible that the author—any author—could plan ahead and set foreshadowings here and there in the text, without expecting a reader to be able to immediately predict how they might be developed later. As Miyoshi says in the same article, "*Watakushi* narrates, taking advantage of the privilege that he knows something that the reader does not know yet."[38] *Watakushi*, as he begins writing the text of Part I, knows that Sensei refers to his close friend as "K," whereas the reader does not. This is simply a classic example of foreshadowing.

Even if we take a methodological step in Miyoshi's direction, we can still answer Miyoshi's question in a way that preserves Komori's intuition about the significance of the problem of naming. Komori and Ishihara, in a 1992 study, attempted to discuss the issue at the level of the "real," or historical, author, Natsume Sōseki, and his primary intended audience. They examined the holograph of *Kokoro* in order to reconstruct Sōseki's writing process and discovered that Sōseki twice rewrote the last two sentences of the first paragraph. This effort suggests the importance of the message of the passage.[39]

Despite these objections to Miyoshi's argument, it does open a number of possibilities for productive discussion of the mission of narrative studies. Another point that Miyoshi makes leads us to a fruitful comparison of his and Komori's outlooks on the analysis of narrative. As is by now evident, the two critics use the term "reader" (*dokusha*) in different senses. For Miyoshi, the "reader" is the historical reader, who existed outside the text and inside the context in which the text was constructed, and who read *Kokoro* in the earliest printed version (although not in the earliest handwritten version that Komori and Ishihara examined). For Komori, however, the "reader" is Wolfgang Iser's "implied reader," someone able to view the narrative as a whole and at one moment. That is, this reader can interpret one section in relation to another, no matter how remote, and without regard to the order in which the two textual instances occur. Komori in this sense has in mind the hypothetical reader whose responses provide the ideal point of departure for formalist/structuralist readings.

Notwithstanding the contradictions that necessarily follow from these different notions of the reader, Miyoshi's response to Komori raises two issues of interest in narrative studies: Miyoshi historicizes readership, and he conceives of reading as a process. As opposed to Komori, who speaks of a "formalist" reader—neutral, unindividuated, and able to see everything in the narrative at any moment—Miyoshi is clearly speaking of historical readers. Miyoshi's readers are bound to a historical context, individual, unable to see anything beyond what they have so far read, and perhaps unable to recollect that which they have previously read. Despite these limitations, Miyoshi refuses to go further than contemporary readers. It is a methodological article of faith with him to privilege the perspective of historical readers. Although he notes the differences between Taishō readers and readers today, he gives no weight to what modern readers might say—he seems to think that only the primary audience is entitled to speak, because they are the ones that the author (the "real," historical author, Natsume Sōseki) intended to address. It is this blind faith in origins that Komori cannot accept.

Naturally, contemporary readers' experience of the serialized *Kokoro* were different from ours, since a complete version is available to us. Thus, we are able to read it through at one setting, read it more than once, read it backward, read it skipping parts, and so on, and transform the crystallized narrative into a process of narrating. Miyoshi's focus on the historical reader suggests possibilities for an analogous exploration of the modern reader, but these have yet to be fully developed. We are now able to think, beyond Miyoshi, of a reader who can contextualize the autonomous text and put it back into the process of making.

Komori Deconstructing Komori

The Komori of 1994, the deconstructionist Komori, is aware of narrative as a process of writing, not in the sense that Miyoshi discussed (the process of the historical author's writing for contemporary readers) but in the sense that the encoded writer *watakushi* writes about how he views what happened, rather than about what happened. To put this more precisely, *watakushi* writes what he wants the reader to believe happened. Komori has changed his position on *Kokoro* constantly, without, apparently, finding himself "faithless." Indeed, he is perfectly justified, as he claims in "'Watakushi' to iu <tasha>-sei: *Kokoro* o meguru ōtokurittikku" (The otherness of "I": Auto-critique regarding *Kokoro*), a deconstructive article, in which he departs from the stance of his previous structuralist analysis. In its self-referentiality, this article can be read as a eulogy for Miyoshi, an autobiography of Komori, and a parody of *Kokoro*.

Komori positions himself in the place of *watakushi* and the late Miyoshi Yukio in that of Sensei and draws a parallel between the asymmetricality of each of the two relationships. *Watakushi* reads Sensei's testament after Sensei's death; Komori reads Miyoshi's writings after Miyoshi's death. It has been, in each case, some years since the reader first read the last correspondence of the deceased, and in writing his own narrative now, *watakushi* shows that he has changed from what he once was. But just as Sensei is unable to read the narrative *watakushi* is writing, or write about him, neither can Miyoshi read Komori's new article or write about him.

Komori differentiates himself from Miyoshi in terms of his ability to transform himself. Miyoshi cannot change any more, but Komori can, and does. Therefore, Komori accordingly differentiates himself from the Komori of 1985, who wrote the groundbreaking article. While still dealing with *watakushi*, the Komori of 1994 focuses on how Sensei might have perceived *watakushi*, how *watakushi* might have sensed this perception, and how *watakushi* intended to reconstruct (or deconstruct) Sensei's perception of him. In so doing, Komori portrays *watakushi* in a completely different light. Previously he was criticized for overestimating *watakushi* at the expense of Sensei, as he contrasted the warmhearted *watakushi* with the cold and detached Sensei. Now it is *watakushi* who is defined as a sleuth, stalking Sensei in Kamakura and in Tokyo, examining every detail of Sensei's life-style, interrogating him about everything that he says, and trying to uncover everything that Sensei seems to hide from him. Komori is consistent with the Komori of seven years earlier in the way he problematizes the quasi-filial devotion of *watakushi* to Sensei. However, Komori now views *watakushi* not as someone who admires and then transcends Sensei, but as someone who threatens and then feels sorry for Sensei. Komori's mistrust of male bonding has not changed, but his hierarchy of evaluation has been turned upside down. Previously, *watakushi* had been a new hero for attempting to dethrone Sensei, a character of "heroic stature" who had been seen as "a little larger than life-size," to use Merivale's characterization of heroes of elegiac romances in general.[40] Now Sensei is made into a victim of the penetrating gaze of *watakushi*, the intruder. Komori may have been thinking as well of himself as "a hero" who turned out to be an "intruder" vis-à-vis Miyoshi, a former hero who is now thought of as a victim.

Komori examines Sensei's perception of *watakushi*'s persistent gaze upon him, and Sensei's polite attempt to discourage *watakushi* from spending more time with him:

It was, I think, on the afternoon of the third day following our swim together that Sensei, when we met at the tea house, suddenly asked me, "Do you intend to stay in Kamakura long?" I had really no idea how much longer I would be in Kamakura, so I said, "I don't know." I then saw that Sensei was grinning, and I suddenly became embarrassed. I could not help blurting out, "And you, Sensei?" It was then that I began to call him "Sensei."[41]

Komori suggests that the reason that *watakushi* did not see Sensei following their swim is that Sensei tried to avoid him and that Sensei could not wait to see the last of *watakushi* when he asked the question. Komori's interpretation seems reasonable, given that Sensei has finally broken his silence in this passage, after having been watched by *watakushi* as he walked, bathed, and talked to the Westerner. Komori emphasizes the fact that it was under such circumstances that the word *sensei*, which *watakushi* says he later used consistently, was first uttered. Although *watakushi* may not have intended to harass Sensei, Sensei clearly feels burdened with this gesture of intimacy, which was unanticipated, if in fact it was welcome at all.

Komori further argues that the "friendship" between *watakushi* and Sensei is one-sided, citing the following passage from near the end of the Kamakura section:

As we were taking leave of each other, I had asked him, "Would it be all right if I visited you at your home now and then?" And he had answered quite simply, "Yes, of course." I had been under the impression that we were intimate friends, and had somehow expected a warmer reply. My self-confidence, I remember, was rather shaken then.

Often, during my association with Sensei, I was disappointed in this way. Sometimes, Sensei seemed to know that I had been hurt, and sometimes, he seemed not to know. But no matter how often I experienced such trifling disappointments, I never felt any desire to part from Sensei.[42]

Komori goes on to examine other textual instances to prove how threatening, though probably unintentionally, *watakushi* was to Sensei. What is more important is that the *watakushi* of the present, as he writes the text of Part I, is aware of what he did not know at the time—that he threatened Sensei. Komori's interpretation of *watakushi*'s intent in writing his relationship with the now-dead Sensei is convincing:

> It is then evident that the "close" [in the original: *ningen rashii atatakai*, lit., "humanly and warm"] and non-"analytical" relationship, that "Komori Yōichi" of the past emphasized, should not be anything but a postscript-like retrospective definition of the relationality—a definition that could be made only after "Sensei"'s death, when no objection or correction could be made by the person in question any longer. [. . .] Only because "Sensei" is dead and because his "letter" has become his "testament" has *watakushi* become able to talk of him, pretending to have come to understand "Sensei."[43]

Komori seems to suggest that *watakushi* quotes "Sensei's testament" at great length because it relieves him from the suspicion that he may have been responsible for Sensei's suicide. It was not *watakushi*'s meddling into Sensei's privacy, the testament seems to say, but the haunting memory of K that led Sensei to his end. It is in this light that Komori interprets the following quote:

> I did not understand then why it was that I should behave thus towards Sensei only. But now, when Sensei is dead, I am beginning to understand. It was not that Sensei disliked me at first. His curt and cold ways were meant rather as a warning to me that I would not want him as a friend. It was because he despised himself that he refused to accept openheartedly the intimacy of others. I feel great pity for him.[44]

Komori suggests that *watakushi* chooses to "understand" the relationship in this way, since it preserves the impression that Sensei did not dislike him. This is the way he wants to think of his relationship with Sensei. But the truth seems different. Despite the intrusive frequency with which *watakushi* visited Sensei and his manifest interest in Sensei's past, *watakushi* is inattentive enough not to respond to Sensei's request by mail that *watakushi* see him and listen to him when *watakushi* is staying in the countryside attending his sick father. *Watakushi* imposes himself upon Sensei, but does not listen to his voice—until it is too late. In regret, *watakushi* has to "rewrite" his memory of "Sensei" and edit Sensei's testament, so as to construct the illusion of a beautiful friendship between himself and Sensei.

The *watakushi* of the past is different from the *watakushi* of the present. *Watakushi,* the subject of action, is different from *watakushi,* the subject of narration of the action. The split in subjectivity in the doer and the narrator is evident here in Komori's new analysis of *Kokoro.* This discovery will allow us to explore other narratives of modern Japan.

As a Point of Departure for Unexplored Territories

The debates on *Kokoro* illustrate a variety of approaches to the texts of prose narratives: one tries to decipher the author's message encoded in the text, as is suggested by Miyoshi most typically, and by other opponents of Komori with lesser degrees of consistency; another anatomizes the order of events, statements, and utterances, in order to see every single part of the narrative in relation to the rest of it, as attempted by the Komori of 1985 and by Merivale; still another, which prevailed in the Komori of 1994, tries to capture the dynamism of the narrator-narratee relationship. A strong interest in the other, an insistence on knowing, the fear of being exposed to the other, an unwillingness to confide in the other, a resigned attitude toward the other's persistence, revenge for the other's intrusion into one's privacy, guilt over violating the other's privacy—these are some factors that affect the way that the narration forms itself and the way that it is interpreted by different agents. The present study uses mainly the third approach, while keeping it in perspective of the other two approaches. This mapping of the variety of approaches to *Kokoro* serves to suggest the orientation of this study, as well as its limitation and the premise that validates it.

Relevant to this theoretical positioning of my methodology is the issue of editions. Handwritten manuscripts, newspaper serials, and books induce different types of reading, as suggested by Miyoshi's mention of the *Asahi shinbun* version of *Kokoro* and by Ishihara and Komori's examination of the *Kokoro* manuscript. The manuscript or the serialized version of a prose narrative should be honored as a version—not necessarily as *the* original version, but as nothing more or less than *a* version—in the same way the authoritative monograph or *zenshū* (complete works) version is. The present study focuses on one later version of the texts studied, while noting major textual discrepancies between the initial and later versions that might affect the narrative contexts in the texts. This is emphatically not to suggest that the later version is more established or authoritative than the earlier one. It is simply a matter of choice in this particular context—a choice made not on the basis of a judgment of inherent qualities (which I believe do not exist outside context) but in light of the fact that completed and perhaps revised versions circulate more widely and have formed readers' responses on a larger scale. Like most readers, my initial contact with these texts was not with the "original" version. Such texts are usually the province of researchers and other motivated readers, who become interested in them only because of their readings of later versions. We may venture to call the "original" version a "digression," rather than the origin, in terms of the act of reading.

The historical circumstances surrounding revisions and editorial changes themselves deserve careful and extensive research. Insofar as this particular study, as stated in the Introduction, deals with intra-textual contexts, references to extra-textual circumstances (such as those Miyoshi mentioned above in regard to *Kokoro*) are kept to a minimum. Again, this is simply to delineate the area that this work plans to cover, and it is not my intent to suggest that such external circumstances are not worth studying. As I maintain in the Introduction, this text itself is a narrative, and as such, it is an act of narration that is not autonomous of a set of conditions which helped form it in a particular way and not in another.

CHAPTER 2

Obsessed with Inscription: Ibuse Masuji's 'Kuroi ame,' or (Re)Writing Memories

"I don't have anything in mind. . . . "

"How about writing a memoir like you used to?"

"But how?"

"Put in words anything that occurred to you. Whatever you might think of."

"But in what style? Should I for example write in the same style as Miki's notebook?"

"That's a thought; it's Miki's style."

"Actually," so saying Miki sat up, "I've begun to write again since I was discharged from hospital."

"Let me read it."

"Do you think I write all right?" Miki opened a drawer of the nightstand, and produced a notebook. There was nothing in the drawer other than it.

Reading a Historical Narrative as a Performance?

IBUSE MASUJI'S *Kuroi ame* is distinct from the rest of the narratives analyzed here in that the narrative has an extra-diegetic narrator—an omniscient narrator outside all the secondary narratives embedded in the text. Another significant feature is that the narrative viewpoint remains consistently that of the protagonist: the secondary narratives of other characters are presented through his reading of them. The two features can easily lead to the interpretation that the work is a variant form of *shi-shōsetsu*—a variation because the historical author's *own* experience is obviously not projected onto the protagonist's. Instead, Ibuse Masuji speaks on behalf of another historical figure, Shigematsu Shizuma, whose memoir of experiencing the atomic bomb and its aftermath is the *urtext* of embedded narrative—namely, Shigematsu's "Journal of the Bombing." Since the process has been publicized by Ibuse and noted by many critics,[1] *Kuroi ame* might be considered a vicarious *shi-shōsetsu*.

Even those who know little of the making of *Kuroi ame* would not miss the fact that the subject matter—the atomic bombing of Hiroshima and its outcome—is no fiction. *Kuroi ame* may thus be called a historical narrative; it deals with a highly publicized historical incident, about which every possible reader is expected to know something from other sources, if not from personal experience. Thus, the reader can be expected to examine the authenticity of the content by testing it against what is known outside the text.

As I have noted above, however, it is not my purpose to seek a connection between the text and the extra-textual circumstances. To draw upon J. L. Austin's terminology again, I resist the "constative" reading—that is, reading in order to determine whether a given statement is a description of truth or not. Instead, I will attempt to read this historical narrative as a web of interactions of intentions and effects of the narrative performance. Needless to say, this choice is not intended as a criticism or a rejection of the reading of this narrative as representation; rather, my aim is to suggest an alternative.

Faith in the Authenticity of Written Accounts

Manji, the subject of the last chapter, is an example of a narrative in which the question is not whether a given account is truthful but rather how convincing it is. Once we see the entire narration of the secondary narrator as an analogue to Catholic confession or to court testimony—as an effort, that is, to tell "the whole truth and nothing but the truth"—we are likely to be struck by how many different versions can be made convincing for listeners within the narrative.

At first glance, it seems that an entirely different state of affairs prevails in *Kuroi ame*. This text seems determined to privilege writing over speaking and to ascertain conclusively what is true and what is not. As we shall see, the protagonist, Shigematsu Shizuma, tends to write down anything he thinks important to prevent its being forgotten or distorted. He feels strongly that one thing in particular has been misrepresented in oral discourse, and that this needs to be corrected in writing. His niece and ward, Takamaru Yasuko, is reputed to have been exposed to radiation, and this has been an obstacle to her marrying:

> That no suitable marriage was in sight for her was a circumstance simple enough in itself. The real trouble was the rumor. Towards the end of the war, it ran, Yasuko had been working in the kitchens of the Second Middle School Service Corps in Hiroshima City. Because of that rumor, the villagers of Kobatake, over one hundred miles to the east of Hiroshima, were saying that she was a victim of radiation sickness. Shigematsu and his wife, they claimed, were deliberately covering up the fact. (9)[2]

The initial motive for Shigematsu to (re)read, copy, and annotate memoirs of wartime experiences—originally written by Yasuko and himself—is to prove that Yasuko was not exposed to radiation, as has been alleged. In the course of this project, he confronts several general problems surrounding the rewriting of memories.

This transition from particular to general, and from personal to public, seems to be mirrored by the change in the novel's title. As almost every scholarly work on *Kuroi ame* mentions, for the first eight installments of its serialization in the monthly journal *Shinchō*, the work was entitled *Mei no kekkon* (Marriage of the niece). The change is usually seen as reflecting the shift in thematic concerns from Yasuko's marriage arrangements to the aftermath of the atomic bombing, represented by the "black rain."[3] A secondary and subsequent shift, involving the question of how to (re)write memories and orally transmitted tales, occurs as the narrative expands beyond its initial focus on Yasuko and becomes more general. The narrative begins to tell us much more than her whereabouts on and after August 6, 1945—the day on which Hiroshima was bombed—and in the process recurrently questions the authenticity of oral discourse and examines ways of reconstructing the truth in written discourse.

The unreliability of oral discourse in this narrative is partly accounted for by its historical setting: although the primary narrative takes place from June to August 1950,[4] many of the embedded narratives are reminiscences of wartime experiences, especially the events of August 6, 1945. The omniscient narrator who, as has often been noted, speaks predominantly from the viewpoint of Shigematsu, describes how people communicated during those years:

> During the war, of course, "irresponsible rumors" had been forbidden by an army edict controlling freedom of speech, and topics of conversation were regulated by means such as the bulletin-boards that were circulated among the inhabitants of each district. Yet once the war was over, rumors and stories of every kind—of holdups, robbery, and gambling, of army stockpiles and men who became rich overnight, of the occupation forces—ran wild, only to be forgotten again, rumors and stories alike, with the passage of time. (11)

During World War II, the old compound *ryūgen higo* (flowing statements, flying words) was applied especially, if not exclusively, to antiwar or antigovernment remarks, which were the object of censorship.[5] It is important to note here, however, that the narrator's criticism is focused not on the control of free speech by the army during the war but rather on how "wild" oral narration can become. False information must have spread from mouth to mouth, not only in 1940s Japan but also in the era when the term was coined. The "irresponsible" and transient nature of "rumors and stories" is contrasted with the "regulated" nature of texts "such as the bulletin-boards." This is not to say that the narrator intends to defend the war or the militarist government. What this quote suggests is a strong concern with the question of truth and falsity and an associated contrast between written and oral discourse. This initial suggestion that oral discourse is unreliable and written discourse truthful seems to linger throughout the narrative. Both narrator and protagonist are always suspicious of the authenticity of oral accounts. Shigematsu tends to collate them with written records of the same events and to trust the texts rather than the oral accounts where there is any discrepancy.

Shigematsu repeatedly mentions in his journal, entitled "Hibaku nikki" (lit., "A journal of being bombed"; in Bester, "A Journal of the Bombing"), how misleading talk during the war was. The following is from the entry for August 6:

> Conversation had sprung up in various parts of the coach, but I could hear what the man in the linen shirt said particularly clearly. He was complaining that the Defense Section of the Municipal Office had been slack in its duties at the time of the bombing. [. . .] (*The Truth About the Atomic Bomb*, a work by Shigeteru Shibata published later, on the tenth anniversary of the bomb, has something rather different to say: [. . .]. The man in the white shirt, in other words, would seem to have been misled by inadequate information. The author of the book, incidentally, subsequently died of radiation sickness himself.) (121)[6]

Similarly, the entry for August 13:

> The middle-aged man who sat next to me on the train was full of hot news. Item: the Soviet army had not only breached the Soviet-Manchurian border, but had rolled on in a great wave southwards and crossed the border between Manchuria and Korea too. Item: [. . .].
>
> He was a perfectly ordinary-looking man in worn, dark blue breeches, but he had an answer for everything I cared to ask about. (It transpired afterwards, though, that his information was full of errors.) (274)

That Shigematsu trusts what is written over what is told is also evident from the following passage, in the entry for August 11:

> It was a bulletin made by cutting rectangular strips off a roll of paper and pasting them onto the iron. In Hiroshima at such a time, only a newspaper company would have used paper like that.
>
> I copied down one of the notices into my notebook:
>
> "Announcement from H. Q., West Japan Military District," it said. [. . .]
>
> Another sheet bore the following notice:
>
> "August 10, from the commander in charge of the defense of Hiroshima to the citizens of Hiroshima: [. . .]."
>
> The piece of paper adjoining this one declared:
>
> "From Imperial Headquarters: [. . .]."
>
> On the blank space at the bottom of the paper somebody, an idle scribbler presumably, had written in charcoal, "August 10: Soviet Union enters the war." He seemed to have written on the paper when it was already fastened against the streetcar frame. I felt sure, from the crude writing and the use of charcoal—of which there was plenty immediately to hand—that it was not an official announcement, yet I also found it impossible to dismiss it as an unfounded rumor. (198)

Note that Shigematsu, on August 11, does not yet know of the entry of the Soviet Union into the Pacific War, which occurred on August 9. Thus, he cannot tell whether or not the scribbled note represents the truth. However, he feels that, despite the crudeness of the writing, it may be true. The very fact that it is written inclines him to believe in the reliability of its content. And that the information was not far from the historical fact suggests that the narrator implies Shigematsu was right in his judgment.

In the case of the emperor's declaration of surrender, we see a similar situation. The last entry of the "Journal of the Bombing," dated August 15, describes the confusion of Shigematsu's colleagues at the factory after hearing the emperor's broadcast:

> After the meal, a factory hand called Yoda suddenly claimed that the Imperial broadcast had been an exhortation to the nation to fight still harder. Everyone looked tense for a while, and neither the manager nor the staff members made any move to leave the table. Then, abruptly, somebody shouted, "Irre-

sponsible rumor!" Encouraged by this, an official from the works section called Nakanishi declared that he had heard His Majesty say quite distinctly, "Should hostilities continue any further, the final result. . . ."

[. . .] Finally, everybody agreed that Japan had really been defeated. The defeat was confirmed over the radio at five that afternoon. (A printed copy of the Imperial message that I saw later said:

> "The enemy is using a new and savage bomb to kill and maim innocent victims and inflict incalculable damage. Moreover, should hostilities continue any further, the final result would be to bring about not only the annihilation of the Japanese race, but the destruction of human civilization as a whole. . . .") (299–300)

The term "irresponsible rumor" (*ryūgen higo*), mentioned above as an institutional term, reappears as a joke here. Again, Shigematsu's point is not to criticize particular instances of government censorship but to point out how intangible oral reports are in general and how easily an oral report may give rise to any number of interpretations. As we see in the passage above, the consensus that the workers reach is first verified by a further radio announcement. But Shigematsu, characteristically, quotes not from this radio report but from a "printed copy."

The Power of Oral Discourse

On the other hand, orally transmitted information, erroneous or otherwise, is effective in swaying opinion. The embedded memoirs of wartime experience occasionally cite propaganda songs. For example, a memoir on the everyday life of Hiroshima citizens by Shigeko, Shigematsu's wife, reads:

The authorities [. . .] used the movies and phonograph records to popularize a song about the spirit of the neighborhood association. I remember the first verse, it went—

> *Tap, tap, smartly at the door—*
> *Now, whoever can it be?*
> *Just a neighbor's well-known face*
> *When we open up and see.*

Pass the board on with a will—
News for you and news for me. (64)

In discussing the neighborhood association's networking (*tonari-gumi*) via the board (*kairan ban*), Shigeko makes it clear that the militarist government intended to influence the population not only from the outside but also from within, in the guise of friendly communality. The melody and rhythm of the song carry the singer away from the purport of the words and into the pleasure of musical performance. However, when the lyrics are written down as a text, as they are here, the audience is given a chance to peruse the text and its context from the perspective of a detached observer rather than as a rapt participant. And under such dispassionate observation, the political intent behind the cheerful tune becomes foregrounded.

Another example of the textualization of oral performance is the following:

On their way to the steel factory, and on their way home again, they marched together, singing in chorus as they went:

A rifle in your hand, a hammer in mine—
But the road into battle is one, and no more.
To die for our country's a mission divine
For the boys and the girls of the volunteer corps!

The girls were employed at the steel works, turning anti-aircraft shells on the lathes. They worked in two shifts, and the later shift would be turning shells until ten at night. None of them, I am sure, ever dreamed of the horror that was waiting to descend on them. (192)

Again, stripped of the immediacy of performance, the song as text is exposed to critical scrutiny from a detached perspective. In this form, the absurdity or crudeness of the songs, which had gone unnoticed when one was singing them, becomes evident. Performance has a ritual or magical aspect that can numb the mind's critical faculties.

From these propaganda songs (which lose their power when transferred from the realm of oral performance to writing), we can see that a text gains power over its listeners when it is delivered orally. Because of a lack of Buddhist monks to conduct funerals for the many dead, Shigematsu is ordered by the chief of the factory to study scriptures and assume the role of a priest. He accordingly visits a temple and asks for instruction. Though seriously sick, the monk in charge of the temple promptly has some scriptures produced for his reference:

> Much of the sense of the scriptures escaped me, but they were written out with signs showing the general intonation to help one in the reading. The "Threefold Refuge" and the "Dedication" were in measured Chinese phrases telling of the Buddha, the Law, the salvation of all beings, and countless aeons of time. The "Sermon on Mortality" was in gentler, homelier Japanese, in a beautiful language that struck home to the heart. (133)

In the original the last sentence contains the clause: "*hikki shite ite* kokoro ni shimikonde kuru yōna utsukushii wabun de aru" (emphasis added),[7] literally, "a beautiful Japanese writing that struck home to the heart *while I was copying it*." Characteristically, Shigematsu appreciates the beauty of the text in the act of transcribing it but not of reciting it.[8]

In contrast, the priest's involvement with the texts is more grounded in their performative context, as we see in his instructions to Shigematsu:

> "Next comes the 'Amida Sutra,' and while this sutra is being read those present offer up incense. Then comes the 'Sermon on Mortality,' but this time one reads facing the congregation and not the departed one."
>
> To show me how to read the scriptures, he recited the "Threefold Refuge" and the "Dedication," his voice unexpectedly strong as he did so. Listening, I made notes on the correct readings here and there alongside what I had copied. Then he read for me from the "Sermon on Mortality." The room was perfectly quiet save for the monotonous chanting of his voice. (134)

Although sick and bedridden, the priest gets up to sit formally in order to recite the texts in the proper way. The words, which Shigematsu has already copied, are meaningless apart from their ritual context. The power of ritual performance strengthens the feeble voice of the priest, for whom the important thing is not necessarily the words themselves but the act of recitation. Shigematsu does not, however, share the excitement of performance at this point—at least he does not say that he is moved.Rather than practicing recitation in the priest's presence in order to master it physically, he takes notes on how to recite the texts—that is, he inscribes the information in a text rather than in his body. For him, knowledge is confirmed only when written down, whereas the effects of ritual performance are transient and thus easily forgotten.

Shigematsu's appreciation of the beauty of the text is shared by his audience, when he recites it at a funeral at the factory:

> The office girls apparently took turns to come and hear me read. Three of them actually asked me to let them copy the "Sermon on Mortality." When I asked why, one of them said she liked the language. "I want to memorize it," said another. "I want to learn what comes after 'Sooner or later, to me or to my neighbor, on this day or the morrow. . . .'" (135)

Indeed, the office girls are moved not necessarily by Shigematsu's recitation but by "the language" of the text. Three of them, as if following in Shigematsu's footsteps, want to copy the text so as to capture what had "sounded good" to them but had remained in the elusive realm of oral transmission. They want, so to speak, to immortalize the transient words, by writing them down. One of them plans to preserve the words in yet another way—by memorization. In this sense, having procured a written text to preserve oral performance, she now hopes to restore that text to orality. Her desire to memorize shows the inseparability of text and performance. Beautiful though the language of a written text may be, it cannot move audience by itself. The beauty of the text, rather, is realized in the act of recitation, and the hearers wish to re-create this experience by reciting it themselves.

In fact, even Shigematsu begins to experience the magic of oral performance as he grows familiar with the text. Busily conducting funerals for victims here and there, Shigematsu gradually learns the sermon by heart.

> I remembered the other body awaiting me, and set off back along the embankment, murmuring the "Sermon on Mortality" to myself as I went. This time, I got through it without so much as a glance at my notes.
>
> CHAPTER 10 [. . .]
>
> All the way back to the factory I continued to recite the "Sermon on Mortality" to myself, but its precepts had no real meaning for me; in my mind's eye,

like a waking dream, I could still see the tongues of fire at work on the bodies of men. (138–39)[9]

The first half of this quote suggests that Shigematsu has internalized the text. His relation to the text, however, remains mechanical; as becomes evident, it has not taken sufficient root in his mind to transcend the visual impact of the actuality before his eyes.

The text seems to grow more organically part of his mind. Observing skeletons everywhere, unidentified and buried in holes without the proper rites, he cannot help reciting the sermon to himself:

> The body on the improvised stretcher lay in a tight huddle, a Pinocchio with every single pin removed. . . .
>
> All unconsciously, I had started murmuring the "Sermon on Mortality" to myself. Hiroshima was no more. . . . Yet who could have foreseen that its end would be of such horror as this? (162)

That he unconsciously begins to murmur the sermon to himself suggests that Shigematsu has outgrown the stage of mechanical recitation. Without being asked to conduct a funeral, he spontaneously begins to do so. However, the power of this recitation is still insufficient to ward off the horror of the massive scale of death. Shigematsu seems to cling to the sermon in desperation, for lack of something better. The reader cannot overlook the deep sense of despair and helplessness in the last sentence.

The final reference to the sermon shows the peace of mind that Shigematsu has at last attained. He is no longer susceptible to the shock of the disaster. He seems calmly determined to mourn the deaths of the people and to cope with what the future may bring:

> The stones of the river bed gradually gave way to sand, then to running water with a slowly shelving bed. As I took my clothes off, I murmured to myself the "Sermon on Mortality." "Sooner or later, on this day or the morrow, to me or to my neighbor. . . . so shall the rosy cheeks of morning yield to the skull of eventide. One breath from the wind of change, and the bright eyes shall be closed. . . ." (277)

In this passage, Shigematsu repeats the part of the "Sermon on Mortality" that the office girl at the factory had wanted to learn. But in the previous quotation, she cited only the words "Sooner or later, on this day or the morrow." No one has repeated these particular words in the text since then. Thus it is here that for the first time we see the words described as beautiful. The effect of the delayed appearance of these words is to suggest that Shigematsu, who earlier had merely read or mechanically recited the text, has at this point finally internalized it. Here the text and performative context—Shigematsu's state of mind, and surroundings—merge, as do orality and writing. As the text is (re)presented in the very act of recitation, text and performance become one.

Stationery—The Contextuality of Narration Preserved in Texts

In fact, written narrations are not free of context. Although they may be devoid of the context of recitation, they do carry their own marks of contextuality. Frequent references to writing implements, types of paper, and styles of handwriting suggest that the characters of *Kuroi ame* are strongly interested in how their texts are inscribed. Shigeko is the first to give evidence of this concern, as she advises Shigematsu as to how to copy his "Journal of the Bombing":

> "About your journal of the bombing—" she began. "You're going to present it to the library for posterity, aren't you? That's right, isn't it?"
>
> "That's right. The headmaster asked me to. It's my piece of history."
>
> "Then you ought to take more care over it. Why don't you write it out with writing-brush ink instead of ordinary pen ink? Writing in pen ink gradually fades away with time, doesn't it?"
>
> "Don't be silly. It may fade a little, but not as much as all that."
>
> "But I've seen a letter written in ink around 1870, and it had turned light brown. A letter grandfather got from someone in Tokyo." (40–41)

Shigematsu, characteristically, does not believe Shigeko until he has seen the evidence with his own eyes. The two delve into the family's "archive":

> The chests [. . .] contained, among other things, a memorandum kept by great-grandfather and various other documents which he had considered worth keeping. [. . .]

"It's in a writing-box in this chest," said Shigeko. "Great-grandfather must have attached a great deal of importance to that particular letter."

She opened the lid of a chest and by the light of the flashlight drew a bundle of papers out of the writing-box. She undid the ribbon and, from amidst letters from the district office and the district officer, a Red Cross membership certificate and sundry other papers, produced the letter in question. (41)

Apparently, Shigematsu's desire for documentation is inherited from his great-grandfather. Although the passage suggests the layers of history folded inside the text of *Kuroi ame*—a topic I return to below—it also describes the layers that physically cover the document in question and suggests the importance the great-grandfather attached to it. And the more valued the text, the more regrettable it is if it becomes illegible:

Shigematsu unfolded the letter and turned the flashlight on it. It was done by brush in excellent hand, but the writing had faded to a pathetic light brown color:

> Sir:
> I am in grateful receipt of the two ounces of *kemponashi* seeds which I begged of you last year on the occasion of our tour of inspection to your village of Kobatake. [. . .] May I mention that this letter, in accordance with my promise to you at the time, is written in the "ink" commonly in use in the West. (42–43)

As Shigematsu later conjectures, his great-grandfather must have requested that the letter of acknowledgment be written in Western ink. The episode reveals both the great-grandfather's strong interest in writing materials and the irony that this valued document is fading due to the very ink that he had so ardently requested.

Persuaded by this visual evidence, "Shigematsu decided to rewrite his 'Journal of the Bombing' using a brush and Chinese ink. He would have Shigeko copy out again the part already written with a pen, and would himself go on with the rest on Japanese-style writing paper, using a brush" (44). This episode, which at first seems to deal with incidental technical details, is echoed by a passage just before the end of *Kuroi ame*: "The transcription of the 'Journal of the Bombing' was finished. Nothing remained but to read it over and give it a cardboard cover" (300). If

Shigematsu had continued copying his journal in a new notebook, he would not have needed to add a cover. This passage about the cover implicitly refers back to Shigematsu's earlier decision to write with a brush on Japanese paper, and thus functions nicely as a marker of closure for the project in which Shigematsu has been engaged. These "marginal" factors thus contribute to the "central" issue of the narrative act.

The choice of types of paper and writing tools can also reflect the style in which a given text is written. A reminiscence of meals during the war, which Shigematsu requests that Shigeko write, is a good example:

> Shigeko had finished writing her account of what she had called "Diet in Wartime Hiroshima." It was done in brush and ink on handmade writing paper, and it ran as follows:
>
> *Diet in Wartime Hiroshima*
>
> What I'm really writing about here is the food situation in Hiroshima before the bomb, but first of all I must just say something about our everyday lives and the way people behaved. (63)

In the original, the paper Shigeko uses is specified as a letter pad (*binsen*). Although this may seem inappropriate for a document destined for a school library, the choice of paper does match her quasi-epistolary style. She writes as if she is addressing someone specific, employing the courteous style of *-desu* and *-masu* endings rather than the impersonal *-da* and *-de aru* style, which serves as a marker of *genbun itchi* discourse—the (allegedly) objective, third-person narrative. Shigeko, clearly conscious of herself and how she writes, does not pretend to be objective; instead she writes from her own viewpoint and in her own way. The description of her stationery shows that the narrator is aware of the particular kind of contextuality of her narration.

Contextuality in the Text, Denied and Sought

Written narration, then, is not without contextuality, but Shigematsu, for his part, prefers a style of narration purged of contextual factors such as the narrator's subjective judgments, motivations, expected audience, and so forth. This is evident in the conditions he sets Shigeko when he asks her to write on meals during the war:

"Say, Shigeko—" Shigematsu called. "I've an idea! You must jot down some notes about our family's meals during the war. A list of all menus for a week would be better still, but I don't expect you can remember all of them. Just jot them down, will you?—tomorrow, if possible."

"'Menus,' indeed! 'Boiled chickweed with soy, wild leek with bean paste and vinegar'—that's about all there is to write, isn't it?"

"But that's just what I mean—that you should write about the abominable kind of stuff we ate. 'The unbelievably meager diet of the Shizuma family in wartime,' you can call it. Then I can include it in my 'Journal of the Bombing.' Why didn't I think of it before now?" (62)

Shigematsu would prefer a "list of all menus" over structured reminiscences, since a list would be free of the narrator's asides or personal impressions that reminiscences would inevitably entail. He does not feel the need for a story, emplotted by the narrator with intent to frame the information within a certain context so as to have a certain effect on the audience. "A list of all menus," in contrast, would be an objective description of sheer facts, and thus worthy of preservation as a historical document. Shigematsu seems to rank fragments of information, freed from the context in which they are produced by and for specific people, above stories, which involve a coherent ordering of the facts in order that a story may emerge, and which are thus inevitably subjective and unreliable.

Having distinguished literary discourse from oral, Shigematsu goes on to create a hierarchy of categories within literary discourse, from the more objective to the subjective, from those that are independent of context to those that are fully contextualized. Eventually, however, he tells Shigeko that she can choose whatever form she likes, and as we have seen, she adopts an epistolary form rather than a list of menus, which Shigematsu accepts, including it as an appendix in his "Journal of the Bombing."

From the audience's viewpoint, however, no list of "facts" can be context-free. Any given audience cannot help interpreting the facts. It is not the "facts" themselves but the impressions that they inscribe on the reader's minds that matters. Thus, in terms of narrative effects, "facts" cannot possibly be autonomous of the human agents involved in the act of narration. Even the dialogue quoted above suggests that the notion of a form of written narration free of any context is fundamentally illusory. For behind even the most neutrally reported fact lies the narrator's decision to include it, a decision for which there can be no purely "objective" justification. Shigeko hesitates to write because she feels that their wartime meals were so poor that there is nothing noteworthy about them. In reply, Shigematsu argues that the very fact that they were so poor is the reason why they should be documented. Although they disagree about what is worth recording, their exchange reveals one common assumption: to choose to record something is to attribute value to it. And such a choice is, inevitably, subjective.

Even Shigematsu begins to feel that itemized records are incomplete, and that it is unfortunate to be unable to reconstruct a lost story. The scantiness of his knowledge about Mitsuda Taka, one of the persons whose funeral he conducts, disturbs him:

I took down details of Mrs. Mitsuda's background in my notebook, just as Mrs. Ariki related them. If we were going to hold a funeral for an outsider, it was necessary to take down her name, address, status, and the names of any relatives, so as to prevent complications later.

Unfortunately, no one knew much about her background, so I had to content myself with the following scrappy notes:

Concerning the Late Mrs. Taka Mitsuda
Address: [. . .].
Age: [. . .].
Height, etc.: [. . .].
Cause of death: [. . .].
Time of arrival at the works: [. . .].
Family: [. . .].
Possessions Found on Deceased by Person who Tended Her: [. . .].

All the above details were given to me verbally by Mrs. Ariki and the chief cook. (140)

Shigematsu is still text-oriented here, eagerly writing down what is related to him orally. But significantly, here he feels that some coherent account of the person's life is needed to conduct a proper funeral, and he regrets that all he has is a fragmentary list of information. A list of facts no longer seems sufficient to him. Instead, he needs emplotment, although that inevitably involves an element of "subjectivity."

Shigematsu's growing interest in narration not only as a medium for "facts" but also as the product of circumstances is evident in the next excerpt from the "Journal of the Bombing":

> The balustrade of every bridge I crossed bore messages written on pieces of paper stuck on the stone, or scrawled on the bridge with charcoal. The number was astonishing. [. . .] The messages were all simple in the extreme, yet they seemed to convey something of the feelings and circumstances of the people who had written them. I jotted down a few of the sentences from pieces of paper stuck on the balustrade of Motokawa Bridge:
>
> *To Kōnosuke: Come to your Aunt's home at Gion—Father.* (189–90)

Most significantly, a change in his understanding of narration is suggested in his attitude toward another document Shigeko writes for him—the "Diary of the Illness of Yasuko Takamaru." We will examine this text more closely below; what is of concern here are the style in which it is written and Shigematsu's view of this style:

> Shigeko described each of the symptoms to him in detail, and showed him the record of the disease that she wrote down every night before going to bed. She wrote it not as a professional nurse would, but as ordinary diary, with occasional descriptions and personal impressions mixed in with it. Even so, they were soon to find that it was well worth the trouble. (225)

Shigematsu, who had previously expressed to Shigeko his preference for a list of facts over a subjective account, is now ready to admit that "personal impressions" have their own merit. After incessant reading, rereading, writing, and rewriting, Shigematsu comes to understand the contextuality of all narration, oral or written.

Well-intended "Censorship": Yasuko and Absence of Communication

Shigematsu's basic belief that facts should be respected and preserved as they are is shaken by Yasuko's reference to the "black rain" in an entry in her diary following the bombing. If the fact that she was showered with this radioactive black rain after the bombing were to be transcribed in the copy for the go-between, it would defeat the very purpose of copying the relevant portion of the diary—to prove Yasuko was not exposed to radiation and thus to help her get married. Thus, Shigeko, whom Shigematsu has assigned to copy the document, consults Shigematsu about what to do:

> "Mightn't it be better to cut out that one place in Yasuko's diary?" she said. "At the time she wrote it you could still talk to people about the black rain without their getting funny ideas, as nobody knew there was anything poisonous in it. But nowadays everybody knows. If we leave that part in when we send them the copy, mightn't they get the wrong idea?"
>
> "How far have you got with the copying?"
>
> "That's just it, you see—I wanted to ask you, so I waited. Don't you realize—it's down there in writing, about her getting rained on." (33–34)

Shigeko is aware of the difference between the context in which the diary was originally written, and that in which she is now copying it. Like most diaries, it was not initially meant to be read by anyone in particular. Now, however, it is being made public—doubly so, for it is being copied by one reader to be read by another.

Seeing Shigeko's point, Shigematsu thinks to himself:

> Ideally, he realized, it would be better to cut out the account of the black rain as his wife had suggested. But what would happen if, when they sent a copy of the diary to the go-between, she asked to see the original? Somehow or other, Shigematsu wanted to put off thinking about that question until another day. (35)

Shigematsu is caught in a dilemma between authenticity and the intended effect of the document—between what is generally commendable and what is specifically being sought in this case. Unable to reach a decision, he "put[s] off thinking about that question"—and in fact he never comes back to the copying of Yasuko's diary, since the Aono family indicates it is no longer interested in discussing the marriage.

This incident raises another issue: does Yasuko have privacy?[10] Why does she not copy her own diary? Why does she silently give the diary to Shigematsu on her own initiative, implying he should read it, if not copy it?

> Slowly and wearily, Yasuko got to her feet and, taking a large diary from the chest of drawers, handed it silently to Shigematsu. It was her private journal for 1945, and the cover had a design of two crossed flags—the national flag, and the Rising Sun flag used by the navy. During their stay in Senda-machi in Hiroshima, she had written up the day's events in it every evening after supper, using the round meal-table as a writing desk. She had written it up unfailingly every day, however tired she might be.
>
> Her way of keeping a diary was to deal with the day's events in a brief five or six lines for four or five days, then, on the fifth or sixth day, to devote one entry to describing the past few days in greater detail. In this she was carrying on Shigematsu's own method, which he had followed for many years past and which he had taught his niece. [. . .]
>
> It occurred to Shigematsu that he must copy out the relevant parts of this diary of Yasuko's and send it to the go-between. Setting to work, he transcribed several days' entries just as they stood, beginning with August 5. (16)

Although Yasuko's actions seem to suggest that she is willing to let Shigematsu read the diary, there is no indication that Shigematsu asked her permission to copy it and send it to the go-between. Nor is there any mention of Yasuko's knowledge of Shigematsu's parenthetical annotations, or his assigning of Shigeko to do the copying, or of their discussion of whether to censor the problematic portion. All this seems to go on outside the knowledge of the diary's author, the very person whose welfare is at stake.

Indeed, as we have seen, Shigematsu is the one who taught Yasuko how to keep a diary. Yasuko's scrupulous following of his instructions suggests her intellectual dependence on him. In this way, Shigematsu mediates Yasuko's narration even as it is produced prior to his reading, copying, or annotating the text.

This is not to say, however, that Yasuko consults Shigeko or Shigematsu every time a chance for personal correspondence occurs. She does write letters herself and read letters addressed to her alone. The most significant example is her exchange of notes with Mr. Aono, who is interested in marrying her.

> That day, Shigematsu was getting the fire going under the bath when the postman brought an express letter addressed to Yasuko. Yasuko herself had gone to Shinichi to do some shopping. The sender of the letter was Gentarō Aono of Yamano village, the young man who had proposed marriage to Yasuko. This was the first time that he had made any approach to Yasuko other than via a go-between. The writing on the envelope was exceptionally neat. It was not a bad sign, thought Shigematsu.
>
> "Put this letter on Yasuko's desk, will you?" he said, giving it to Shigeko. "I don't know what it says, but the fact he's written at least shows that the young man himself is interested. I wish everything was done in the same way. . . ." (126–27)

Neither Shigematsu nor Shigeko tries to read the letter on Yasuko's behalf. There is thus some indication that they respect her privacy.

Significantly, however, her privacy is shielded not only from her relatives but also from the reader of *Kuroi ame*. The letter is never transcribed or paraphrased in the text, by Yasuko or by the omniscient narrator. Her reading of the letter and her response to it are not presented in the text. The narrative does not develop from her viewpoint, nor in her voice, and the reader is able to learn only what lies within the reach of Shigematsu. Hence, when she acts without Shigematsu's knowledge, the reader is left to speculate, along with Shigematsu, about her behavior and her motives. Without the reader's knowledge, Yasuko seems to have been writing to Mr. Aono and eventually to have told him that she was affected by radiation, most likely before she told Shigeko or Shigematsu. Shigematsu includes the following note in annotation to his "Journal of the Bombing," which is all that the reader learns regarding Yasuko's contact with Mr. Aono: "Yasuko, it seems, has sent the young man a despairing letter saying she has started having symptoms. I wonder whether it was love for him that made her decide on this honest course? Or did she do it in despair, on the impulse of a moment?" (219). We do not know whether Yasuko's lack of candor toward Shigematsu or Shigeko about her thoughts or feelings is a reaction to their interference. The omniscient narrator says:

> Yasuko's illness grew rapidly worse. The blame lay partly with Shigematsu and his wife for not having kept a more careful eye on her behavior, and partly on her own excessive reluctance to confide in them. The trouble had started before the young man's family rejected the marriage, just as the match seemed on the verge of being settled. She had clearly ascribed her symptoms to some disturbance of the feminine organism caused by a mixture of acute happiness and bashfulness, and she had been too shy, even, to have a woman-to-woman talk about it with her aunt. [. . .]
>
> "It was so silly," said Shigeko to Shigematsu, who was out in the garden when they got back from the hospital. "Her keeping everything to herself like that."
>
> "I'm sorry, uncle," said Yasuko. She went past with her head bowed, her eyes on the ground. (220–21)

Yasuko is a paradoxical being who establishes her independence not by expressing herself but by being silent. Indeed, surrounded by well-meaning yet meddlesome relatives, secrecy may be her only weapon in her struggle to think and act independently.[11] Rather than an example of repression, her silence is an action she has chosen to make herself, rather than a passive state imposed upon her by authority. As seems to be the case here, silence does not always mean a surrender to the dominant voice. As the poet and critic Adrienne Rich says, "All silence has a meaning,"[12] and Yasuko's is no exception. It can be a strategic choice to defend one's mind from the inquisitive, if not threatening, audience, or from "detectives," the role that, from kindness and concern, Shigematsu and Shigeko assume. The two are indeed no different from the unidentified people who spread the rumor about Yasuko's condition or the go-between who visited the village to collect information about Yasuko.

Yasuko's silence can also be interpreted as her response to her chaperons' secretiveness as well as their inquisitiveness. Earlier in the story, Shigematsu and Shigeko discuss what to include in the copy of Yasuko's diary they will show the go-between, without consulting Yasuko. Later, when Yasuko is being nursed by Shigeko in a wing of their house, Shigeko tries to communicate with her husband about the doctor's opinions without being overheard by Yasuko:

She closed the shutter behind her and, crouching down on the edge of the veranda that projected into the garden, whispered in Shigematsu's ear.

"Yasuko may not be asleep yet for all we know. Let's have a quiet talk somewhere outside." (222)

Shigeko and Shigematsu, who complain that Yasuko should not have kept her secret from them, are themselves ready to conspire in secret.

Another and even more surprising example of Yasuko's secretiveness is described in the "Diary of the Illness of Yasuko Takamaru," kept by Shigeko as she watches over the patient. In the next section, I discuss the complex embedding of this narrative; for the moment, I focus on the course of events related in the following excerpt:

We decide in the end to let Yasuko herself choose, and after lunch she says she feels well and her temperature is normal, so she goes off to find a doctor. I want to go with her, but do not insist when she says she doesn't need to be accompanied everywhere she goes. [. . .]

About four o'clock, the old man from the general store comes hurrying over to our house.

"We've just had a telephone call from the young lady," he says. "She asked us to give you a message. She's decided it would be best to go into a hospital, the Kuishiki Hospital in the next village. But there's nothing particularly serious, and you're not to worry, she said."

"Are you sure it was her?"

"It was Miss Yasuko."

A bolt from the blue that leaves me stunned. (229–30)

Here, Shigematsu and Shigeko let her have her own way, and Yasuko takes advantage of the freedom. Yasuko is aware of the fact, and her guilty conscience is evident when Shigeko visits her in the hospital:

> The bed is half screened by a curtain. As soon as she sees me, Yasuko starts weeping. She doesn't sit up. "I'm sorry to be so selfish," she says, and buries her face in the pillow. I make no comment, just talk about the broiled eel I've brought, then go on to give her what little information I've picked up about the rearing of carp. I might have saved my breath for all it does to bring her out of herself. (231)

Shigematsu and Shigeko solidify their secret "conspiracy" not to inform Yasuko of anything negative and to encourage her only with good news and diversions.

Keeping secrets is a recurrent motif in the narrative. "The Diary of the Illness of Yasuko Takamaru," a portion of which is quoted above, is not intended for Yasuko's eyes: "For the sickroom, the doctor selected a room in the separate wing where Shigematsu's mother had lived. Shigeko was to do the nursing, and they decided, without telling Yasuko, that Shigeko should keep a daily record of the progress of the disease" (224). Whereas Shigematsu and Shigeko read Yasuko's wartime diary and even consider editing it, Yasuko is denied access to this diary and indeed is never even informed that it exists. Her narration is intruded on, even as theirs is not, although both narratives deal with Yasuko. She is insulated by Shigeko and Shigematsu from the voices of the world. She is confined in a vacuum of narrative contexts, in which she neither speaks nor hears. She not only commits verbal suicide but also is verbally exiled by others.

Memory Eroded by Narration

As should be obvious by now, the narrative of *Kuroi ame* is not monolithic. The primary narrative of the third-person omniscient narrator embeds many secondary narratives, as characters read what has been written or write something new. Some of these accounts, such as Yasuko's wartime diary and Shigematsu's "Journal of the Bombing," are introduced as transcriptions as they are copied and edited by Shigematsu. Others, such as Shigeko's report on meals during the war and Dr. Iwatake's memoir of his recovery from radiation disease, are presented as Shigematsu reads them. An exception is the "Diary of the Illness of Yasuko Takamaru," which is presented neither as it is originally written by Shigeko nor as it is copied and edited by Shigematsu, but as a third party, Dr. Hosokawa, reads it.

Shigematsu plays a crucial role in these narratives, since he is involved in some combination of reading, rereading, writing, and rewriting most of the accounts in the novel. He is active in the story time of the primary narrative—identified with a historical period of time from June to August 1950—and since he is largely concerned in this period with rewriting the past (including his own), the reader follows him through a variety of alternating chronological perspectives. As has frequently been noted, besides reflecting on the past, Shigematsu engages in other activities, such as trying to arrange his niece's marriage, cultivating carp, socializing with people in the village, and helping Yasuko recover from radiation disease. These activities are occasionally described, along with the copying of the journal, fragments of which are sometimes inserted in the main narrative. What is interesting is the way in which these secondary narratives, which appear in *Kuroi ame* only as they are written or read by the novel's characters, end by eroding the primary narrative. The "Journal of the Bombing," in particular, gradually overwhelms the primary narrative, not only by its volume but also by its power.

Here I will examine only three of the intersecting and occasionally bewildering flows of time that coexist in and around specific secondary narratives: the "Journal of the Bombing," the "Diary of the Illness of Yasuko Takamaru," and the journal of Dr. Iwatake. This examination of temporal flows also includes a consideration of the reasons behind a given character's decision to tell, or read, a given story at a given time.

The time at which Shigematsu decides to copy (and edit) his "Journal of the Bombing" can be specified as June 1950:

> This was four years and nine months after the end of the war, when Yasuko had the chance of a match which seemed, if the truth be told, almost too good for her. The prospective husband was the young master of old family in Yamano village. He must have seen Yasuko somewhere, for a tentative proposal was duly made via a go-between. (15)

Shigematsu decides to show his journal to the go-between when a medical certificate fails to convince the matchmaker that the rumors about Yasuko's health are unfounded:

"Shigeko!" he yelled, his frustration finding outlet in his voice. "Get out my journal of the bombing, will you? Shigeko! You remember—you put it away in your chest of drawers, didn't you? I'm going to show it to the go-between, so get it out for me."

Shigeko, who was in the next room and could have heard perfectly well without being shouted at, brought the diary at once.

"I should have had to copy it out decently soon at any rate, if I'm going to present it to the Primary School Library for its reference room. I'll show it to the go-between before I give it to them."

"Surely Yasuko's diary will be enough for the go-between, won't it?"

"Yes, but this will be a kind of appendix to it. Either way, if it's going to go in the school reference room, it'll have to be written out properly sometime."

'Won't you just be making yourself more work?"

"I don't care. It's my nature to keep myself occupied. This diary of the bombing is my piece of history, to be preserved in the school library." (36)

It appears, then, that Shigematsu has two motives for copying the journal. He first conceived of it with the idea of submitting the copy to the library as a historical document for future generations. At this point he finds a more personal motive, when it occurs to him that the journal might facilitate Yasuko's marriage. This double motivation becomes important later, as one of his reasons for copying the journal is made moot.

The first scene in which we see Shigematsu copying his diary is very instructive:

He went and got out a fresh notebook, then set about rewriting his own account of the bombing.

Document entitled "A Journal of the Atomic Bombing," written by Shigematsu Shizuma in a room of a rented house in the town of Furuichi, in the district of Asa, Hiroshima Prefecture, during the month of September, 1945.

August 6. Fair.

> Every morning *until yesterday* [emphasis added] the familiar voice on the radio would say "A squadron of eight B-29s's is proceeding northwards over the sea." (36–37)

The preface tells us that Shigematsu wrote of his experiences of August 6 to August 15 in retrospect, in September 1945—it suggests that the text was written, rather than revised or copied, at that time. The first entry, however, makes us wonder if this inference is correct. This entry, like many that follow it, uses words such as "yesterday" and "today," which suggest that the diary was written day by day, rather than retrospectively in September of the same year, when the whole incident was over. The next quote, from the entry for August 11, reinforces the impression that the diary was kept every day, almost simultaneously with the experiences it reports:

> I excused myself, *as I had to get up early the [tomorrow] morning,* and I went to bed in the small room next door. But I could still hear them talking. [. . .]
>
> [*The above is a description of what happened last night.*] *This morning, I got up early* and started to write a letter for them to take to my mother, but so many emotions crowded in upon me that I gave up the attempt. (188; emphasis added; trans. modified)[13]

This excerpt suggests that Shigematsu stopped writing to sleep and then resumed the following morning. Two distinct references to the same span of time, the morning of August 12, as "tomorrow morning" and then as "this morning" clearly indicate a progression in the discourse time in which the narrator writes. This further suggests that the writing, along with a range of other activities, occurred more or less contemporaneously with the events described, contradicting the impression given in the preface that the writing looks back on those events from the historically distinct time of September 1945.

The three temporal frames of reference—the contemporary one reflected in some of the entries, the retrospective one of the September 1945 preface, and the period of copying and revising the diary in the summer of 1950—are thrown together in a way that often produces ambiguities. The text of the "Journal of the Bombing" presented in *Kuroi ame* includes a number of parenthetical notes, some of which begin with the phrase "gojitsu chū" (note added later). Given that the diary seems to have initially been written in August 1945, either September 1945 or the summer of 1950 would qualify as "later" than the original entries. The notes themselves, however, give little clue as to the time they were written.

More significant for our interpretation of the narrative, the story time of the primary narrative coincides with the discourse time of the secondary narrative. The confusion produced by these overlapping time frames is not limited to readers of *Kuroi ame*. When Shigematsu gets carried away with his writing, absorbed in recollecting the past, he tends to forget that he is living and writing in 1950. He writes more and more, and the text of the journal occupies most or all of many of the novel's chapters, seeming, at times, to continue unbroken from one chapter to the next. Hence, Chapter 3 ends with an entry from the journal, without any reference to 1950, but Chapter 4 begins by bringing Shigematsu back to 1950:

> I feel compelled—unnecessary though it may be—to set down here some of my memories of them, just as they come back to my mind today:
>
> [...]
>
> CHAPTER 4
>
> Shigematsu had reached this point in his copying when Shigeko called from the kitchen: "Shigematsu! Whatever time do you think it is? I'd be grateful if you'd call it a day and come and have your dinner."
>
> "Right! Just coming." Getting up, he went to the kitchen. He had been putting off dinner until now, staving off hunger while he copied out his journal of the bombing by munching home-made salted beans. (57–59)

Here, it is the narrated past in which Shigematsu dwells, and from which he must forcibly be drawn to return to the present in which he writes, eats, and interacts with the people around him. It is easy for the reader, as well, to forget the 1950 setting in which Shigematsu writes, and to become absorbed in reading his old journal rather than the novel *Kuroi ame*. Thus the need for reminders such as Shigeko's interruption at the opening of Chapter 4.[14]

The converse of this is that events in the story time of the primary narrative can affect Shigematsu's writing of the secondary narrative. When he realizes that the go-between has secretly visited a neighbor to ask about Yasuko, for example,

> he felt intolerable pity for Yasuko at being exposed, as it were, to the public gaze like this. There was only one thing for him to do: he must finish copying out his journal of the bombing as soon as possible. He must show it to those concerned, and let them compare it with Yasuko's diary. It was a matter of normal self-respect. By now, he realized, he had been driven into feeling it as his own personal problem.
>
> For dinner, he had a simple bowl of rice mixed with green tea and pickles, then got down to his transcription again. (75–76)

Shigematsu is impelled to write by the hope of protecting Yasuko's marriage prospects, and his impatience to write costs him a relaxed meal—again the motif of eating frames the act of writing. He similarly sacrifices a present pleasure in order to pursue his project of rewriting the past, when Yasuko's prospective husband sends her a letter: "He abandoned the bath and went off to his room. He must get the copying of his 'Journal of the Bombing' completed quickly. He worked at it all the evening, without even going to see the Lantern Festival" (127).

The positive influence of events in the narrative present on Shigematsu's writing about the past, however, eventually ceases. The reason for this is unknown to the reader until Shigematsu reveals something that happened to Yasuko, not in the primary narrative, but in the secondary narrative of the journal. The following note appears in the entry for August 12: "What follows is another addition that I am making now to this diary. I want to make it in order to correct erroneous reports previously included as fact, and for one further reason that I shall explain later" (215). The section introduced by this note was not in the original journal, and quite likely not in the September 1945 version either. The original omission was not deliberate; Shigematsu simply did not know it at the time. But his subsequent reasons for writing down new information are another matter. There are in fact two reasons, as Shigematsu explains. The first is his desire to give a faithful representation of the facts. Another is that he no longer needs to withhold anything, as becomes clear later in this same note:

> Having no need to keep silent any longer, I have described these things, right down to the nurses' superstitious resort to moxibustion, just as they occurred. In the same way, I have set down the exact statistics of deaths among those who wandered about the bombed city.
>
> My reason is that the talks on my niece Yasuko's marriage, which were rapidly approaching agreement, have quite suddenly been broken off by the Aonos—the young man's family. (219)

The reader now understands that Shigematsu may not have been copying and updating the journal according to the best of his knowledge. It seems that prior to this point he may have cut the original text, or refrained from including in notes, any information that might have cast doubts on Yasuko's health. As we saw earlier in his discussion with Shigeko about the black rain, Shigematsu has been torn between the desire to give a truthful account of what he knows, and his intent to prove that Yasuko is well.

From this point on, however, Shigematsu seems determined to relate all he knows and thinks important for a general audience to know, for the copy of the journal is no longer meant for the go-between to read. In a self-reflexive and paradoxical moment, the author, within the text, confesses that his text has lost its primary audience and that he has lost his primary motivation for writing it. To whom, then, is this statement addressed? Shigematsu had two motives for copying the journal. One was to show it to the go-between; the other, to submit it to the school library and make it available to everyone. The first of these motives is gone, but for the sake of the second, the project continues. The primary audience will never read the text, but a secondary, wider audience will. Although this is a pivotal moment in terms of the motivations for writing, Shigematsu's copying and editorial work continues uninterrupted.

From the reader's viewpoint, it is quite surprising that embedded narrative relating events that happened five years prior to the primary narrative should suddenly reveal new information on a character in the primary narrative. Although we may succumb to the illusion of seeing the characters from an omniscient viewpoint, as readers we actually have access to neither Shigematsu's nor the omniscient narrator's knowledge. Such gaps in the information provided in the primary narrative force us to rely more on the secondary, embedded narratives. The secondary narratives in *Kuroi ame* are not always securely framed within the primary narrative. They step out of the frame, reversing the chronological order of discoveries, and inverting the hierarchy between primary and secondary, present and past, as well as between the novel's characters and its impersonal narrator.

Another case in which the narrative present is overwhelmed by the narrated past is the "Diary of the Illness of Yasuko Takamaru," kept by Shigeko, edited by Shigematsu, and read by Dr. Hosokawa. This time the chronological inversions are even more complex, as significant gaps in the reader's knowledge in the narrative present are filled in with information from the narrated past in the diary, which the reader reads along with Dr. Hosokawa.

Before we as readers of the novel see the diary, we learn of a visit by Dr. Kajita, the family doctor, to Yasuko. We also learn that Yasuko moves to a wing of Shigematsu's house, and that Shigeko begins to keep the diary without Yasuko's knowledge. Then we read the following:

> On the second day after she had moved into the separate wing, Shigematsu, going in to put an early-blooming pink in the vase in the alcove, was shocked to see how rapidly she had weakened. Catching him staring at her, she shut her eyes. In the past few days her color had deteriorated badly; the white, transparent-looking skin of her face was a clear sign of anemia.
>
> Shigeko described each of the symptoms to him in detail, and showed him the record of the disease that she wrote down every night before going to bed. She wrote it not as a professional nurse would, but as an ordinary diary, with occasional descriptions and personal impressions mixed in with it. Even so, they were soon to find that it was well worth the trouble. Shigematsu, at a loss for further ideas on the illness, decided in desperation to go and consult the head of the Hosokawa Clinic, where he himself had been operated on, and to take the record with him as the best account available of the progress of the disease. (224–25)

As we learn by collating the primary narrative with the diary transcribed later in the novel, "the second day" proves to be July 25. Two references in the primary narrative to circumstantial events (an afternoon thunderstorm and a subsequent visit by Dr. Kajita) in the primary narrative are also noted in the entry for July 25 in the diary. What is initially unclear is just when Shigematsu shows the diary to Dr. Hosokawa. This is revealed in the following passage:

"But I'll have a look at the diary if you like—tonight, if I can. So I'll keep it for the moment."

The doctor having agreed so readily, Shigematsu left with a promise to come back in a few days' time.

The diary covered a period of seven days, beginning on the first day that Dr. Kajita had come from the hospital to see Yasuko. Shigeko had written it in untidy scrawl, so he copied it out neatly onto ruled paper, altering the style to suit his own taste wherever he felt like it:

DIARY OF THE ILLNESS OF YASUKO TAKAMARU

July 25. Thursday rain. Festival of the Tenjin Shrine. (226)

The diary covers seven days, and the events it relates have already happened in the primary narrative by the time Shigematsu gives the text to the doctor. Moreover, the experiences of these seven days have already been written by Shigeko, and then read, copied, and edited by Shigematsu. But all of this has occurred without the knowledge of the reader. The text appears in *Kuroi ame* only as the doctor reads it. As we read, we learn of an important change in Yasuko's life:

July 28. Fine and sunny. A shower around noon, then sunny again.

[. . .] "We've just had a telephone call from the young lady," he says. "She asked us to give you a message. She's decided it would be best to go into a hospital, the Kuishiki Hospital in the next village. But there's nothing particularly serious, and you're not to worry, she said." (229–30)

That Yasuko has put herself in the hospital, without Shigeko's or Shigematsu's knowledge, comes as a surprise to the reader, for there has been no previous hint of such a change in her life. The last we had heard of her was Shigematsu's impressions of her on his June 25 visit. Our knowledge has not kept pace with that of Shigematsu, Shigeko, or the narrator. Shigematsu and Shigeko knew that Yasuko was in Kuishiki hospital. The reader, however, learns of the fact only by reading the journal that they wrote and edited. Thus, crucial aspects of the story unfold not within the primary narrative of 1950, but within one of the many embedded narratives. The reader's knowledge, in other words, corresponds not to that of the novel's omniscient narrator, nor to that of the secondary narrators Shigematsu and Shigeko, but to that of the audience Dr. Hosokawa.

Another startling discovery is revealed in the following entry, in which the reader learns how Shigematsu decided to consult Dr. Hosokawa:

> *July 30. Fine.*
>
> [. . .]
>
> A sudden squally wind this afternoon. The wife of the man at the watermill [. . .] tells me what happened at Dr. Hosokawa's place in Yuda village. The doctor's younger brother[-in-law], himself a doctor of medicine, was at the army hospital in Hiroshima when the bomb fell. [. . .] Once he even stopped breathing, and seemed to be dead. But Dr. Hosokawa went on looking after him, and in the end restored his health remarkably. (232–33)

Shigeko, then, must have told this to Shigematsu, who decided to ask for the doctor's help. But none of this is related to the reader of the novel. The omniscient narrator simply states that Shigematsu had previously been treated by Dr. Hosokawa (225), by way of introducing the doctor into the narrative. Again, information shared by Shigematsu and Shigeko is withheld until the reader reads the diary entry along with Dr. Hosokawa.

A third embedded narrative is the journal kept by Dr. Iwatake, Dr. Hosokawa's brother-in-law, which is introduced into *Kuroi ame* as follows:

> One day, a letter with enclosure came from the Hosokawa Clinic in Yuda village. Dr. Hosokawa was an elderly man, and the letter had an old-fashioned formality:

> My Dear Sir:
> [. . .]
> I have had my brother-in-law send me the notes which he made on his experiences, and am sending them to you under separate cover. [. . .]
> I should be grateful if, after perusal, you could return the manuscript to me. [. . .]
>
> The account was entitled "Notes on the Bombing of Hiroshima by Hiroshi Iwatake, Medical Reserve." (236–37)

As Shigeko had heard from the woman at the windmill, Dr. Hosokawa's brother-in-law had recovered from radiation disease. The memoir of this person is transcribed for the reader, not as the author wrote it, but as Shigematsu and Shigeko read it. Here again the reader's knowledge develops, not with that of the narrator but, rather, with that of the narratee. In this case, however, the reader is less taken aback by this reversal, since the primary narrative has not focused on Dr. Iwatake.

This document, however, is not presented to the reader neutrally. Shigematsu's response to it is described prior to the transcription of the journal itself, thus forming a frame for it: "Shigematsu read it seated by Shigeko's bedside, exclaiming 'A miracle,' 'Yes, a miracle' over and over again as his reading progressed. 'We must let Yasuko read it too,' said Shigeko. It was all there, just as the woman from the water mill had said" (237). Thus before we read it, we can guess that Dr. Iwatake's journal conveys a message that Yasuko will find encouraging as she tries to recover from the disease.

The intervention of Shigematsu as a previous reader is signaled occasionally, with Iwatake at times the narrator and at other times the object of narration. The text of his journal is sometimes paraphrased, and sometimes transcribed directly. At first, the text is seemingly presented as is:

> The notes began in the following fashion:
>
> My draft card, summoning me to the Second Hiroshima Unit barracks, arrived on July 1, 1945. I hastily set my affairs in order and boarded a westbound train from Tokyo. (237)

The text of the journal continues to be presented as a first-person narration, until it is suddenly interrupted by a passage in the third person: "In due course, Iwatake was posted to infantry unit, where for fifteen days he received basic infantry training" (240). This mode of narration, in which Iwatake is referred to as "he," alternates with one from Iwatake's own perspective. To give some examples: "'It was more like a forced labor camp than a training unit,' Iwatake wrote"; "As Iwatake himself put it, 'His face displayed unconcealed perplexity and disappointment, like a father being bullied by his own son'"; "What follows is Iwatake's own account of what happened"; and, "The following is Iwatake's own account of conditions that day" (241–42, 247). These frequent changes in the mode of narration suggest that the narrative is being presented to us not necessarily in its original context, but in the new context in which Yasuko's recovery is the issue. This shift is effected by Shigematsu as he reads and transmitted by way of the novel's omniscient narrator.

Iwatake did not write the journal with Shigematsu in mind or to suggest remedies for radiation disease. It is Shigematsu who is responsible for the way this journal is "edited" for the reader of *Kuroi ame*, since he reads the journal from his own perspective. Shigematsu focuses on two points—how Dr. Iwatake came to be affected by the A-bomb and the details of Iwatake's fight with the disease and his recovery—the rest of the story is summarized. The context in which the narrative is read controls the presentation of the text itself. Shigematsu's response to the journal is restated at the end of the paraphrases and excerpts, thus framing it within its new context:

> These reminiscences of Iwatake's wife, taken together with Iwatake's own account of his experiences, suggested that no proper treatment for radiation sickness had been discovered yet. The only measures taken in Iwatake's case were blood transfusions and large quantities of vitamin C, with a diet of peaches and raw egg. With him, that seemed to have done the trick—that, and an enormous will to beat the disease. Such, at least, was Shigematsu's conclusion after finishing his perusal of the document. (266)

Another reader of Dr. Iwatake's journal in *Kuroi ame* puts it in yet another context. Shigeko takes the text to Dr. Kuishiki, the director of the hospital in which Yasuko is being treated, thinking it may give him some ideas. She tells Shigematsu of an unexpected response from Dr. Kuishiki:

"The hospital director read the journal while I was there," she said, dabbing inside her blouse to dry the sweat as she spoke. "It was interesting to watch the changes in his expression as he was reading."

"Did he say anything about the treatment? That's the important thing."

"Twice while he was reading he said 'Now this *is* useful.' After he'd finished, he told me that he himself had gone into the Second Hiroshima Unit under the punitive medical draft. He joined the same unit as Mr. Iwatake, on the very same day."

"But he's alive, isn't he?"

"It seems he was sent straight home the same day as a result of the physical examination. He had a plaster cast round his middle at the time, because of caries of the ribs. It's funny what a difference such details can make, isn't it? He was frowning all the time he was reading, and once he swallowed rather hard."

"I'm not at all surprised," Shigematsu said. "I shouldn't wonder if he wasn't fighting back the tears." (272–73)

At this point the reader may recall a passage from Dr. Iwatake's journal that appeared earlier in the novel:

As a result of the X-rays and sputum tests, a number of the new recruits were sent home the same day. Others were sent back because their absence would have left their hospitals without a doctor. I envied them as they shouldered their rucksacks and went off with pious expression on their faces, barely able to restrain their glee. (239–40)

Recalling this passage, the reader can understand Dr. Kuishiki's reaction. Shigematsu read the journal for a very personal reason; Dr. Kuishiki, who begins reading for a professional reason, in the end cannot help reading it personally. The intentions of the writer Iwatake, the transmitter Shigeko, and the two readers are all different, and each affects the way the text is presented.

Old Calendars: Time Recovered

Outside the narrative present of the primary narrative and the various pasts of the secondary narratives, another flow of time intermittently rises to the surface of the narrative—the time marked by old almanacs. The primary narrative periodically gives the date according to an old calendar or almanac and reflects on the significance of the date. The present and the recent and remote past are superimposed, creating the impression that time flows not in a line, but in cycles.

> The Mass for Dead Insects was a rite performed on the day after the festival, when farmers would make rice dumplings as offering to the souls of the deceased insects they had inadvertently trodden on as they worked in the fields. On the same day, custom also demanded that they should return any articles that they had on loan from their neighbors. (71)

Tradition requires that Shigematsu return the things he has borrowed from his fellow villager Kōtarō. On his visit to Kōtarō, Shigematsu comes across the go-between asking Kōtarō about Yasuko. In this way the remote past intrudes into the present. In a more general way, the insect and worm metaphors that Shigematsu employs to describe victims of the atomic bomb seem to find an echo in this Mass for Dead Insects.

The next reference to old annual customs is even richer in its associations with human life, past and present:

> Still Shigematsu continued the transcription of this "Journal of the Bombing." This month, he reflected, was a succession of festivals. The Mass for Dead Insects had gone by already; the Rice-Planting Festival came on the eleventh, and the Iris Festival, by the old lunar calendar, on the fourteenth. On the fifteenth there was the River Imp Festival, and on the twentieth the Bamboo-Cutting Festival. In all these countless little festivals he seemed to sense the affection that the peasants of the past, poor though they were, had lavished on each detail of their daily lives. And as he wrote on, and the horrors of that day came back to him ever more vividly, it seemed to him that in their very insignificance these farmers' festivals were something to be loved and cherished. (101)

Shigematsu not only observes the old customs faithfully but also feels connected to the peasants. For Shigematsu, their customs are not dead, but alive, because he is also one who "lavish[es]" "affection" "on each detail of" his daily life, such as changing the flowers in the vase in the alcove. It is also because they have been inscribed and documented that Shigematsu can revive the customs and connect to the peasants. Memories need to be inscribed and read by future generations. The references to old almanacs seem to reconfirm Shigematsu's faith in documentation.

The following entry is particularly poignant in retrospect, for we later learn that it was soon after the date that Yasuko's marriage plans were ruined:

> June 30th was the day of the Sumiyoshi Festival in Onomichi harbor. In Kobatake village, the occasion was marked by a festival at which lanterns were set afloat on the river to call the attention of the god of Sumiyoshi and invoke his protection against flood. Four small floats, named after the four seasons, were made of plain, unvarnished wood, lighted candles were placed inside them, and they were set afloat on one of the pools of calm water that occurred along the mountain stream. The longer they drifted about the dark surface of the water, the more favorable the omens were said to be. If the autumn float, for example, was promptly carried away out of the pool, it was believed that there would be a danger of floods in the autumn. (126)

It is as if the lantern of Yasuko's fortunes were not afloat long enough to bring a favorable outcome. The reference to the old religious act suggests that Shigematsu's writing has the nature of a personal prayer. At the time of devastation, he cannot take superstitions lightly; indeed, he feels closer to the people of former times who tried to foresee their fortunes through such media.

The last reference to an old almanac weaves together strands of the remote past, the recent past, and the present:

> When he arrived home, Shigematsu got out an almanac—Daigaku Katō's "Treasure Almanac" it called itself—and studied it carefully. It was the seventeenth of the sixth month by the old lunar calendar—the "seventeen-day old moon," when it was appropriate, according to the almanac, to sow certain varieties of

giant radish, kidney beans, and a particular kind of Chinese cabbage on the soil where one's carrots, marrows, and the like had been. A good piece of advice that, thought Shigematsu—it was obviously based on the farmers' experience in taking advantage of the Indian summer that regularly occurred in September. On the same principle, carp fry should do nicely, too. It also occurred to him that there were only three days to go to the anniversary of the Hiroshima bomb, which occurred on the sixth and was followed on the ninth by the anniversary of the Nagasaki bomb.

"I'd forgotten," he said to himself. "Only three days to go. I must get on with copying the journal." (272)

These references to plants and vegetables suggest the recurrence of the seasons, and the perennial revival of flora and fauna. Perhaps Shigematsu's attention to these matters embodies his prayer for Yasuko's recovery. The advice about raising carp relates directly to his life as well, since he has taken up this pastime. The relatively new anniversaries of the Hiroshima and Nagasaki bombings take their place among these timeless, recurring events. And though there is no particular reason why the anniversary of the Hiroshima bombing need serve as the deadline for the completion of the copying of his "Journal of the Bombing," Shigematsu feels compelled to finish the job by that date. The three temporal perspectives coexist in Shigematsu's mind, interconnected by a web of memory and impulse, like ripples on the surface of a pond. As John Treat interprets the passage above:

In this brief passage, the cosmological world of calendrical observances, the inherited lessons of human history, the animal life cycle of carp, and Shigematsu's diary with its need to memorialize Japan's incinerated cities are all juxtaposed to combine in a complex wheel of ritual dynamism. The two atomic bomb anniversaries become old, taking their cue from the "valuable bit of knowledge, learned from the peasants' experience."[15]

Time's flow is neither linear nor homogeneous. It can leap forward or back, repeat, or appear as superimposed layers. Time emerges from the perspective of the observer—the reader or writer of the narrative. A historical perspective may give unique meaning to specific dates and perhaps encourage reflection on the causal relationships among incidents. A mythical view of the past, however, sees affinities and repetitions linking historically distant times. The voices of the measureless past begin to be heard, mingling with the voices of the recent past, and present, creating a consoling and revitalizing cycle.

We began this chapter with the understanding that *Kuroi ame* is based both on an individual's memoir and on a commonly known historical incident. We also saw that the purpose of writing a number of documents within this narrative is to confirm and preserve facts. Given that, *Kuroi ame* surprises us by showing how performative such narratives can be (as they should be). The persistence in specifying writing tools, the postures and other physical attributes of writers and readers, and the activities they engage in or suspend while writing and reading corresponds precisely to Barbara Herrnstein Smith's first group of conditions that shape and constrain narratives, namely, "circumstantial variables," including the "material setting" of the narration (see the Introduction). Her second group of conditions—psychological—is represented in *Kuroi ame* by clear definitions of writers' and readers' motives for writing and reading, their past experiences both in writing and reading and in activities relevant to the narrated content, and the ways they remember and restore or reject their memories. All these suggest that narratives are formed in response not only to exterior contexts but also to the internal contexts of characters' speech acts.

Kuroi ame, unlike other narratives, retells a well-known historical incident, whose significance is not, and should not be, forgotten. The reading in this chapter is intended not to refute such a perception of the work, but to add a new layer to it. We are moved not only by the significance of the incident that is retold but also by the passion and persistence of the writers and readers inside the text, which are so conspicuous in this narrative. It is not simply a conglomeration of secondary narratives connected by the omniscient narrator's remarks. Rather, the text consists of acts of writing and reading by which incorporated texts come into the action. It is with the particular circumstances under which people write and read that texts are generated. Texts are not produced to exist; texts "happen." And it is only when texts "happen" that we get connected to the past—the past does not sit in the text, restored or to be restored. We make it happen, by our acts of writing and reading.

CHAPTER 3

Unmaking the Tableau: Natsume Sōseki's 'Kusamakura' and Gender/Genre Politics

Shame on the folks who would try to attach words to Miki and drag her into the presence of the audience. I'd rather use words to make Miki transparent and erase her. But to assume the minimal responsibility [of the narrator], let me sketch the Miki of the day [of our first encounter].

Like a Painter, Like a Poet: 'I' as Transparent Agent

Kusamakura[1] IS CONSISTENTLY narrated by a first-person narrator who refers to himself by the pronoun *yo*. The pronoun indicates that the narrator is a male intellectual who both is able and chooses to write in literary Japanese. He sounds a bit snobbish, if not pompous for his age (he reveals near the beginning of the work that he is almost thirty years old), in addressing himself in this way, albeit only in writing. (*Yo* uses another first-person pronoun, *watashi*, in conversation, which sounds free of gender and class connotations, although it is, for that very reason, very much a mark of a modern education.) This hint of aloofness proves to match his personality, because, as we will see, he thinks more highly of himself than the rest of the characters in intellectual terms. People of different educational background, class, and gender do speak, but their speeches are first heard by him and then transcribed or represented by him for the reader. Indeed, *yo* assumes responsibilities appropriate for his perceived status.

Also important, although easy to overlook, is that the narrator seems to have conceived his narration as if it were written, if he did not actually inscribed it himself. (Other than a few references by *yo* to poems he has written, there is no self-reflexive reference to the act of writing in the text.) The style of the text clearly suggests that the written discourse is distinct from the oral discourse; this is evident, for example, in the use by *yo* of different first-person pronouns when quoting his own utterances and when narrating. In short, there is no inclination toward *genbun-itchi* in this text; this is not irrelevant to the issue of the genre discussed below in this chapter—this is not a *shōsetsu* but an example of *bun*, or "high literature." Although the text contains no personified trace of an "implied author," *yo* seems the sole candidate for the roles of both narrator and author of this narrative.

To whom does he address this narration? And how is his audience expected to receive it? Although there is no specification of the intended audience or indication of the medium of communication with it, the hyperbolic discourse used in a portion of the narrative makes it reasonable to assume that he is expecting to be heard or read by those with a level of education similar to his own. His narration seems to be almost a soliloquy (or "interior monologue" to use the technical narratological term used by Dorrit Cohn in her extensive exploration of monologues)[2] and is meant to be shared by his own kind, if by anyone. The audience should be understood as either reading the inscribed version of the narrative or hearing *yo* recite the narrative.

However monologic the narrative may appear, *Kusamakura* unfolds as a polyphony of narration, because the first-person narrator is also an intra-diegetic narrator, to use Gérard Genette's terminology.[3] Unlike third-person narratives, the reader knows that the narrator is not a hypothetically neutral or omniscient entity, but someone specific. Moreover, since *yo* lives in the same space as the other characters and engages in other activities in addition to narrating and inscripting, he moves beyond the status of a disembodied voice and takes on a tangible, corporeal presence for the reader. In the words of Ōtsu Chisako:

> The travel of *Kusamakura* begins light-footedly, according to the pleasant rhythm of the painter's words. How comforting the beginning is, which many readers favor and like to recite! As we read along, we are somehow lured by the beautifully performed melody of words into the pleasure of reading itself.
>
> The next moment, however, the reader, or the painter himself, stumbles over a stone in the road and falls out of step.[4]

Kusamakura is indeed famous for the aesthetic appeal of its first few paragraphs, whose five- and seven-syllable clauses mimic the predominant rhythms of traditional Japanese poetry. The reader not only is "lured" into the text, as Ōtsu suggests, but also is lulled into overlooking the agency of narration by such well-established expressions. The narrator's subjectivity grows invisible in literary convention, and we lose sight of him as a tangible, fleshy presence. This mode of narration is in keeping, in its effect, with the traditional style of the text. The narrator, who has not referred to himself yet, speaks in an ostensibly general way, about human nature and the human world. Not until the seventh paragraph does he refer to himself in any way. He talks about what he has learned, at the ages of twenty, twenty-five, and thirty, yet these statements do not convey a concrete sense of the narrator as a human being.

It is only in the eighth paragraph that the narrator makes an appearance, in a literal sense, to the reader.

> It was just as my meandering thoughts reached this point, that my right foot came down suddenly on the edge of a loose angular rock, and I slipped. To compensate for my left foot, which I had hastily shot out in an effort to keep my balance, the rest of me—dropped! Fortunately I came down on to a boulder about three feet across, and all that happened was that my colour-box, which I had been carrying slung from my shoulder, jerked forward from under my arm. Luckily no damage was done. (14)[5]

Ōtsu points out that this passage is a focal point at which the narrator is transformed from a "mind" to a "body":

> The reader of *Kusamakura* comes to encounter the body of the painter who is the narrator for the first time at this point of stumbling. To look backward, the travel presented by the purple prose up to that point is that of consciousness only, so to speak, or of the spirit separated from the body. But the travel in *Kusamakura* is not that of words only. What travels is nothing but the body of the painter.[6]

At this point the reader realizes that he or she can not only read the narrator's words but also watch him act as a human being. This revelation allows the reader to contextualize the things that *yo* says. The reader learns that the narrator's words, although predominant within the text, do not issue from an ultimate authority; rather, they are uttered from a particular position, itself susceptible to changes of perspective or reversals. As Ōtsu suggests, "from the viewpoint of the reader, who is positioned even beyond his reach, the narrator is only 'a figure in the picture.'"[7]

The narrator is visible, moreover, not only to the reader but also to the other figures in the text. Far from being the sole observer, who exists only in observing, he is also an object of others' observation. His vision is limited—as is evident, for example, in his inability to see in advance that the stone in his path is not stable. Things that happen beyond the ken of the narrator are reported in the text as hearsay. The first-person narrative thus becomes heterogeneous, built on the implied polyphony of the speeches of others. The other side of this coin is that the observations of others remain under the textual control of *yo*. Not only does the narrator exert power over the formation of the narrative, but the limitations of the narrative itself are made evident through the existence of this first-person narrator, who speaks (and/or writes) to himself. In other words, the bias of narration, which is theoretically self-evident, is given textual confirmation as well. Since the narrator is not a theological "creator" whose discourse the reader is not entitled to question, but rather a human being, the reader is made aware of the need to contextualize his account and examine it from different angles. The reader is given license to suspect that there may be things left out of the narrative, and that the things that are included may not represent the final word.

This does not mean, however, that there is no hierarchy between *yo* and the others. Indeed, the narrator is preoccupied with establishing his status as a neutral, objective, and detached onlooker in a superior position relative to others, and free of any personal interest.

> In order to appreciate the poetry, you must put yourself in the position of an onlooker, who being able to stand well back, can really see what is happening. It is only from this position that a play or novel can be enjoyed, for there you are free from personal interests. You are only a poet while you are watching or reading, and are not actually involved. (18–19)[8]

Yo likes to stand outside the frame of a picture and observe the figures inside. If such a position could ever conclusively be established, then *yo* would be shut off from any communication with the others. In the interest of avoiding the potentially distorting effects of involvement, the observer must not take part in a dialogue with those he observes.

Yo goes so far as to renounce all movement, as is appropriate to his position as a neutral and detached observer. He wishes to remain simply an eye, without moving or even breathing. He wishes to become invisible, as still and selfless as a "plant":

I knew if I were to think, I would be dragged off along some side track. It was dangerous to move. Had it been possible I would have even stopped breathing. I just wanted to stay there quietly for about a fortnight, as though I were a plant which had pushed its way up through the matted floor. (61)

If he were able to realize his wishes, he would relinquish all control over his surroundings. There would be no communication; *yo* would simply watch, as he does, with his breakfast before him:

On the table was a wooden bowl, and a plate of broiled fish garnished with parsley. Removing the lid, I saw that the bowl contained clear soup at the bottom of which I could see the pink and white of shrimps lying among some young ferns. I thought the colours so lovely that for a while I just sat there staring into the bowl.

'Don't you like it?' the girl asked.

'Oh yes, I like it. I'll eat it in a moment,' I replied; but to tell the truth I thought it a great pity to eat something which was so delightful to look at. (61–62)

The maid's question is only natural. For her, food is something to eat, not just something to look at. For *yo*, however, the delicate-looking soup arouses his desire to observe, rather than his appetite. He wishes to sustain a moment of beauty and delight. He is reluctant to affect the shape of the food, to make it disappear into his mouth, be consumed, or lost.

Metaphor Versus Metonymy: The Disciplines of Text Construction

Once he has established his own position outside the picture frame, *yo* likes to associate the human beings within the frame with images from works of literature and art. This is more than a pedantic gesture, a display of intellectual superiority. In comparing those he observes to artistic images from the past, *yo* negates the temporal dimension of his portrayal. His characters are crystallized into immortal but lifeless images that reject the flow of time and resist change.

At a teahouse on the way to Nakoi, *yo* sees the face of an old woman and thinks it beautiful. But it seems beautiful to him not in its own right, but because it resembles a face in his memory—the face, not of a real person, but of a *noh* mask:

> Two or three years ago I went to see Takasago at the Hosho Noh theatre. I remember thinking at the time that it was like looking at some beautiful painting which had been brought to life. The old man in the play, carrying a broom over his shoulder, took five or six paces along the *hashigakari*, and very slowly and sedately turning his back on the audience, came face to face with the old woman. To this day I can still see their postures as they stood there facing one another. From where I was sitting I was able to see the old woman almost full-face, and I thought how beautiful she looked. In that instant her features were indelibly imprinted on my mind. The likeness between the old woman in the tea-shop and that image in my mind was so striking that it quite took my breath away. (28–29)

The only link between the old woman and the *uba* mask in the *noh* play *Takasago*[9] is the fact that *yo* associates the two "in an instant." This instantaneous association occurs with no chronological or causal relationship to support it.

Shortly thereafter, *yo* overhears the old woman and a horseman named Gembei who drops by the teahouse speaking retrospectively of a bride going to her bridegroom. Without knowing much of the bride and groom, or of their wedding, *yo* is inspired by the mental picture that he immediately draws, and he appends a haiku to it:

> Once again I opened my sketch book. Such a scene as the old woman had described would make an excellent subject for either a picture or a poem. I could visualize her as she was on that day, and with a look of satisfaction I wrote:
>
> Wise is the bride who goes horseback
> After the blossom has all fallen from the bough.
>
> Strangely enough, although I had a clear impression of the clothes, the hair-

style, the horse and the cherry tree, the one thing I just could not picture was the bride's face. I was searching my mind for a face that would fit, trying now one type, now another, when suddenly the face of Millais' Ophelia came to me, and slipped neatly into place beneath the high 'Shimada' hair-style. (35)

"Neatly," indeed. The narrator's definition of the bride, who we later learn is Nami, is indeed too "neatly" made to represent the story of a life behind the face. Whereas the old woman and Gembei recall Nami's past, exchange information about her present life, and are concerned about her future, *yo* is preoccupied with selecting the most suitable artistic image for Nami the bride at the particular moment on the particular day when her horse paused under the cherry tree on the way to her future husband's house. In short, the two local people are engaged in the development of events and incidents—story and plot—whereas the narrator is primarily interested in the instant that produces a poetic image.

The contrast between the modes of observation of the narrator and the old woman is reinforced by the following dialogue, which occurs shortly after the passage quoted above:

'Shioda's daughter is so much like the maid of Nagara,' continued the old woman.

'In looks, you mean?'

'Oh no, I mean the course of their lives.' (37)

The old woman, too, links Nami and the maid of Nagara associatively, rather than causally or chronologically. The two have no relationship, consequential or genealogical. But the old woman associated them because of similarities in "the course of their lives" or their story, whereas the narrator's link is based on their "looks," or the image. The two observers exemplify two different modes of text construction: metaphoric versus metonymic; paradigmatic versus syntagmatic; poetic versus narrational. As Roman Jakobson and the narratologists inspired by him have suggested, narrative is primarily metonymic, since it develops on the basis of contiguity (causal and temporal) between one section and another of the narrative, rather than on the basis of similarity (the metaphoric).[10]

The narrator is conscious of his lack of interest in the chronological development of events as opposed to the paradigmatic, atemporal exfoliation of images. In the following interior monologue, *yo* observes:

Perhaps time was a contributory factor to the happiness which reached right down to the innermost depths of my soul. There was, however, no element in my present condition which had to follow the course of time and develop successively from one stage to another. My happiness was not due to the fact that one event arrived as another left, and was in turn followed by a third whose eventual departure heralded the birth of number four. It was derived from the atmosphere which pervaded my surroundings: an atmosphere of unvarying intensity which had remained with me there in that one place from the very beginning. It is those words 'remained in that one place' that are important, for they mean that even if I should try to translate this atmosphere into the common medium of language, there would be no necessity for the materials which had gone into creating it to be placed in any chronological order. All that would be necessary surely is that they be arranged specially as are the components of a picture. (93)

This passage succinctly outlines the aesthetic ideal of the narrator. The object has to be arranged in the right place, to remain still and unchanged over time. In this picture, misplacement, disturbance, and transformation are all unwelcome.

Insistence on Integrity, Resistance to Heterogeneity

The figures within the frame of a painting cannot move on their own. They must occupy their designated places and properly represent the roles assigned to them. Both the figures and the gaze upon them have to be static, as in a painting or in a poem of a certain kind—not an epic, which requires the flow of time, or a lyric, which is based on human emotions. It is no coincidence that *yo* admires Wang Wei, a renowned classical Chinese poet and painter who drew parallels between paintings and poetry. According to Stephen Owen,

In addition to being a poet, Wang Wei was an important Tang landscape painter (though all the original versions of his paintings have been long lost). In an often-quoted couplet, Wang wrote:

Born in this age, I mistakenly turned out a writer;
in a past life I was surely a painter.

Critics have often remarked that Wang's poetry shows something of the painter's attention to space, shapes, and the pattern of relationships formed by objects in space.[11]

The only acceptable forms of change are cycles, or rhythmical repetitions, which guarantee that objects will remain within a predetermined framework.

After a mild earthquake, *yo* observes a cherry tree and its reflection in a pond:

Outside, the spring rainwater which filled a hollow in one of the rocks had been goaded into drowsy motion by the earthquake. Since, however, the tremors which passed up through the rock had set the body of water moving as a whole, the surface remained unruffled save for a filigree pattern of lightly etched lines. The impression this gave was one of passive activity, so to speak. The reflection of wild cherry blossoms which had hitherto bathed in the pool undisturbed was now spreading and contracting, writhing and squirming in sympathy with the ripples. What struck me as extremely interesting, however, was that in spite of all its contortions it was still clearly recognisable as cherry blossom. (128)

Determined to maintain his aesthetic stance, *yo* deplores any movement that results in a change in arrangement, a disturbance of harmony, and loss of the original (and thus ideal) form:

Were the figure to move, all the great dignity of mankind which is dormant in the enormous potential force would be expressed. In the course of expressing this, however, the figure would be forced to change to some other position in which a different set of conditions prevailed. Admittedly every one of these new positions would have its own original state of harmony. Any new situation would be as ugly as that resulting were a beautiful river to subside suddenly, revealing a bed of mud. It is for this reason that I think that wherever you have motion, you must also have vulgarity. (54–55)

It is evident that *yo* makes such observations on the basis of a series of opposed concepts—harmony versus vulgarity, stillness versus motion, original versus new, the beautiful versus the ugly—and privileges the first element in each pair.

Yo applies a similar theory in observing Nami's face:

> There was absolutely no consistency in her expression. She was a person in whom understanding and bewilderment were living together under the same roof and quarrelling. This lack of consistency in her expression was evidence of the conflicting nature of her feelings, which in turn reflected the instability of the life she had lived. Hers was the face of one who is oppressed by misfortune, but is struggling to overcome it. She was undoubtedly a very unhappy woman. (56)

The authoritative connoisseur determines that Nami's face represents unhappiness, simply because it does not represent harmony, the ultimate criterion of beauty for *yo*. Further, *yo* is as concerned with the contextual vacuum in which the picture is to be placed as with the internal organization of the picture. He requires no explanation of the context in which the picture came about. For him nothing exists outside the frame of the picture—not even his own selfhood—for his subjectivity is hypothetically nonexistent. When the forces for contextualization seem irresistible, he resolutely sweeps them away.

When the narrator is invited to tea by the abbot of the Kankaiji Temple, he happens to be seated next to a cousin of Nami, Kyūichi, who will soon join the Japanese imperial army fighting the Russians in Manchuria. Although one might expand on the significance of this occasion in any number of ways—by discussing the historical import of the Russo-Japanese War, by glorifying Kyūichi as a nationalistic hero, or by romanticizing the encounter of two young men close to Nami—*yo* instead comments: "Fate had brought these two together under the same roof, and then had left without a word" (121). To ascribe an encounter to fate is to abandon any search for a reason behind it. Fate is not accountable for its actions; it negates causal or chronological order and thus does not narrate—it simply *shows* "without a word," or claims to show the truth, rather than tell a story. It is thus mimetic (showing) rather than diegetic (telling), to apply the Aristotolean-Platonic contrast between the two modes of verbal communication.[12] Fate does not claim to speak on behalf of any particular agent; it is faceless and positionless. It reveals a single crystalline view and silently annihilates other voices; in this it resembles the presentation of a "picture" or a "poem." The contextuality of narration is negated by the introduction of Fate, and static "truth" is left to occupy the entirety of the scene.

When such an aesthetic stance is challenged, *yo* feels uneasy and acts quickly to reassert his status as a proper artist. The first night *yo* spends in Nakoi, at the residence of Mr. Shioda, Nami's father, he dreams of the legendary figure of the maid of Nagara, and of the two men who pursued her. The maid's image is somehow juxtaposed with that of Ophelia, which automatically entered the picture of Nami as a bride that *yo* had in mind:

> There was the maid of Nagara with her long billowing sleeves, riding a white horse through a mountain-pass, when out leapt the two men Sasada and Sasabe, and each tried to drag her off. Suddenly the girl turned into Ophelia; first climbing out along the branch of a willow, and then being carried away by the stream, singing in a beautiful voice. Thinking to save her, I grabbed a long pole and ran after her along the shore of Mukōjima. She did not seem in the least unhappy, but smiling and singing drifted with the current down to wherever it would take her. I put the pole on my shoulder, and yelled, 'Hey, come back! Come back!'
>
> At this point I awoke to find that I was damp with perspiration under the arms. What a strange conglomeration of the poetic and commonplace that dream had been, I thought. [. . .] It must have seemed to a man who had devoted his whole life to the arts, that not to be able to dream beautiful dreams was a sign of still being shackled by the world. I felt that most of my last dream was material for neither a picture nor a poem. (43–44)

Yo feels ashamed of himself for having had a dream inappropriate for a painter or a poet. It is not only "strange" and "conglomerat[e]," a challenge to the ideal of homogeneity, but also crowded with dynamic motion and commotion: "leapt," "drag," "climbing," "being carried away," "grabbed," "ran after," and "yelled." These verbs and verbal phrases suggest little of the harmony or composure that *yo* values.

Despite *yo*'s determination to reject any disturbance to homogeneity, harmony, and stillness, *Kusamakura* unfolds how his poetic and "artistic" discourse is eroded by others' prosaic and "colloquial" discourse. His text, which would occur in the void of a single first-person narrator, is infiltrated by hybridity.

Hierarchizing Literary Genres: 'Kusamakura' as a Meta-novel

In meta-fictional moments in *Kusamakura*, *yo* reflects on literary genres, privileging poetry over the novel and classical over modern and Chinese over Western literature. To him, the first element in each pair is freer of human affairs and emotions and thus preferable.

> Within the space of these few short lines, a whole new world has been created. Entering this world is not at all like entering that of such popular novels as *Hototogisu* and *Konjiki Yasha*. It is like falling into a sound sleep, and escaping from the wearying round of steamers, trains, rights, duties, morals and etiquette.
>
> This type of poetry, which is remote from the world and its cares, is as essential as sleep in helping us to stand the pace of twentieth-century life. Unfortunately, however, all the modern poets, and their readers too for that matter, are so enamoured of Western writers, that they seem unable to take a boat and drift leisurely to the realm of pure poetry. [. . .] Moreover, this type of poetry appears to me to be more palatable than *Faust* or *Hamlet*. (20–21)

Here, *yo* refers in an explicitly negative way to two Western works of drama, rather than to any Western novels, as representing modernity and worldly concerns. But he also mentions two best-selling *shōsetsu* from the Japan of Sōseki's day, both of which deal with romantic love and the social and economic constraints from which lovers suffer. This suggests that the narrator is also distancing himself from the Western-inspired genre of the psychological novel.

This implicit critique of the psychological novel has struck some readers, among them Leslie Pincus, as self-contradictory: "The narrator reserves his harshest criticism for the genre under whose sign he himself has so unwillingly appeared, the Western psychological novel and its Japanese imitators."[13] Is *Kusamakura* a psychological novel? If so, it is a defective one; it does not delve into the depths of its characters' psyches and lacks a tightly knit plot. Moreover, as far as authorial intent is concerned, the text was not written as a novel in that sense. In the conversational essay "Yo ga *Kusamakura*" (My *Kusamakura*), Sōseki characterized his work as follows: "I wrote *Kusamakura* in a sense entirely opposite to what is generally called *shōsetsu* nowadays. All that I intended is to give the reader a certain impression—a beautiful impression. I didn't have any purpose other than that. Therefore, there is no plot or development of incidents."[14] If we can take Sōseki at his word, *Kusamakura* is not a *shōsetsu*—the genre comprising, in Pincus's words, "Japanese imitators" of "the Western psychological novel"—and thus would escape the criticism of self-contradiction.

Sōseki's genratic consciousness has been noted by, among others, Karatani Kōjin. Karatani argues that Sōseki's earlier works do not fit the category of the *shōsetsu*, not because he failed to write *shōsetsu*, but rather because he did not try. A scholar of English literature, conversant with novels from Jane Austen to George Meredith, as well as with a range of works in other genres such as poetry and drama, Sōseki could not have been ignorant of generic distinctions:

> It is important to note that Sōseki began [his literary career] with *bun* [literary discourse]. [. . .] He was fully aware that the novel, i.e., "Literature" was progressive and predominant not only in Japan but also in the West. It is nothing but an anachronistic self-definition to write *bun* with such a consciousness.
>
> A tentative definition of *bun* is a writing prompted by a consciousness that aims at preserving language. [. . .] If one is to define *bibun* not as a form of writing but as a consciousness that does not address the object but rather the language itself, then Sōseki was always conscious that he wrote *bun*.
>
> The [Japanese] naturalist writers did not have such a consciousness of *bun*. They considered language as a transparent medium [to express something].[15]

In the context of his view of Sōseki as an idiosyncratic writer, resisting the then-canonical Japanese naturalism, or *shizen shugi*, Karatani characterizes Sōseki's linguistic and genratic consciousness as the joint product of a premodern tradition of *bun* and a knowledge of Western literary history.

Maeda Ai's interpretation is in keeping with Karatani's, insofar as he does not believe that *Kusamakura* defines itself as a novel or *shōsetsu*. Maeda, however, is more explicit in identifying, behind the genre-consciousness of the text, Sōseki's critical intent: Maeda reads *Kusamakura* as a work of literary criticism in the form of fiction. *Kusamakura* refers to literature self-reflexively not only in *yo*'s manifesto as putative author—in which he distances himself from authors of emotion-oriented literature—but also in his "lecture" on how to read a novel. Indeed, *yo*'s conversation with Nami in the following excerpt constitutes a prescription of how to read a novel. Whereas Nami thinks it only natural to read a novel from the beginning to the end, *yo* suggests another way of reading:

> 'What's wrong with reading a novel from the beginning?'
> 'Because if you start reading from the beginning, you have to go on to the end.'
> 'That seems a peculiar reason. What's wrong with reading to the end?'
> 'Nothing at all, naturally. I do it myself when I want to read the story.'
> 'But if you don't read the story, what else is there left?'
> 'Yes, she's a woman all right,' I thought, and decided to test her a little. (123)

The narrator's disparaging comment on a female reader, his view of femininity itself as determining that particular reader's attitudes, and the authoritative gesture he makes as a man of letters are all in keeping with the colonizer / male chauvinist attitude I will discuss below. Here, I focus on his theory of reading. What *yo* is hinting at here is his view that a novel should be read as an anthology of poems. The effect of such an approach would be to fragment the story; the text would not make sense or reveal any conclusion. In return for this loss of coherence, however, the reader would appreciate momentary beauty at each textual "moment," as if gazing at a picture or a "poem." For this narrator, the paradigmatic dimension of prose is far more important than the syntagmatic dimension, or the story, which Nami sees as the sole reason for the existence of a novel.

The mode of reading that *yo* recommends is intrinsically related to the aesthetic distance he wishes to maintain from the human emotions and human affairs around which novels tend to organize themselves and to his detachment from the genre itself, as this famous passage suggests:

> 'And because I am an artist I find any passage of a novel interesting even when it is out of context. I find it interesting talking to you—so much so in fact that I'd like to talk to you every day while I'm here. I'll even fall in love with you if you like; that would be particularly interesting. But however deeply I were to fall in love with you it would not mean that we had to get married. If you think that marriage is the logical conclusion to falling in love, then it becomes necessary to read novels through from beginning to end.'
>
> 'What an inhuman way of falling in love you artists have.'
>
> 'Not "*in*human"; *non*-human. It is because we read novels with this same non-human, objective approach that we don't care about the plot. For us it is interesting to flip open the book as impartially as if we were drawing a sacred lot, and to read aimlessly at wherever it falls open.' (124)

Yo's mode of reading seeks after momentary, coincidental, and unschematized events, a quest that he describes as "non-human" (*hininjō*) in terms of the degree of the reader's psychological involvement in the story. One might also call this type of reading "poetic," in the sense that the reader is concerned more with the image of a given moment than with the progression from one moment to the next.

Maeda considers the "poeticization" of the novel that *yo* is aiming at not a shift from one genre to another, but an anti-modern reformation of the novel:

> By this nonchalant conversation, Sōseki tried to present a critical statement about the novel inside a novel. Though it has not been much noted that *Kusamakura* is a novel which contains within itself criticism of the genre of the novel, the scene of the novel reading undoubtedly resonates with the following passage of "My *Kusamakura*," the text of an interview.[16]

Maeda then quotes the passage from "Yo ga *Kusamakura*" we looked at above, and continues:

> "A novel without plot or development of incidents" reminds us automatically of the disputes over the "plot in the novel" between Akutagawa Ryūnosuke and Tanizaki Jun'ichirō, but Sōseki was furnished with the perspective of reader-

response criticism, which the two younger writers lacked. Drawing on Lessing's *Laokoon*, a radical question into the form of the novel as a temporal art occurred to Sōseki.[17]

Maeda's reference to the famous dispute in 1927 between two of the most acclaimed storytellers of modern Japan about whether the novel should have a plot succeeds in showing how progressive Sōseki was in his critical awareness. The contrast between the temporality of the novel and the spatiality of poetry or painting is made evident not only in *yo*'s statements as putative author but also in his conversation with Nami on their respective attitudes as readers.

From Impersonal 'I' to Private 'Eye'

Even as *yo* challenges, both as narrator and as reader, the temporal and syntagmatic development of the novel with his vision of the spatial, timeless, and paradigmatic expansion of poetry, his high-brow "poetic" discourse is constantly eroded by the colloquial and prosaic discourse of the local people in and around Nakoi. The literary discourse of *yo*, austere and free of disturbing elements, is threatened, along with his privileged position, by the other characters in the mountains. *Kusamakura* seems open to a "postcolonialist" reading, as it maps out positions along a polarity running between the urban/central (the Tokyoite) and the rural/marginal. The contrasting values on this scale are played out not in the sense that *yo* loses battles with native residents as he tries to persist in his own theory but rather that, seemingly without being aware that a change is taking place, he finds his own position eroded by the impulses he had resisted: active involvement in the affairs of others and in developing and reading stories.

The self-acclaimed detachment that *yo* boasts of at the beginning of the narrative offers one advantage that is neither noted nor explicitly desired—an advantage, in fact, that seems in blatant contradiction to the unconcern for human affairs that *yo* claims for himself. The position of disinterested observer would allow *yo* to collect information about the people around him without making his own personal life the object of scrutiny. He enters the mountains as nobody in particular—a requisite condition for a "private eye." No one in this other world must know him or know of him. It is significant that no other Tokyo intellectual is present in the story. The barber is from the city, but is from a different social stratum. Nami says she used to live in Tokyo, but only temporarily. *Yo* is the only one who belongs to the intellectual milieu of the center, and it is he who is most truly set apart from the rest of the people in the mountains.

This, of course, must have appeared to *yo* as a great advantage. Should he have come across another of his kind in Nakoi, his privilege as outsider would be shared, and the pleasures of that status correspondingly diluted. If he were to travel with a friend from the same class and district, as male characters often do in other works of Sōseki (e.g., *Gubijin-sō* [Poppies; 1907]), he would refrain from investigating the personal lives of the locals, for fear of dismaying his companion with his indecent curiosity. As it happens, however, this narrator is "alone" in the mountains. He encounters only locals, who are not of the same intellectual sphere, and thus qualify to be potential figures in his sketches. They may be viewed, not necessarily as fellow human beings, but as objects to be depicted.[18] Indeed *yo* is what Trinh T. Minh-ha calls an "anthropologist-nativist," who claims to disclose "a confidential truth" about other people "that requires commitment from both the speaker and the listener." Although, as we saw, there is no "listener" who shares the same cultural background with *yo* inside the text, his literary discourse is meant for an equally educated audience, which is expected to enjoy with the narrator the "gossip" about "them"—the local people of Nakoi. The "colonized" or the "native[s]," who are silenced and not expected to hear what *yo* has to say about them, are "scientifically comprehended" through "a pretentious discourse" of *yo*, the "anthropologist" or "the industrialized man." *Yo*'s observations of Nakoi residents thus leave them "barely present in [their] absence" and attempt to determine them as the "subject of discussion" rather than the "discussing subjects."[19]

Yo hierarchizes cultures and treats the local people as "noble savages"—"noble" in that it is evident that he has a certain kind of aesthetic appreciation of the people in and around Nakoi. The most conspicuous example is his conversation with the barber and his subsequent reflections on that figure. The conversation between the intellectual and the working-class man is not only dissonant in terms of vocabulary and diction but also hilariously incongruous, as the two speak at cross-purposes. *Yo* succeeds in making the barber realize that he is off-track but fails nonetheless to put him back on track. For example, when the barber begins to tell *yo* about how Nami embarrassed a young priest who fell in love with her by revealing his romantic advances to his mentor-abbot, the barber says:

> 'I'm so scatter-brained, I'm always jumpin' from one topic to the other, without ever finishing a story properly. Well, as I was sayin', the priest fell head over heels in love with her . . . .'
>
> 'What priest?'
>
> 'Why, the young novice up at the Kankaiji temple.'
>
> 'You haven't mentioned anything about a priest yet, novice or otherwise.'
>
> 'Haven't I? I'm so terrible hasty. Well this priest was good-lookin' in a rugged sort of way. 'E was the type that women go for. Anyway, he fell head over heels in love with old Shioda's daughter, and at last wrote a letter to her.—Hang on a minute. Did he write, or did he go and see her? No, that's right, he definitely wrote her a letter. Now where was I?—Er. . . What was I goin' to say?—I'm a bit mixed up. Oh, yes. That's right, that's what happened. It came as a shock see, so. . . .'
>
> 'Who was shocked?'
>
> 'The woman, of course.'
>
> 'When she received the letter?'
>
> 'If she was the sort of woman to be shocked by a letter, it would at least show some modesty. But she don't shock that easy.'
>
> 'Then who was shocked?'
>
> 'Why he was when he went to tell her he loved her.'
>
> 'But I thought you said he didn't tell her.'
>
> 'Give me strength. You got it all wrong. It was gettin' the letter that was a shock.'
>
> 'Then it must have been the woman who was shocked after all.'
>
> 'No, no, no, the man!'
>
> 'Well, if it was the man, it must have been the priest.'
>
> 'That's right it was the priest.' (78–79)

The barber is somewhat lacking in lucidity and is self-contradictory. He makes many grammatical mistakes, and frequently interrupts himself with questions, for his memory is not reliable. As he admits himself, moreover, his story is also elliptical, leaving out important pieces of information that *yo* has to try to get by asking questions. The barber's speech is a perfect example of oral discourse.

After a few pages of transcription of this dialogue, *yo* suddenly inserts a few paragraphs of narratorial comment. These are written in a highbrow diction, with many Chinese locutions, in clear contrast to the barber's colloquialisms. Then, *yo* evaluates the barber as an aesthetic object against the backdrop of the spring scenery:

> This scenery and the barber had nothing at all in common, and had he been a more forceful personality, strong enough to impress me as powerfully as my natural surroundings, then I would surely have been struck by the incongruity of their co-existence. Fortunately, however, he was not a very striking character, and for all his brash city ways, and his caustic wit, he was certainly no match for the perfect harmony and serenity of Nature. He had persistently tried to shatter this aura with his interminable chatter, but so formidable was his opponent that he had been reduced to the level of a barely perceptible speck of dust hovering in a ray of spring sunshine. (81)

Although the barber, with his vulgarity, does constitute a disturbance in *yo*'s "picture" of spring scenery, *yo* reasons to himself that this disturbance is too small to upset the picture. In fact, *yo* seems to suggest that the noisy barber in fact serves to remind him of the perfect beauty of the scenery before his eyes. Here, *yo* not only draws a contrast between the "poetic" and the "prosaic" but also hierarchizes the two on a scale of values.

In a similar vein, *yo* listens to the old woman at the teahouse telling the folktale of the maid of Nagara and her two lovers.

> Just before her death she composed this poem
>
> From leaves of autumn flushed with love,
> A pearl of dew shakes free
> And falls to shatter on the earth beneath.
> So too must I, to flee Love's stifling folds
> Drop from the world.

> I had little thought when I arrived at that small mountain village, to meet an old woman such as this, and to hear from her such a charming tale, told with such old-fashioned elegance. (37)[20]

Yo's response to this retelling of the legend with its embedded *waka* poem reveals his prejudice against the quaint, the rural, and, perhaps, the female. He had not expected to find literary refinement in the mountains, or in an elderly person, or, moreover, in a woman. His surprise notwithstanding—and in line with his prejudices—*yo* reconfirms his superiority to the amazing lady. When *yo* notes the final words of the old woman, "'This is more than enough for the tea, thank you very much.—Mind how you go,'" uttered in response to the "silver ten sen coin"[21] he has thrown on the table, his economic superiority is highlighted as well. *Yo* is a man of power, both economic and linguistic, imposing his system on a local population without wealth or education.

Yo addresses Nami in a similarly patronizing vein, though to a lesser degree. When he reads Meredith's novel aloud to Nami, she keeps interrupting him with questions on the identities of characters, their whereabouts, and the process by which they have come to that point—in short, the context. As we saw above in a different context, this irritates *yo*, who does not read the text for the sake of the story.

> 'Who are the man and woman in the story?'
>
> 'I don't know either. That's what is so interesting. It doesn't matter what their previous relationship might have been. Don't you see that there is something interesting about that situation, which is independent of what comes before or after, just as there is about you and I being together here?'
>
> 'I suppose so. They seem to be on a boat.'
>
> 'It's immaterial whether they are on a boat or the top of a hill; just take it as it's written. And before you ask why, as I can see you're going to, I'll tell you. It's because if you probe for these details you turn yourself into a detective.' (125–26)

The word *tantei*, or "detective," that *yo* uses here reveals a split between the narrator's self-definition and his real identity. It is understandable that, wearied of human emotions and human affairs, *yo* must detest detectives and counsel others against acting like them. Sōseki uses the term "detective" repeatedly in *Kusamakura*, as well as in other works.[22] The vexation that this class of people inspire in the narrator of *Kusamakura* is evident in the following tirade, delivered in an ostensibly humorous tone:

> The world is full of the most terrible people who are importunate, coarse, niggling and, to crown it all, brazen. [. . .] They will set a detective on your tail for five or ten years to reckon up how many times you break wind, and they think this is Life. Moreover, they will, on occasion, leap out in front of you and impart such unsolicited information as, 'You farted x number of times'. When they tell you this face to face, you may listen and make a note of it for future reference. But the refrain, 'You farted x number of times' often comes from behind. (146)

Yo is also prompt to give an anti-civilization lecture to an abbot who naïvely expresses an interest in tools of civilization such as steam trains:

> 'If you live in Tokyo for any length of time, you have your farts reckoned up.'
>
> 'How do you mean?'
>
> 'If that were all it wouldn't be so bad, but they do such unwarranted things as examining your backside to see whether your anus is triangular or square.'
>
> 'Ah, you mean the sanitary inspectors, I suppose.'
>
> 'No, I do not mean the sanitary inspectors. I mean detectives.'
>
> 'Detectives? Oh, I see, the police. What in the world is the use of the police? Are they really necessary, I wonder?'
>
> 'Well, artists certainly don't need them.' (154–55)

Artists do not need them, insofar as they are uninterested in other people's business. Obviously, *yo* left Tokyo to get away from snoops; he has come to the mountains, where, presumably, he is free from such inquisitiveness.

Ironically, however, *yo* turns out to be a private eye himself, playing the very role that he tries to teach the locals to avoid. The revelation occurs early on in the text, after he has spent only one night at the Shiodas' house. As a young maid serves him breakfast, *yo* begins his "investigation" by questioning her persistently about the identity and activities of the woman who had been roaming outside his room the night before—Shioda Nami:

'There's a young lady living here, isn't there?' I asked, replacing the bowl on the table.

'Yes, sir.'

'Who is she?'

'The young mistress, sir.'

'Is there another older mistress then?'

'There was, but she died last year.'

'And the master?'

'Oh yes sir, he's still alive. The mistress is his daughter.'

'The young lady, you mean?'

'Yes, sir.'

'Are there any other guests?'

'No, sir.'

'Just me then?'

'Yes, sir.'

'What does the young mistress do with herself every day?'

'Well, she sews . . .'

'And?'

'She plays the samisen.'

This was both unexpected and interesting.

'What else does she do?' I asked.

'She goes up to the temple.'

Another unexpected answer. I found this samisen playing and going to the temple rather strange.

'Does she go there to pray?'

'No sir, she goes to see the priest.'

'Is he learning to play the samisen then?'

'She goes to see Daitetsu, sir.'

[. . .]

'[. . .] By the way, why does she go to see Daitetsu?'

'I'm afraid I don't know.'

'What else?'

'I beg your pardon?'

'I mean, what other things does she do?'

'Many other things.'

'Such as?'

'I don't know.' (62–64)

Despite his earlier protestations of detachment from human affairs, *yo* cannot help digging into Nami's personal business and is intrigued by some of the details. *Yo*'s questions on who, what, and why and the maid's replies or failures to reply occupy a page and a half in the original. In his lecture to Nami, which occurs later in the text, the narrator says that she should not ask "why," lest she become a "detective." In this lengthy "interview" of the maid, however, *yo* is no less a detective than Nami is in the book-reading scene. Again, a quotation from Trinh T. Minh-ha might well be an interpretation of *yo*'s behavior:

> The anthropologist-nativist man who seeks to perforate meaning by forcing his entry into the Other's personal realm undertakes the desperate task of filling in all the fissures that would reveal the emptiness of knowledge. On the lookout for "messages" that might be wrested from the object of study, in spite of its opacity or its reticence in sharing its intimacy with a stranger, this knowledgeable man spends his time spying on the natives, in fear of missing any of these precious moments where the latter would be caught unaware, therefore still living.[23]

Whether anthropologist or detective, *yo* seems eager to collect information about Nami from the locals, in order to reconstruct her life story.

A conversation between *yo* and Gembei the horseman as they sit beside the Kagami pond makes us wonder if *yo*'s apparent absorption in the timeless beauty of nature and in the immortality of literary figures is indeed genuine. *Yo* begins by asking Gembei:

> 'By the way, this pond is extremely old, isn't it? How long has it been here, for heaven's sake?'
>
> 'For ages.'
>
> 'For ages? What do you mean by ages?'
>
> 'Well, from a very long time ago.'
>
> 'A very long time ago. I see.'
>
> 'I know it's been here for years and years, because this is where the Shioda girl drowned herself.'
>
> 'Shioda? At the hot spring, you mean?'
>
> 'That's right.'
>
> 'You say she drowned herself? But she's still alive and well.'

'No, no, no. I'm not talking about the present Mr. Shioda's daughter. This was years ago.'

'Years ago? How long?'

'Oh, way back in olden times.' (139–40)

Here it is *yo* who sounds more like a detective, eager to determine the dates of events and identities of those involved, rather than a poet, who enjoys associating images from ancient Chinese poetry with those before him, no matter how great the historical distance between them. *Yo* here seems completely caught up in the linear flow of historical time. It is rather Gembei, a man presumably of lower rank and less book learning, who is able to appreciate the mythical time of the "poet," in which the verification of time and persons is not an issue.

Yo, for his part, feels that folktales and gossip alike are as noise to a musical melody, disturbing the wholeness of the nascent picture: "I had come to this pond to paint, but it was clear that if I continued musing and listening to such tales I would not produce a solitary picture even if I remained here for days" (141). Such introspection does not, however, prevent *yo* from listening to gossip, especially about Nami's private life. His interest begins with his attempt to pin down, define, and crystallize the image of Nami as a bride. Gembei the horseman and the old woman at the teahouse chat about Nami's present, worry about her future, and become absorbed in recollections of the Nami of the past. As soon as the horseman leaves the teahouse, *yo* begins to question the old woman regarding Nami:

'Who was the bride he brought on horseback through the mountain pass?'

'Shioda's daughter. He mounted her on his grey, and led her down to the town at the time of her marriage.—My, how time flies. That was, let me see, five years ago.'

[. . .]

'She must have been very beautiful,' I said, 'I wish I'd been here to see her.'

'Ha, ha, ha. You can still see her now. If you stay at the hot-[s]pring resort, she's bound to come out to welcome you.'

'[Is she back at her parents' place then?] It would be wonderful if she were still wearing those long billowing sleeves, and had her hair done up in a high "Shimada" style. . . .'

'Well, perhaps she'll dress up for you. Ask her and see.' (36)

As observed above, in this scene *yo* is preoccupied with the momentary beauty of the image of Nami the bride, whereas Gembei and the old woman focus on her sad fate. But what is important in the present connection is that Nami herself comes to hear of this conversation between *yo* and the old woman.

As a traveler from nowhere, at least as far as the locals are concerned, *yo* should be able to remain neutral, free from responsibility, and uninvolved in others' business. Indeed, it is evident from the following excerpt that he had not expected his conversation with the old woman at the teahouse to reach Nami's ears. When *yo*, in conversation with Nami, mentions the night she walked to and fro in the hallway outside his room, clothed in her wedding kimono, Nami asks for a return favor. This surprises *yo*, who had assumed Nami could not have known that he had wanted to see her in these clothes:

'[. . .] That business of the wedding gown . . .' I began accusingly.

'Will you give me a nice present [in return for the favour I did for you]?' she asked suddenly in a coaxing voice.

'Why?'

'Well, you said you wanted to see me in my bridal gown, so I put it on for you specially.'

'Who, I did?'

'I was told that a certain artist who had come across the mountains was kind enough to make such a request to the old lady up at the tea-house.'

I could not think of any appropriate reply to this. (128–29)

When *yo* asks "Why?," he is unaware that Nami knew of his desire and that she is hinting at an exchange of favors. He is unwilling to admit that he wanted to see her in her wedding outfit even when Nami tells him she knew of his desire. It is only when Nami cites concrete details that he is left with nothing to answer. He had not expected the old woman at the teahouse to have told Nami of their chat.

There is another instance in which the locals' information network is hinted at, although so subtly that the narrator gives no indication whether he has noticed it. *Yo* chats with the barber, who relates to him how Nami embarrassed the novice priest by embracing him in front of the abbot (see above). The barber goes on to mention Nami's elder brother and the *honke*, or "main branch of the house."

> 'Stands to reason. I mean she don't get on with her elder brother, who lives in the [main] house, either.'
>
> 'Is there a [main] house?'
>
> 'Yes, it's up there on the hill. You ought to go up an' pay 'em a visit some time. There's a lovely view from up there.' (76)

Yo does not have a chance to visit them till close to the end of the story. After Nami discovers that *yo* has been clandestinely observing her meeting with her ex-husband, *yo* follows her to an unfamiliar place:

> 'There's a beautiful white-walled house down there on the hillside where all the orange trees are. It's nicely situated. Who does it belong to?'
>
> 'That's my elder brother's house.' (173)

In the original, Nami says: "Are ga ani no ie desu"[24] rather than the expected "Are wa ani no ie desu." The difference between the two particles *ga* and *wa* in these two alternatives is subtle but crucial. *Ga* suggests that the speaker knows that the information that follows in the sentence (in this case, *ani no ie*, or "my elder brother's house") is familiar to the addressee, whereas *wa* suggests that the speaker believes that the addressee has no previous knowledge of it.[25] To render explicit by paraphrase what is implicit in the original, what Nami is saying is: "That is my elder brother's house, of which I understand you have already heard."

As we have seen, *yo* collects information on Nami not only by interrogating the locals, but also by spying on her. Nami, however, becomes aware of this activity as well. *Yo* even hides himself as he observes Nami meeting with an unidentified man, who later proves to be her ex-husband. Typical of "detectives," he seems to concentrate on doing his job well, convinced that "the more indiscreet the research, the greater the value of its revelation."[26] He never displays any sense of guilt for his voyeurism, as the man of letters he claims to be should, until Nami uncovers *yo*'s hidden role of detective:

> She was coming towards the place where I was lying, and soon was standing immediately in front of me.
>
> 'Sensei. Sensei,' she called.
>
> Oh Lord, that's done it, I thought, and wondered when she first realised that I was there.
>
> 'Yes, what do you want?' I asked, raising my head above the quince and losing my hat in the process.
>
> 'What on earth are you doing there?'
>
> 'I was lying down composing poetry.'
>
> 'Don't tell fibs. You were watching what happened just now, weren't you?'
>
> 'Just now? Just now, over there, you mean? Well, yes. I did just have a peep.'
>
> 'Ha, ha, ha, ha. You should have had a long look.'
>
> 'Well, to tell you the truth—I did.'
>
> 'There you are, you see! Oh please come out from among all that quince.'
>
> I obeyed meekly. (171)[27]

All along *yo* has been watched by Nami, when he thought he was watching her unnoticed. The privileged position of the "anthropologist-nativist" is usurped by the native. The detective is investigated by the suspect, and the objectifier is objectified. The panopticon, in which *yo* was the watchman in the center, turns out to be an amphitheater with him as the spectacle and the locals as spectators.

Subversive Intent: The De-colonization of Nami

Beyond the information she derives from the local information network, Nami also seems gifted with clairvoyance, which allows her to look directly into the psyche of *yo*. Although she is one of the natives and, with the other local residents of Nakoi, subverts the "colonial" authority of the Tokyoite *yo*, Nami's subversion also suggests feminist resistance to male narrative authority. A powerful piece of evidence for this is the way in which she comes to know of his fantasy about Ophelia.

I believe it was Swinburne who, in one or other of his poems, described a drowned woman's feeling of joy at having attained eternal peace. Looked at in this light Millais' 'Ophelia', which has always had a disturbing effect on me, becomes a thing of considerable beauty. [. . .] There is certainly something aesthetic in the sight of a figure being carried along by the current free from all pain, whether it be floating, beneath the surface, or rising and sinking by turns. (102)

This must represent an interior monologue by *yo*. No one could have heard it, although the passage following it suggests the possibility that Nami is physically proximate:

Still floating in the bath, I composed the following eulogy on drowning.

> Beneath the earth where all is black as night.
> The drenching rain seeps down
> And frost descends to chill;
> But in spring water,
> Buoyed by waves or lying in the deep,
> There is no pain.

As I lay there absently murmuring the lines over to myself, I heard the sound of a samisen. (103)

From the comments of the maid who served the narrator breakfast, we know that Nami plays the samisen (63). When Nami enters the bathroom, the narrator observes, "the samisen had stopped playing at some time or other" (105). Thus it may have been Nami who was playing as *yo* sang to himself. If so, she may have caught some words of the song.

Except for this hint, there is no evidence that Nami could have had any knowledge of the narrator's fascination with the motif of a peaceful, watery death. Nonetheless, to judge from the following passage, Nami knows that *yo* wants to paint his own version of Millais's "Ophelia":

'Will you paint a beautiful picture of me floating in the water?—Not in any pain you understand—but floating easily and peacefully in my eternal rest.'

'What!?'

'Aha! That startled you. Go on, admit it. That startled you, didn't it?'

The woman slid gracefully to her feet, and having walked the three paces to the door, paused on her way out to look back at me with a trace of a smile hovering about her lips. For a long time I just sat there gazing vacantly into space. (130–31)

Nami knows, then, of the narrator's fantasy, and knows, furthermore, that *yo* would be surprised if she were to hint at her knowledge—in other words, she knows of his ignorance. If knowledge is power, Nami is doubly empowered over *yo*.

It is true, as Seki Reiko suggests, that Nami stays within the male fantasy that associates her with the legendary feminine role of Ophelia: "In contrast to *I Am a Cat* in which the historical notion of gender is visibly inscribed, *Kusamakura* realizes a situation that neutralizes the conventional constellation of males and females, while nonetheless being bound to the already constructed notion of gender."[28] Nami cooperates with *yo* to the extent that she does not refuse to play the role that he ascribes to her. On the other hand, she has chosen to perform the role, and hence she is not necessarily enslaved to *yo*'s fantasy. As Ōtsu puts it, unlike Ophelia and the other archetypal female figures with whom she is compared, Nami chooses to "display" (*miseru*) attributes of Ophelia rather than "be observed" (*mirareru*).[29] As Judith Butler maintains, "gender proves to be performative—that is, constituting the identity it is purported to be. In this sense, gender is always a doing, though not a doing by a subject who might be said to preexist the deed. [. . .] There is no gender identity behind the expressions of gender; that identity is performatively constituted by the very 'expressions' that are said to be its results."[30] Nami is responsible for the performance, not *yo* or any authority (Nature?) that he tries to represent. If she plays feminine roles such as Ophelia, it is not because she is essentially female but because she chooses to be feminine.

Nami's subversive intent becomes more obvious and also textual. An earlier occasion, in which *yo* finds revised versions of haiku he has written, may be even more telling of the reversed power relationship between him and Nami, although she is not explicitly identified as the author of the new poems:

I wondered how those poems that I had feverishly scribbled down last night would look in the cold light of day.

> Aronia blossoms decked with dew:
> Fool would he be who shook the bough.
>
> I was surprised to see that beneath this someone had written:
>
> Aronia blossoms decked with dew:
> Disturbed as dawn's light perches on the bough.
>
> This had been written in pencil, and was therefore rather difficult to read. The writing looked too firm to be a woman's, and too graceful to be a man's. I looked at my next poem.
>
> The shadows of a spring night blend and blur,
> But there beneath the blossoms I feel sure
> A woman stands.
>
> Underneath this had been written:
>
> The shadows of a spring night blend and blur
> And blossoms and woman are as one.
>
> Fox or woman, woman or fox
> That figure in the misty moonlight standing?
>
> This had been amended to:
>
> Lord or lady, lady or lord
> That figure in the misty moonlight standing?
>
> Had these been written in an attempt to copy my poems, to improve them, or as an expression of agreement with my taste? Were they foolish, or were they meant to make me feel foolish? I just did not know. (57–58)

The topic of *yo*'s haiku is Nami, whom he had glimpsed hovering outside like a ghost. The writer of the new versions is presumably Nami. What is happening here is a meta-fictional paradox, in which the object is objectifying the subject. *Yo*'s interior monologue at the end suggests that he is concerned with the intellectual hierarchy between himself and the author in pencil. Obviously, his sense of his own superiority, until then unshaken, is threatened; he would very much like to hang on to his pride as the lone intellectual in an area otherwise inhabited by "noble savages." Unfortunately for him, however, there is another educated person, who happens to be a woman, and who appears to be more confident, if not more skilled, in composition—the very mark of literariness and education.

The gender distinction that *yo* attempts, and fails, to make here between male and female handwriting is suggestive of Nami's androgynous temperament. In another passage, she poses an even more radical challenge to conventional notions of gender. When *yo* mentions the maid of Nagara, to whose fate the old woman at the teahouse had likened Nami's, she states that she would not have reacted in the same way to the situation of being simultaneously pursued by two men. Her strategy for resolving the difficulty calls into question not only the parallel between herself and the legendary maiden but also conventional ideas on the relations between men and women:

> 'But that's a sad song isn't it?'
>
> '[Do you think so?] I would never have sung a song like that. In the first place the maid of Nagara gained nothing by throwing herself in the deep river, did she?'
>
> 'No that's true. Well, what would you have done in her position?'
>
> 'What would I have done? I should have thought that was quite simple. I would merely have taken both Sasad[a] and Sasabe as lovers.'
>
> 'What both of them?'
>
> 'Yes.'
>
> 'That's very clever.'
>
> 'Not at all. It's the obvious thing to do.' (71, modified)

A love triangle involving one man and two women would not be expected to end in the man's suicide; the suicide of the maid of Nagara is thus a specifically "feminine" solution. The "obvious" solution for a man would be to take both women as concubines, and this is the solution that Nami opts for. In the original, "lovers" is *otoko mekake*, or "male concubines," which highlights even more clearly the subversive nature of Nami's proposal.

Nami not only challenges commonsense notions of gender relations, but actually surpasses *yo* in the application of his own aesthetic theory—or rather, proves so adept at practicing this theory that, by contrast, *yo* appears to have renounced it. When the two arrive at Nami's elder brother's house, they spend a long time looking at the natural surroundings.

> The garden which faced south, contained three or four hemp-palms, and was bordered by a mud wall. Sloping away beyond this was an orange orchard. Sitting down on the edge of the verandah, O-Nami said, 'It's a lovely view. Look.'
>
> 'You're right, it is lovely.'
>
> The room bordering the verandah was shut off by a line of shōji. I listened, but nothing stirred within. O-Nami showed no signs of announcing our arrival, but seemed quite content just to sit on the verandah and look at the orange orchard below. I thought this strange, and wondered what had brought her here in the first place. (173–74)

Here it is Nami who seems better qualified to be a poet or painter. Whereas she is "quite content" simply to "look at" the beautiful scenery, *yo* cannot help wondering *why* Nami has come to visit her brother's house, and *why* she is lingering outside without even announcing her arrival. By this point in the text, the narrator has completely reversed his stance on appreciating natural beauty. He had observed, on an earlier walk in the mountains:

> I felt not the slightest trace of pain or sadness[. . .].
>
> I wonder why this should be? I suppose the reason is that, looking at the landscape, it is as though you were looking at a picture unrolled before you, or reading a poem on a scroll. The whole area is yours, but since it is just like a painting or a poem, it never occurs to you to try and develop it, or make your fortune by running a railway line there from the city. You are free from any care or worry because you accept the fact that this scenery will help neither to fill your belly, nor add a penny to your salary, and are content to enjoy it just as scenery. (18)

Sitting outside the house of Nami's elder brother, however, *yo* wants a reason for being there; he finds something strange in being "content to enjoy" scenery for its own sake. Thus, *yo* proves self-contradictory, inconsistent, prone to change—the very characteristics he had tried to exclude from his aesthetics.

Becoming a Story?: Conflicting Interpretations of the Picture's Final Touch

In light of Nami's usurpation of the narrator's authority near the end of the narrative, one might wonder if the taut "poetic" nature of the text has at that point ceded place to "narrativity." Many have tried to answer this question by analyzing the last section, in which Nami and *yo* join others in seeing off Kyūichi and Nami's ex-husband at a railroad station outside Nakoi.

The shift of scene from Nakoi to the town, along with a notable change in Nami's expression, seems to invite the reader to conclude that the text has become a structured story with a conclusion. Among those who have argued for this interpretation is Leslie Pincus:

> "In that instant," concludes the narrator, "the picture in my mind received its final brush stroke." We are left with the fictional consummation of a fictitious painting, the final touch on a fragmented and disrupted story. The descent down the mountain back into the world of historical time signals one last shift in the balance between art and life, between aesthetic detachment and involvement in human affairs.
>
> The expansive aspirations of the inner text have been tested with irony and excess, humor and tragedy; and in the end, though the inner text is neither effaced nor recontained, it recognizes the claims of historical time, of human engagement, and of novelistic emplotment.[31]

Pincus thus focuses on the (re)emergence of civilization, the (re)placement of the text in historical time, and the completion of the picture in the mind of the narrator as evidence of "narrativization" of *Kusamakura*.

Although she reaches a similar conclusion, Ōtsu's approach is clearly different from that of Pincus. After examining a number of references to characters' bodies, especially *yo*'s, she sees a special significance in *yo*'s final gesture to Nami:

> It seems that the end of *Kusamakura* depicts the "[disappearing] train" and the woman's "look" inside our eyelids, and conveys the sound of the painter's

"whisper[ing]" voice to our ears, and the touch of his hand on [Nami's] shoulder to our hands, as if to narrate the story that has hidden itself underneath the surface of the text.

"Compassion" is not a type of expression that is easily focalized. Lacking a strong intent or plan to display, it is hard to depict in a "picture." [. . .]

The painter, who has by this point learned to feel in his own body the strain of the other, makes it possible not only to create a patchwork of high points of condensed performance, but also to reconstruct the undulations of living emotions of a woman named Nami. To focus attention not only on the instances where performance has been planned, but also all the points of the undulating line should mean to look at the other as a multifaceted human being, without distorting her.

The painter pats Nami on her shoulder, touching the body of the other for the first time. At this moment, perhaps the two have succeeded in transcending both the "human world" and the "in-human world," as well as the past they have been caught up in, facing each other as human beings, and standing, as self and other, within hands' reach.[32]

Though perhaps convincing in its interpretation of human behavior in sexual terms, this conclusion seems a bit hasty. To touch someone is not necessarily an expression of intimacy; rather, it may confirm the sense of distance that makes it safe to touch the other's body. To cite a counterexample, both Nami and *yo* are careful to avoid skin contact when they observe the garden at the time of the earthquake.

'A pheasant,' I said looking out of the window.

'Where?' asked the woman relaxing still more and leaning her body against me. Our faces were now almost touching, and I could feel the breath coming from her delicate nostrils lightly brush against my moustache.

'Objectivity, remember?' she said firmly, and quickly sat upright again.

'Of course,' I replied promptly. (127–28)

This scene takes place after *yo* has seen Nami naked. The tension that springs from an awareness of the potential for romantic involvement serves to keep the two apart, rather than pulling them closer. Thus, bodily contact can be interpreted in opposite ways: as the confirmation of intimacy or of distance.

I tend to agree, rather, with Maeda Ai, who draws the opposite conclusion from *yo*'s mention of a "picture"—a recurrent motif throughout the text—which seems to suggest *yo*'s return to the original framework:

> The picturesque poem that the painter idealizes, which does not necessitate the arrangement of materials in chronological order, is homologic with the whole text of *Kusamakura*, which "dispenses with a plot or event." If Nami in the scene of the "conversation on literature" is assigned a role of the "implied reader," then this monologue of the painter reveals his role as the "implied author." At least, the last remark of the painter who discovers, unexpectedly, an expression of "pathetic beauty" ["*aware*" in the original (171); in Turney's version, "compassion" (184)] in Nami's face as she sees off her ex-husband leaving for the continent—"it was at that very moment that the picture in my mind received its final touch" [Turney 184]—suggests that the text of *Kusamakura* closes with the "atmosphere of unvarying intensity which had remained with me there in that one place" [Turney 93]. The first impression that the painter had derived from Nami's face was a lack of "consistency" [Turney 56]. [. . .] The screen that has been left vacant is suddenly made available for the completion of a picture at the moment that this expression of pathetic beauty shines in Nami's face. [. . .] It seems as if a variety of images of Nami, recurrent in the text, were intentionally varied and deferred so as to be summoned at this last moment. In this sense, the text of *Kusamakura* has a cyclical structure, with the end internalizing the beginning.[33]

In contrast to Pincus, Maeda thinks that the completion of the picture closes the long search for the ultimate image of Nami. Rather than ending the story by introducing a temporal dimension to the narrative as Pincus argues, this closure brings us back to the beginning. The process of search leading to the discovery of the right image is not really a temporal one, but rather a paradigmatic expansion, a catalogue of images parallel with one another, that never unfold into a story. Karatani also argues against the ultimate shift from poetry to narrative in the end: "Indeed, *Kusamakura* not only lacks a 'plot'—it actively rejects one. Sōseki rejects a plot at the very moment when the mysterious person of Nami looks as if she were read as a plot or a story. The reality that surrounds Nami is once again reduced to a 'picture.'"[34] As Pincus points out, the departure from Nakoi and the suggestion of historicality seem at first to show the story finally beginning to flow out of the reservoir of mythical time, and ending with a definite sense of conclusion. The narrator's last remark, however, stops the story, bringing back the timelessness of poetry and tableau.

Karatani, as we saw in the discussion cited above on the author's consciousness of genre and on *Kusamakura*, thinks the final touch proves Sōseki's resistance to the predominance of the *shōsetsu*, by resorting anachronistically to the genre of *bun*. Along the lines of Karatani's argument, Maeda Ai, while fully aware of Sōseki's position in the Japanese literary tradition, proposes an even more radical view of *Kusamakura* vis-à-vis contemporary Western literature:

> Regardless of conventional-sounding labels such as *yoyū-ha bungaku* [literature at leisure] and "haiku-esque *shōsetsu*," *Kusamakura* harbors an intent of experimentation with deconstruction of the story and abolition of linear temporality in the text, which is rather reminiscent of [Stéphane] Mallarmé's *Un Coup de dés* and [Michel] Butor's *Mobile*. In other words, *Kusamakura* tries to convert a digital text, to be read along the axis of temporality, into an analog text, which expands along the axis of spatiality.[35]

Although such a claim may seem out of keeping with the historical context in which Sōseki worked, in fact the author himself also expressed an intent to break a new ground in the genre of the novel, as the concluding remark of his "Yo ga *Kusamakura*" shows:

> So if this haiku-esque *shōsetsu*—strange as that name might sound—were to materialize, it would open a new territory in the world of literature. No such novel has been produced in the West, either, to set Japan aside for a moment. For a work of this type to appear in Japan would mean that a new movement in the novel had originated in Japan.[36]

Not only on the level of reader-response criticism but also on the level of authorial intent, we could read *Kusamakura* as a postmodernist text, questioning the norms of prose fiction, as well as the canonicity of the genre of the novel altogether—and simultaneously as a postcolonialist attempt at dethroning Western literature.

The combination of the literary style of discourse in the narrator's statements and colloquial styles in which his dialogues with others are given seems to suggest the incongruity, if not the incompatibility, of the oral and written languages—not *genbun itchi* but *genbun fu-itchi*. This does not necessary confirm the conventional hierarchy between the high (written) and low (oral) discourse. Rather, the narrator's sense of a ladder, whose top rung he imagines his place is to be, is challenged by others. They accomplish this usurpation of the perceived superiority of the narrator by speech acts—chatting—which are significantly made absent in the narration, which is presented as though written. The framing of *yo*'s text by the textualized fissures within his text effectively undoes its completeness and highlights its context-boundedness.

CHAPTER 4

Thinking Beauty, Unseeing Scholar: Displaced Narrative Authority in Mori Ōgai's 'Gan'

The manuscript is still in my possession. I don't know why I keep it; I have just lost the reason to return it to the Writer. It was written in a synoptic style, about "he" and "she"—and it is interrupted where "he" arrived in a hotel "she" had been staying in, and spent some hours with her. When I first read this, I wondered if this "he" was myself. Why in the first place did the Writer call me to the hotel by telegraph?

Reading 'Gan' Through Genette

THE NARRATIVE STRUCTURE OF *Gan* (1911–13, 1915)[1] has intrigued scholars both in Japan and in the United States. Stephen Snyder, for example, deals with the structure—"order" and "voice" in particular—of the narrative, drawing on the ideas of Gérard Genette.[2] Earlier, in Japan, Takemori Ten'yū pointed out the discrepancy between what could roughly be translated as "story time" and "discourse time," to use Genettean terminology,[3] in the text, as well as the manipulative hand of the first-person narrator, who is not only a character within the story time but also the encoded author writing the text thirty-five years later.[4] The complexity of the narrative structure is, indeed, one of the distinctive features of this novel—a structure that involves a number of distinct but mutually interrelated speakers, a narrator who speaks both inside and outside the main narrative, and many scenes that include acts of writing, narrating, and observing. Drawing partly on structuralist analyses of narrative, I focus on the multilayered and multifaceted contextuality of narration in *Gan* in this chapter.

The opening sentence of *Gan* reveals much about the context in which narrative is generated within the text:

> This story happened long ago, but by chance I remember that it occurred in 1880, the thirteenth year of Emperor Meiji's reign. (OG 13)

It is made clear from the outset that *Gan* is a first-person narrative, recounted in retrospect after the passage of many years. This brings to mind features of *Kokoro* and *Kusamakura*. First, there will be limitations and biases in the narrator's viewpoint. Second, the narrator will tell what he (*boku* is a gender-specific first-person pronoun, like *yo* in *Kusamakura*)[5] did, saw, or heard in a past from which he maintains a certain distance and perspective—and we are thus given notice that the narrator will be representing different temporal perspectives and assuming various roles, as agent ("character"), narrator, and perhaps, as proves to be the case here, encoded author.

The retrospective mode in *Gan* gives rise to a distinct array of relationships between narrative and story, narrator and narratee, and the subject and object of reading. The narrator enjoys a privileged understanding of the events he narrates and is better able to tailor the mass of information garnered at the time to make the narrative more appealing. "Story time" and "discourse time" are thus clearly differentiated, unlike the case in *Kusamakura*, in which events are related in the narrative present. The retrospective narrator occupies a privileged position in relation not only to his former self (who is present in the story as a character) but also to the reader, whose knowledge he is accordingly able to manipulate. Again, this is in contrast to *Kusamakura*, in which the reader "travels" with the narrator and shares his experiences of wondering, being surprised, and gaining new knowledge. Hence the reader comes to know the heroines of the two stories in quite different ways; Nami's mind remains a mystery to the reader as well as to *yo*, whereas Otama's mind is presented in such a way that the reader might sympathize with her.

What complicates the structure of *Gan* is that, as many have noticed, *boku* is not the only narrator. He may always remain the encoded author, as I explain below, but at times he yields his position as narrator to an impersonal, omniscient narrator, who represents the speech of all the other characters except Okada. Unlike the narrator of *Kusamakura*, who is consistently present as an interviewer of others and a transcriber of their speech, *boku* is elusive, and the act of "interviewing," if it does indeed take place (as it apparently does in the case with Otama, from whom *boku* says that he heard a part of the story), is not reflected in the text. Instead, other characters speak to each other and to themselves, with no account, explicit or implicit, of how the transcription was made.

As noted in the surveys of Stephen Snyder, Dennis Washburn, and others, this inconsistent narratorial stance has been criticized by both Japanese and American scholars as proof that Ōgai's fiction—if not the whole of modern Japanese fiction of that period—is structurally deficient and underdeveloped. However, the occasional use of the omniscient narrator enriches the narrative; not only can the story then portray many different social strata of people who live in the same area and around the same time as *boku*, but also the discourse of the privileged male intellectual can be placed in perspective, if not objectified, by the presence of speeches otherwise off limits to him. *Boku* as encoded author relativizes the authority of *boku* as narrator, in showing things he does not see or sees differently. In other words, the reader is shown conversations among the Other, such as those that must have taken place beyond the narrator's ken between Nami and the old woman at the teahouse, Gembei, and the barber in *Kusamakura*, complementing the narrator's discourse and completing the narrative. Nor is this all. Paradoxical as it may sound, the incomplete authority of *Gan* narrator's screens him from the kind of subversive reaction to narrative control deployed against *Kusamakura*'s *yo*.

How much credit can we give the narrator of *Gan*? If the sole aim were to present speeches that could not have been heard by *boku* or by any single agent of narration for that matter, then why not have an omniscient narrator consistently tell the story in the third person? The reader would still have access to the speeches of *boku* and his comrades, through the medium of this omniscient narrator's report. What would be lost if *boku* did not appear in the first person at all? Indeed, the presence of *boku* as partial narrator embodies the rupture between the acts of narrating and writing, since he also assumes the role of encoded author. This rupture is reflected in *Kusamakura* through shifts in linguistic register—*yo* uses literary discourse for his interior monologues and oral discourse for dialogues with other people. (In *Manji*, the topic of the next chapter, the two acts are carried out by different persons, the primary narrator and the narratee, who is also the encoded author; there the rupture between the two functions is rather sharp.) *Gan*, on the other hand, draws the line between literary and oral discourse subtly. When *boku* narrates the story directly, describing things or reporting his conversations with Okada, the distinction between literary and oral discourse is minimal. It is only when other characters speak under the direct control of the encoded author that this disjunction becomes evident, as different levels of formality, publicity, and cultural background are chosen, depending on the degree of authorial intrusion. The encoded author's role merits careful attention since he frames common discourse in elite discourse, thereby highlighting the contextual nature of what is ostensibly an unmediated, objective report. The following discussion therefore begins by examining the ways in which the encoded author's written discourse exercises control over the narrators' oral discourse.

I then go on to consider the multivalence of the narrative. I propose to read the text as a polyphony of interacting gazes, of desire, and of interpretive discontinuities between characters of opposite genders and different generations, levels of education, degrees of wealth, and social strata. Such characteristics define the positions of addresser and addressee, their relationships, and their motives and expectations in narrating and hearing. The polyphonous nature of *Gan* foregrounds the contextuality of the act of narration, which is in fact far from a simple telling of the truth. An examination of these interactions serves to demythicize intellectual male comradeship in the Meiji period, which is generally regarded as based upon trust and propriety. The male intellectual author, subtly and yet relentlessly, foregrounds ruptures in the stereotype of bonding based on mutual trust between virtuous men of letters *(bunjin)*. Such ruptures are sometimes noticed by characters in the text, sometimes not. It is arguably when they remain unnoticed by any of the characters and are thus naturalized that the myth reveals itself most clearly as myth.

Gan's sarcastic view of male homosociality is even more significant if one compares this text with *Kokoro* (1914), a contemporary work that has won a more secure canonical status in studies of modern Japanese literature. *Kokoro* appears to glorify male friendship (between Sensei and the narrator *watakushi*) while leaving room for the reader to question it; *Gan*, on the other hand, actively suggests rivalry and even betrayal between the two central male characters, the first-person narrator and Okada (to whom the narrator assigns the role of protagonist).

Another question that bears on the privileged position of elite male comradeship is that of subversive female spectatorship and narratorship. In *Kokoro*, as Oshino Takeshi, among others, has convincingly argued, the desire and voice of the heroine, Okusan, are essentially eliminated from the text. In *Gan,* by contrast (although its encoded author is again male), the heroine, Otama, the mistress of a moneylender, narrates the story of her crush on the university student Okada from her own viewpoint and in her own voice. Her observations of Okada and her master, Suezō, not only complement the narratives of male characters by offering a female perspective but also, and more important, remind us of the engenderedness of any narrative. The gender of the narrator is one of the factors that define a given narrative in a specific way.

So is the class of the narrator. The narratives of Suezō and his wife, Otsune, are significant in decentralizing the voice of the male intellectual. Narration is not the monopoly of the male or the intellectual. Nor is any narration context-free.

The Authorial Gesture of the Narrator

Gan seems to invite the reader to believe that it is an autobiographical writing by the historical author, Mori Ōgai. Many critics have noted correspondences between autobiographical and fictional details. Tanaka Minoru, for example, has pointed out that Mori Ōgai, or Rintarō as he was known in real life, lived in a boardinghouse in the same location as the Kamijō in *Gan,* in the same year of 1880:

> Not only did *boku* "lodge in the Kamijō, a boardinghouse that was just opposite the Iron Gate of Tokyo University" in the thirteenth year of Meiji [. . .] the subject who wrote the book version of *Gan* with the signature Mori Rintarō also lodged in the same boardinghouse. It is not only in the memory of "Ōgai" but recorded in writings such as *Ōgai no keizoku* [Relatives of Ōgai] that he was "one of those who lost all of their possessions when the Kamijo burned to the ground" "in the fourteenth year of Meiji."
>
> In short, just as the narrator begins to narrate his "story," the story extends outward in reference as far as the "writer" as a real person.[6]

Also, the fathers of Mori Ōgai and *boku* in *Gan* both lived in Kita Senju. The narrator of *Gan* writes: "My father, now no longer living, was busy growing autumn flowers in the garden of our Kitasenju house" (W 111). As recorded in a number of biographical writings[7] and reconfirmed by

Kishida Yoshiko,[8] Ōgai's father, Mori Shizuo, moved his house and clinic (he was also a medical doctor) to Kita Senju in 1880.

Kishida further examines a series of biographical details shared by the encoded authors of *Vita sekusuarisu* (1909; trans., *Vita Sexualis*, 1972) and *Gan*, which leads to the identification of the fictional female characters whom the two narrators see and fantasize about on their way to and from their fathers' places in and around Kita Senju. The woman in *Vita Sexualis*, the mistress of a Buddhist monk in the neighborhood, living with her father, had been a source of fantasies for the narrator until he left for Germany. Her circumstances closely resemble those of Otama. In a similar vein, Masao Miyoshi notes affinities between these two female figures: "Otama was evidently modeled after a girl Ogai himself saw occasionally, but only as Okada and the narrator saw Otama. In a more explicitly autobiographical, if rather parodic, story, 'Vita Sexualis' (1909), the narrator-author presents a girl just like Otama."[9]

But *Gan* shares more with *Vita Sexualis* than the characterization of this woman. What is more important in the context of this study is that both narratives play with the notion of transparency in autobiographical writing. The myth that the narrator is identical with the "real" author is reinforced in both narratives, as if to mock the myth itself. Indeed, at the end of the narrative, the narrator of *Gan* says that thirty-five years have passed since the incident in 1880, suggesting that the telling of the story was completed in 1915. This is the same year in which Mori Ōgai completed *Gan* by adding the last few chapters to the portion previously serialized in *Subaru* (The Pleiades) in 1911–13 and publishing the text in one volume through the publishing house of Momiyama shoten. *Boku* thus lures the reader into the belief that the encoded and historical authors are identical.

One could choose to read *Gan*, in whole or in part, as a series of autobiographical statements by the historical author, Ōgai. In this chapter, however, I will read the narrative not as a product of the historical author but rather of the encoded author, *boku*. Setting aside any parodic intent on Ōgai's part to write a fictional narrative that would mislead some readers into taking it for autobiography, I will read *boku*'s intentions as an attempt to step outside the frame of fiction and pretend to be a "real" person identifiable with Ōgai. The narrator of *Gan* is fond of periodically claiming authorship of the text. He frequently refers to the entire narrative as "kono hanashi," or "this story," which no one else within the text does. Furthermore, he calls the narrative "*Gan* to iu monogatari"[10] or "the story entitled *Gan*," suggesting that it is this act of his that gives the story its name. *Boku* is the only character who is free to trespass the boundaries of the text outward, making such meta-fictional statements as these.

Moreover, *boku* assigns the status of protagonist to Okada, although Okada in fact rarely appears or does or says much, in comparison with the heroine (see below):

> My room was right next to that of the hero of the story. (OG 13)

> Although the events of this story that have Okada for their hero took place before I learned the earlier history of the woman of the window, it will be convenient to give an outline of that history here. (OG 21)

Who but the author could define Okada as the hero? *Boku* is clearly assuming authorship, with its attendant authority, here. In addition, *boku* delineates the frame of the text, distinguishing what is to be told from what is not to be told: "Just as great events happen because of a peg, a dish of boiled mackerel at a Kamijo supper prevented Otama and Okada from ever meeting each other. This is not all of that story. But the events beyond it are outside the present narrative [entitled *Gan*]" (OG 119). *Boku* reserves the right not to tell what he does not feel is properly part of this particular narrative—a right only the "author" should possess.

In yet another notable authorial gesture, *boku* is obviously conscious of the existence of a prospective audience:

> Some of *my readers* may ask: "How did you get to know Otama? And when did you hear the story from her?"
>
> But as I said before, the answers to those questions are beyond the scope of my story. It is unnecessary to say that I lack the requisites that would qualify me to be Otama's lover; still, let me warn *my readers* that it is best not to indulge in fruitless speculation. (OG 119; emphasis added)

It is evident here that *boku* expects his narrative, once written down, to be read by others unacquainted with any of the characters. In other words *boku* writes the narrative with the intention of publishing it—a mark of authorship more distinct than any other.

Polyphonic Narrative and Authorial Control

As noted above, the narrative of *Gan* occasionally leaves the domain of its first-person narrator to report the speeches and interior monologues of other characters. The voices of the characters with whom we would not expect *boku* to have immediate contact, such as Suezō, Otama's father, and Suezō's wife, are either transcribed or paraphrased by an omnipresent narrator, who it is difficult to identify with *boku*, given the apparent practical limitations of the latter's knowledge.[11] Such characters' speeches appear in the text in three forms: indirect speech (that is, in the impersonal narrator's paraphrase, in which each character is referred to in the third person, and verb tenses are geared to the context of narration rather than to that of the original statements); free direct speech (each character's speech is given without quotation marks, in the first person, and with tense markers geared to the context of the original utterance); and tagged direct speech (the speech of characters is demarcated from narratorial comments by quotation marks or similar conventions). The diction of each speech portrays the background of the speaker, the context in which the speech act took place, and the degree of authorial intrusion in the process of transcription. One would expect the instances of indirect speech to show the greatest signs of authorial control. Suezō's feelings, for example, are presented by the author in foreign words that Suezō would not himself use—such as *fête, solannel,* and *tête-à-tête.*[12]

The author's words also appear in an interior monologue of Otsune, Suezō's wife, as she is absorbed in speculating (with good reason) on the possibility of her husband's infidelity. Although not framed in quotation marks, her speech is in the first person and can be distinguished from the narrator's statements by the direct speech markers "konna koto o omou" (she thought as follows) and "konna koto o omotte iruto" (as she thought as above).[13] Otsune's interior monologue seems free from authorial intervention. However, the way in which she refers to Suezō hints at a rewriting of her discourse. *Otto*,[14] a noun meaning "husband," may be used, as here, to mean "my husband." This is formal usage, however, more appropriate for elite or written discourse, and it seems somewhat odd coming from a speaker like Otsune. Another form of reference that she uses elsewhere, *ano hito* ("that man," commonly used for "my husband" or "my lover"),[15] is specifically feminine and more colloquial, and thus seems more natural coming from her. Otsune's interior monologue has apparently passed through a layer of authorial intervention.

In contrast, Suezō's interior monologue, presented in the first person and within quotation marks, exhibits a higher degree of distance from the author's discourse. As Suezō weighs two possible lodgings for Otama, he looks at the sleeping Otsune. Here is the passage in Burton Watson's translation, which maintains the direct speech found in the original:

> Yes, it better be the Muenzaka place!
>
> Then in the evening, after I've been to the bath and changed into some better looking clothes, I'll think up some tale to tell the old woman so she won't suspect anything, and off I go! What will it be like, when I open the lattice door and step inside? There will be Otama, a kitten or something on her lap, sitting there lonely, waiting for me to come! Of course she'll be carefully made up. And I'll see she has whatever she wants in the way of kimonos. . . .
>
> But wait a minute! No use throwing money away! You can get perfectly good items at the pawnshop. Why act the fool by lavishing kimonos and hair ornaments on a woman the way other men do? (W 26–27)

In the original, the orality is even more pronounced. "It better be the Muenzaka place!" is "Muenzaka ni shiyō, shiyō"—the repetition of *shiyō* is a uniquely oral mannerism that would be out of place in literary discourse. "There will be Otama" is "Otama no yatsume," which suggests that Suezō's stream of consciousness pauses at the picture of Otama for a moment, and that he gazes at it with affection and with a gesture of intimacy. Again, one gains a vivid sense of the exact manner in which Suezō thinks to himself.

Similarly, Otama's father's interior monologue is presented in the first person and framed by "konna koto o omou koto ga aru" and "konna koto o omotte,"[16] which function, as we have seen, like quotation marks:

> Then he started looking at it this way: If I stay in the house all the time I think too much about things. It would be better if I went out. If Otama comes when I'm out, she'll at least think what a waste of time it was to have come all the way over here for nothing. Let that be a lesson to her! With such thoughts in mind, he began going out more. (W 49)

The first-person pronoun that the old man uses in this interior monologue is the informal *ore;* this is apparently his customary usage, since it is also the pronoun he uses to refer to himself in conversation with Otama, which is framed within quotation marks.

This is significant when we contrast it with the same man's speech as represented by the old woman and heard by Suezō:

> Even the glib old woman who was acting as go-between in the arrangements found herself stymied on that point, as she realized that Otama would invariably second her father's stand on any matter, and that if pressure were brought to bear to keep the old man away, all the negotiations could end in failure.
>
> The old man's position was this. "Otama," he told the go-between, "is an only daughter and very precious to me. [. . .]
>
> "Whatever happens," he insisted, "I don't want to see her become somebody's mistress or kept woman. But you tell me that this gentleman of yours is perfectly trustworthy. Otama will be twenty next year and it doesn't do to put such things off too long. So I guess I'd better listen to your proposal. But since she means so much to me, I want to be sure to go along when she meets the gentleman."
>
> Suezo was anything but delighted when he heard of these remarks. (W 31–33)[17]

It is evident that the old man does not speak in a contextual vacuum. He employs *watashi,* a more formal first-person pronoun, to refer to himself, which shows that the presence of an addressee makes him feel that some degree of formality is required. But the logical and succinct flow of the argument may at least be partly attributed to the mediation of the old woman as she passes on the old man's words to Suezō. The original context of the utterance aside, neither the old man's nor the old woman's speech is rendered exactly. The *-ta* and *-da* endings are not usually used in conversation, formal or informal, and thus mark the passage as written discourse. Since neither of these two characters could have spoken this way, we are alerted to some degree of authorial intrusion. The author's keen consciousness of the contextuality of the narrative and its multiple layers is most conspicuous in the variety of ways in which he refers to Otsune. In addition to her name, the terms *nyōbō, kakā, kamisan, okamisan,* and *okusan* are used. Even though all these terms mean "wife" or "housewife," they are appropriate to different speakers and different contexts. *Nyōbō* could be used either by Suezō or by the impersonal narrator (as in this case), but others might hesitate to use it, unless they take their social superiority to Otsune for granted. Thus, for the impersonal narrator to refer to Otsune as *nyōbō* suggests a distance as well as a hierarchy between them. Only a husband is entitled to use *kakā*, which suggests a degree of familiarity that leaves no room for romanticizing. Thus, this term is appropriately used by Suezō as he observes his snoring wife, while planning to move his mistress into a house. *Okusan* is used only by Otsune's maid when she directly addresses her mistress, which is appropriate given that the term is both respectful and conversational.

The use of *kamisan* and *okamisan* is indicative of a shifting viewpoint, as these terms alternate with *nyōbō* in the scene in which Otsune first quarrels with Suezō. One could perhaps use *kamisan* to refer to someone else's wife, although it would be more appropriate to use in public, with a hint of shyness, to refer to one's own wife. When this term occurs in the narrator's voice, it indicates either his sympathy with Otsune or his descent into the sphere of fictional characters of low social status. *Okamisan,* a colloquial and yet polite way to refer to someone else's wife, cannot possibly be used by a husband. The shifting use of these three terms suggests the viewpoint from which a given scene is being described. When Otsune's psyche and her reactions to Suezō's words, such as grasping his hand, are described, *okamisan* or *kamisan* is used. This suggests that the impersonal narrator is taking her part. When Suezō observes his wife, tries to look into her mind, or frees himself from her grip, *nyōbō* is used, implying that Suezō's perspective is adopted in those instances. The shifting viewpoint allows the narration to adopt different perspectives and to penetrate the characters' interiors when necessary.

Dissolution of Male Comradeship

As has been noted by Stephen Snyder, *boku* as the author exhibits his authority most conspicuously when he observes Okada from a vantage point of superior knowledge.[18] Even as a character, sharing the same time and space as Okada, *boku* is better informed about Otama and is thus able to put Okada's story in perspective. Further, as the encoded author, writing of Okada thirty-five years after the fact, *boku* is able to see at what points Okada was not entirely frank with him and how Okada tried to hide this lack of candor from him. But what is *boku* trying to tell the reader by noting or implying Okada's dishonesty? *Boku* betrays his own critical gaze and the possibility that he could have deceived his friend.

The second conversation between *boku* and Okada appears in Chapter 18, following the relating by the omniscient narrator of the story of Otama, Suezō, and his wife (the first is their discussion of Chinese fiction in Chapter 1).

One Sunday evening I returned from Kitasenju to my room in the Kamijo. The other students were all away and the house was completely still. Entering my room, I sat for a while, my mind a blank, when in the next room, which I had assumed was empty, I heard a match being struck. Feeling somewhat lonely, I immediately called out, "Is that you, Okada?"

I heard something like a grunt, though I could not be sure if it was meant as a reply. Okada and I had become quite chummy and no longer bothered with the usual formalities, but this was not his customary way of answering.

If I was in a vacant mood, it appeared that Okada was too. Perhaps he's got something on his mind, I thought, and *I had a sudden urge to see what his expression would be like*. I called out once more. "Mind if I bother you a while?"

"Why would I mind? I just got back myself and was sitting here thinking about nothing when I heard you rattling around. Then I decided to get up and light the lamp." *This time he spoke distinctly.*

> I stepped into the hall and opened the door to his room. The window that faced the Iron Gate was open and Okada was sitting, his elbows propped on his desk, gazing out the window. Beyond the vertical bars of the window, a few dusty cypresses growing in the area between the outer wall and the street were visible in the dusk. (W 112; emphasis added)

When *boku* senses something odd in Okada's manner, his reaction is not concern but curiosity. *Boku* is acting as a "detective," like *yo* in *Kusamakura*.

Okada, for his part, does not remain an inert object to be studied by this Peeping Tom. His second reply reveals how eager he is to talk, despite the ambiguous nature of his first answer. Okada does not want to appear anxious to tell the story he is about to tell, but nonetheless cannot help telling it; the arrival of *boku* at just this moment in the deserted boarding house is, for Okada, a stroke of luck. His initial hesitation is due to the nature of his story: it is about an encounter with a beautiful woman, which makes him, as a decent man, feel a bit shy. The reason for his eagerness to tell the story, however, is that it concerns a beauty—for *boku* and Okada are both young men, interested in beautiful women.

Okada's shyness persists, as is evident in the facts that he does not begin telling the story immediately on *boku*'s entry, and that he avoids the gaze of *boku* for a while, staring into the darkness outside his room.

> "Then I felt so groggy in the head I went out after lunch and met with this strange adventure." Okada did not look around but kept staring out the window as he spoke.
>
> "What adventure is that?"
>
> "I slew the dragon—or rather, the snake." Okada turned to face me.
>
> "And rescued the beautiful lady?"
>
> "No, I rescued the birds. But it had something to do with a beautiful lady."
>
> "Sounds interesting. Tell me about it." (W 113)

Okada's urge to tell *boku* of his encounter with Otama is matched by *boku*'s interest in the story—one needs a confidant; the other, like a detective or tabloid informant, thirsts for inside information about the suggested "romance." Okada then recounts his experience: he took a walk at an unusual time (his usual time is after supper) and encountered Otama, her maid, and her neighbors in a commotion as Otama's finches are being attacked by a snake.

Okada's story is framed by two references to Okada's role in telling the story: "This is what Okada told me" (OG 85) and "Okada had gone this far"(OG 91)—in a manner similar to that in which the interior monologues of Otama's father and Suezō's wife are framed. What is different in this case—significant for our purposes—is that Okada's references to himself are not rendered in the first person; rather, Okada is referred to as "Okada" or "kare" (he). Okada's real voice is heard only three times, in three different short sentences. Thus, the direct impact of his speech is minimized. To a greater extent than are those of the other characters, Okada's voice is mediated by *boku* as author, thus marginalizing him in terms of discourse, if not in terms of the story, and Okada is largely expunged from what ostensibly began as his story. However, *boku*, as Okada's original interlocutor, does not intrude either, until the end of the retelling. In this sense, the scene is deprived of a sense of orality. *Boku* as encoded author, on the other hand, does intrude twice during the process, by annotating Okada's remarks with information that *boku* has come to know by the time he writes the story. This increases the literariness of Okada's story and serves to remind us of the retrospective viewpoint from which *boku* rewrites the story.

> When he came to the stone wall of Iwasaki's mansion on the right where the slope begins to descend, he saw a group of people on the left. They stood in front of the house he always looked at in passing. This was the only fact that Okada didn't tell me at that time. (OG 86)

Boku, as the character hearing Okada's story for the first time, cannot have known that Okada was in the habit of looking at Otama's house. Okada, for his part, does not seem to think that his special interest in this house is known to his listener and thus feels safe in making no mention of it. But *boku* as author knows what *boku* as character does not. So does the reader, who at this point has read Chapters 2 and 3, in which

Okada's daily encounters with Otama are narrated by the omniscient narrator. Thus, *boku* as author successfully conveys his message: Okada was not entirely forthcoming with his good friend.

There is a further thing that Okada kept from *boku*. As *boku* himself notes: "When Okada was telling me this, he said: 'The woman was quite beautiful.' But he didn't say that he had seen her before and that he had greeted her each time he passed her house" (OG 87). Snyder interprets these repeated references to Okada's failure to tell the whole truth as a proof of the narrator's skepticism about Okada's candor:

> In telling the story of the finches, the narrator comments on Okada's lack of candor in relating what has happened, implying that he, the narrator, has another source as well. Here the reader begins to detect an ironic distance opening between the narrator and his characters: "When Okada told me this story, he said that the woman was quite beautiful, but he did not mention that he had seen her before [this incident of the finches] nor that he had been in the habit of greeting her each time he passed her house." Okada, in his own role of narrator, demonstrates the art of narrative bad faith that becomes pandemic in the modern novel. In response, the *boku* narrator is increasingly skeptical, and encourages the reader to be skeptical, of Okada's story. The narrator himself, since he is filling in what Okada omitted, is by implication more trustworthy (or represents himself as such).[19]

It is true that *boku*'s persistent foregrounding of Okada's secretiveness suggests that Okada is an unreliable narrator. Indeed, Okada even tells *boku* toward the end of the narrative that he has told *boku* "everything" about Otama. The reader, who knows that Otama is being disingenuous, will interpret this as further evidence of Otama's unreliability, although *boku* does not note it as such in the text.

The reader will not be convinced, however, that *boku* is more trustworthy than Okada. For as both the encoded author of the entire narrative and a character who converses with Okada, *boku* reveals his own lack of candor. One instance of this occurs immediately after Okada's story. Although he knows Otama's identity, *boku* does not share this information with Okada:

> All the students at the university, including those who never borrowed from Suezo, knew the usurer, the money-lender who had risen from the position of a school servant. But there were some who didn't know that the woman at Muenzaka was his mistress. Okada was among these. At that time I hadn't learned any of the details about her, yet I did know that the woman living next to the sewing teacher was Suezo's mistress.
>
> *In this instance I knew a little more than my friend.* (OG 92; emphasis added)

Just as Okada kept his daily encounters with Otama secret from *boku*, *boku* withholds his own knowledge of Otama's circumstances from Okada. Not only in the time he enjoys a privileged position as author but also in the time in which he listens to Okada's story, *boku* exults in his superior knowledge over Otama.

Another instance occurs later in the narrative, when *boku* and Okada take a walk together in the direction of Muenzaka. Knowing Suezō will not visit her that night, Otama stands in front of the house, waiting for Okada to pass by.

> Just as we were about to go down Muenzaka, I nudged Okada, saying: "Look—there she is!"
>
> "Who?" he asked in spite of knowing whom I meant, for he turned to the left side to glance at the house with the lattice door.
>
> Otama was standing in front of her house. [She was beautiful even when she was ill.] But a young, healthy beauty is made even more beautiful by using make-up, and she was just that. I couldn't tell why, but there was a difference from her usual appearance. *I thought she was lovelier than ever.* And the radiance of her face dazzled me. (OG 108–9; emphasis added; trans. modified)

At first glance, this passage simply seems to reveal Okada's stubborn resistance to admitting his special interest in Otama. He pretends not to realize whom *boku* is referring to as "she" (in the original, the verbal phrase "iru-ze" [look, (she) is there] has no explicit subject),[20] but his pretense is so transparent that the narrator *boku* cannot help pointing it out. The following paragraph, however, makes *boku*'s own affectation of ignorance equally transparent. To be able to compare Okada in good health and in sickness, and her usual self and the Okada of this particular occasion, *boku* must have seen Otama frequently before, both in more makeup and in less, and paid close attention to her appearance on each occasion.[21] But *boku* never admits to Okada, even when Okada tells him the story of the finches, that he knows her. Their reserve is reciprocal.

Both as a character in the story and as its encoded author, *boku* seems to revel in the luxury of better knowledge and to draw pleasure from the ignorance of others. As *boku* and Okada take a walk together before Okada's departure for Germany, they pass Otama on their way to the Shinobazu Pond. *Boku* mentions Suezō to Okada, without telling him that Suezō is Otama's master.

I looked at the two-storied houses on the side of the street and said as though talking to myself: "Those houses belong to Fukuchi and Suezo."

"They're a fine contrast. Though I hear the journalist hasn't much integrity either."

"He's a politician too, and a politician," I said without giving much thought to the question, "no matter how he may live, is not free from slander." Perhaps I wanted to make the distance between these two men as wide as possible. (OG 110)

Although *boku* speaks "as though talking to" himself, he of course intends Okada to hear what he says. But his purpose is not to make his addressee understand what he really means. *Boku* is aware that Okada does not know of Otama's link to Suezō and does not expect him to react in any particular way. *Boku* wants to enjoy Okada's ignorance of the hypothetical love-triangle involving Okada, Otama, and Suezō, about which only *boku*, and Otama, is in a position to fantasize.

The name of the journalist Fukuchi has occurred at two earlier points in the narrative. In the first, Otama's father encounters him in a theatre. Later, Suezō contrasts his own financial security with Fukuchi's extravagance, reflecting to himself that, in financial matters at any rate, he is superior to this famous intellectual:

How stupid to squander money like some men, like Fukuchi for example. Suezo suddenly saw his famous neighbor Fukuchi strutting openly on the streets and followed by his expensive geishas. The students would see the writer and be envious, but Suezo knew that the dandy was actually ill off. He was supposedly an intelligent man, a writer. But was he? If a clerk did the same kinds of nasty tricks with his pen as Fukuchi did, he would be discharged. (OG 28)

Although presented as part of Suezō's interior monologue, the passage is related by *boku* as encoded author, probably a deliberate foreshadowing of the dialogue between Okada and *boku* discussed above. There is no way that *boku* as a character could know Suezō's opinion of Fukuchi; nor could he have taken any interest in the question. The only reason to present Suezō as one who thinks disparagingly of Fukuchi is to anticipate structurally the contrast later to be drawn between the two, and it is *boku*, in his role as encoded author, who chooses this arrangement. In this way the authorial *boku* emplots the story, tailoring his characters' thoughts and speeches to aspects of the story of which the characters themselves may not be aware.

The authority of *boku* as author extends as well over the character *boku*. In fact, the author *boku* caricatures the character *boku* as a man of letters who agonizes over the dilemma between his desire to be a hero and his sense of decency. When *boku* and Okada pass by Otama, *boku* enjoys the privileged bystander's perspective, while at the same time feeling a nagging sense of regret that he does not qualify as a lover of Otama.

I felt she was transformed as she fixed her eyes on Okada. When he took off his cap, I noticed how upset he was, and I saw him unconsciously quicken his step.

Having the liberty of a third party, I looked back several times and saw that she continued to watch Okada.

He went down the slope with his head bent and without relaxing his hurried gait. I followed him in silence. Opposing thoughts tumbled inside me. They arose from the desire to put myself in Okada's place. But the idea sickened me. Denying my wish, I thought to myself that I couldn't be that base—yet I was annoyed at not being able to repress it effectively. (OG 109; emphasis added)

Snyder sees *boku*'s subversive intent here—he wants to dethrone Okada and replace him as a romantic hero:

This remarkable flight of the narrator's fancy accomplishes several things: it convinces the reader of Okada's coldness and effectively ends the story of his encounter with Otama; it allows us to imagine Otama's feelings although we are no longer in the presence of the omniscient narrator; and it rhetorically substitutes the narrator for the hero. As the only place in the novel where a character directly relates his own feelings in his own voice, the passage has considerable immediacy and power. The narrator, at least in his imagination, has ceased to be a bystander. The actual ending of *Gan*, like the killing of the wild goose that serves as its symbol, is a story of crippling inaction and thwarted desire; the narrator proposes here an alternative scenario with himself as hero. The narrator, however, quite obviously feels considerable ambivalence (and is practicing considerable self-deception) at the idea of supplanting Okada, ambivalence apparently rooted in his uncertainty about how to deal with (that is, in his case, how to write) his own sexual desire.[22]

This is entirely true of *boku* the character. When we consider *boku* as an author and try to interpret his reasons for writing of his jealousy of Okada, however, self-righteousness is not his only quality. He is motivated by a desire to marginalize himself as a character. At the expense of his autonomy as a character, *boku* gains the authority with which he controls the narrative. Even as he enviously disqualifies himself from acting as a hero, *boku* takes advantage of his marginal position to subvert the power hierarchy. Indeed, *boku* is a "detective" like *yo* in *Kusamakura;* he is a paparazzo who follows, observes, and reports details of the private life of Okada, the star figure. Okada, the acknowledged protagonist, is only an object to be observed. He is never allowed to observe *boku* in turn and is deprived of insight into *boku*'s psyche. Okada's unawareness and his naïve attempts to manipulate *boku* are themselves observed and circumscribed by *boku* from the margins.

Telling in Order to Erase: Narrative Manipulation

Male intellectuals are not the only characters who try to manipulate each other by giving and withholding information. Dialogues between characters of all sorts, as transcribed by the omniscient narrator, suggest that telling is never a simple act of revealing the truth but is, rather, a performative act aimed at producing some effect in the hearer—blinding the hearer to certain facts the speaker wants to hide or misleading the hearer into believing something that is not the case.

Suezō manipulates Otsune in this way when she confronts him with her suspicions that he has been betraying her. His strategies include reticence, a mapping of the other's territory by interrogating her before answering her inquiries, and making up a story that makes sense of the information she has.

> Suezo looked at her sharply, but remained silent. He realized that she had learned something, but since he couldn't measure its range, he could say nothing yet. He wasn't the kind of man who gives bait for the opposition's advantage.
>
> "Now I know everything!" she cried, her voice shrill and trembling at the end of her words to the point of tears.
>
> "You sound so mysterious. What do you know?" he said, like a man who is surprised by the unexpected but who still retains a gentle tone.
>
> "You ask too much of a person! How can you pretend like that? Even without any shame!" Her husband's calm so excited her that her voice broke, and she was forced to wipe her eyes on the sleeve of her underwear. (OG 58)

Otsune responds to Suezō emotionally, and his lack of emotion outrages her all the more. However, his mental calm makes it easy for Suezō to convince her that her information is wrong.

> "Who told you?" he asked again.
>
> "Forget about that so long as it's true." The pressure of her breasts increased.
>
> "But it's not true, so I do mind who's misinformed you. Tell me."
>
> "All right. The wife of the fish dealer—Uwokin."
>
> "What? What? I can't understand you chattering away like a monkey! Who's that? Who?"
>
> Otsune pulled herself away from him and smiled in spite of herself.
>
> "Uwokin's wife." (OG 59)

The joke Suezō makes to assuage Otsune's anger—"chattering away like a monkey" (in the original, the simile is "like a badger" which, in Japanese, conveys a folktale-like overtone)—produces its desired effect, as seen in Otsune's involuntary smile. The simile also implies that Otsune is as inferior to Suezō as a badger is to a human being. This level of implication is echoed by another simile that Suezō uses for Otsune elsewhere in the text—"like an animal" or "a kind of beast" who has been "raised to a human level" (OG 74)

Suezō takes advantage of Otsune's lack of sophistication and browbeats her with the intellectual tone of his talk, rather than with its content.

> His wife felt as though she were stumbling in a fog, yet she wondered if she weren't being duped by his words, and she remained alert. Watching him closely, she tried to follow him carefully. But when her husband used the difficult words of a newspaper as he had done in speaking about public opinion, she was overwhelmed and submitted without comprehension. (OG 60)

Such recourse to vocabulary beyond Otsune's comprehension has little bearing on Suezō's fidelity, but what is at issue is not the truth or falsehood of what he says but how his speech sounds to her. Her inability to comprehend does not present an obstacle to the speaker; rather, it helps him achieve his goal of deceiving his wife. This classic example of the performativity of narration challenges naïve notions of narration as a medium for conveying a message or revealing the truth.

Suezō's triumph over Otsune, however, is short-lived. For one thing, Otsune is not completely convinced; rather, she is swept away by the momentum of his words. Suezō's success relies on the issue being closed, but as Otsune's sources of information increase from one to many and their intrusion grows more frequent, he is left with less room to maneuver.

> Suezo's explanation, a mixture of truth and fiction, reduced his wife's jealousy temporarily, but since its effect was naturally only palliative, the gossip and grumbling never stopped as long as the woman lived at Muenzaka. Even the maid told Suezo's wife about the scandal, saying among other things at different times: "Today, so-and-so saw our master go there." But Suezo was never at a loss for an excuse. (OG 61–62)

Indeed, like the *yo* of *Kusamakura*, Suezō is threatened by an information network that is beyond his control. As Takemori Ten'yū notes, the same network that had helped him find Otama now works against him, and many people are antagonistic to him because he is a moneylender.[23]

Finally, a chance encounter with Otama, who is carrying the very same kind of parasol that Suezō bought for Otsune, convinces her of her husband's infidelity. By this point, Otsune has herself matured as a participant in narrative performance.

> When she had returned home, she had wanted to go to her husband immediately, but what would she have said? She knew her own limitations, and her words would have been meaningless. And then her husband would have invented some tale to trick her and would have succeeded. "I'm not his match in a quarrel. He's too shrewd." She wondered if she weren't better off to keep quiet. But then what would the result have been? (OG 67)

Otsune weighs her own strength against her husband's as a narrative performer. She also considers in turn the likely effects of keeping silent and of confronting her husband. To the extent that she wonders not whether her suspicion is right but whether a particular choice of strategy is likely to be effective, she shows a new awareness that narration is performance. It is ironic for Suezō that it is his own tactics that teach his "enemy" not only how to deal with him, but also how to place what he says in perspective: "Before this she had let him take advantage of her with his lying, but now, as though she were vividly seeing the affair acted out in front of her eyes, nothing could make her feel that her husband's words were convincing enough" (OG 70). Otsune is no longer naïvely convinced by Suezō's pseudo-intellectual discourse. She has outgrown it, although she does not quite know how to deal with it.

Otama, on the other hand, learns not only how Suezō manipulates her but also how she can manipulate him in turn.

> During their talks Suezo would get her to speak for a time, usually on *trivial and sentimental* matters about the years she had lived alone with her father. In spite of himself, *Suezo would listen with a smile, not so much to what she was saying but rather to the pleasant melody of her voice*. It was as though he were hearing *the*

pure tones of a bell-insect. Then Otama would suddenly become self-conscious, blush at having run on about herself, and *dash off the rest of her sentence before lapsing into her usual silence.* With his *penetration* Suezo could see that her speech and behavior were so *totally innocent that she seemed as transparent as fresh water in the bottom of a flat vase.* [. . .] The experience of this delight, quite a new one for him, had been giving him unconsciously a sort of "*culture*" since the start of his visits to her. After all, *a primitive beast can be subdued by sensitive hands.* (OG 48; emphasis added)

This looks almost like a reversal of the pattern we observed in the quarrel between Suezō and Otsune. Just as Otsune is duped by the highbrow nature of Suezō's talk without understanding what he is talking about, Suezō listens not to the content of Otama's talk but to its tone. What is different here is that, thoroughly convinced of the insignificance of what Otama is saying, Suezō feels superior enough to compare her to "a bell-insect"—weak, small, and far below a human being in the chain of creatures—just as he compares Otsune to a badger.

Otama, however, is much more clever and complex than Suezō expects:

"Something's bothering you. What is it?"

"No," said Otama, her eyes widening, "there's nothing wrong."

[. . .] She began to search for an item when obviously she had nothing to look for. Suezo could tell that her eyes could not keep very great secrets.

In spite of frowning unconsciously, he brightened instantly. "Come, Otama, you know you're worried. It's written all over your face. I can just make out the words. Let me see," he said, looking at her sharply. "Oh, yes! 'I'm all confused. What'll I do? What'll I do?'"

Otama was embarrassed, and for a while she sat in silence as though she did not know how to begin. Suezo could clearly perceive the motion of this delicate instrument.

"I—well—it's my father. I've been thinking about visiting him—one of these days. . . . And it's been long since. . . ." (OG 48–49)

Despite her appearance of innocence and transparency, Otama does know how to hide things. She hides her thoughts not by directly concealing them but by revealing something else. With a multilayered mind, she is capable of disclosing one thing so as to conceal something else. She narrates for the sake not of what she wants to tell but of what she wants to hide.

Although Suezō is indeed perceptive enough to sense that Otama is hiding something, his information is limited, as in the case with Otsune, and he is left in ignorance:

> As for Suezo, he had caught an image at the bottom of Otama's mind, had sounded her out regarding it, and had found it a childish trifle. But as he walked down Muenzaka after eleven that night, it seemed as though something were behind what he had already discovered. He was shrewd enough to locate part of the trouble. "Something," he conjectured, "someone's told her something. Something about me. And she's holding it against me."
>
> But he did not know who had told what. (OG 50)

Although Suezō has a professional stake in maintaining a wide-ranging information network, his monopoly is challenged by his women, who now have channels of information independent of him.

Otama employs this strategy of telling one thing to hide another when she visits her father for the first time. One reason for this visit is to share an unbearable fact she has recently discovered—the fact that Suezō is a moneylender. But she grows hesitant about revealing this when she sees how content her father is in the house Suezō provides for him. This hesitancy is expressed in the pauses that precede her responses to her father's questions and leave him baffled.

> "We're managing," she said after a pause. "You shouldn't worry about me. Please don't."
>
> "Everything's all right then—" His daughter's reply had not quite satisfied him, and the two of them unconsciously began speaking as though their mouths were full of paste. They had never kept anything from each other but now they were speaking with formality, like unrelated persons having secrets to conceal from each other. [. . .] They became painfully aware of a barrier thrown across their former intimacy. (OG 53–54)

The paradise of complete transparency, of freedom from any need for secrecy, is lost for father and daughter now, not because of some evil intention but because of Otama's concern for her father's happiness. Their lives have parted, and mutual consideration is now expressed not as candor but as the hiding of unpleasant information.

This is a new dilemma for Otama, and she naturally feels uneasy.

> The old man looked puzzled. "Hum—why should he be a *bad* man?"
>
> She looked at her father, her heartbeat increasing. She realized that she now had her chance to tell him what she had learned, yet it pained her to bring him any new problems. She had put him at ease now. He was comfortable. And she suddenly decided: "I won't tell him!" She would keep the matter to herself, an unopened secret behind the one they shared of her serving as a mistress, even though in doing this she was aware that the gap between them was widening. (OG 54)

Just as she replaced her concern with Suezō's occupation with concern for her father's well-being, Otama replaces the shocking news of Suezō's occupation with the news of his marital status, since that information seems less devastating to her:

> "You never have to worry about that, Otossan. How often you used to say: 'Ta-bo's honest.' I know I am. But lately I've made up my mind, and I won't let myself be tricked again. I won't lie to anyone. I won't deceive anyone. But at the same time no one's going to deceive me either. I'll see to it that they don't."
>
> "All of this, I suppose, means that you don't trust Suezo?"
>
> "Just that. He treats me as though I were an infant. I'm not surprised that his type takes that approach with me. He thinks he can go through somebody's eye and nose without being seen. But I'm not as much of a child as that."
>
> "You don't mean that he's lied to you?"
>
> "Yes, he has. You remember, the go-between said he was a widower left with some children and that the woman he took under his care would be just like his wife though not in name. [. . .] Well, he has a wife. He told me so himself. He didn't even hesitate. He didn't even feel ashamed. I was shocked."
>
> The old man was shocked too. "Is it true? Then—then what she said was only a matchmaker's trick?"
>
> "So I must be kept strictly secret from his wife. Since he's lying to her, how can I trust him completely?" (OG 55–56)

Whereas Otama's father takes everything that he is told as truth, Otama, at least the Otama of the present, is aware that people say things not because they are true but because they want to achieve their goals. The last statement ironically suggests that although Suezō thinks he is controlling both his wife and his mistress, the two women have independently reached the same conclusion—that he is a manipulative speaker.

The Invisible/Silent Woman and the Man Without Eyes or Ears

Like the acts of writing and narrating, the act of seeing is also important in this narrative. The first and most distinguished object of observation is the house in which Otama lives. Suezō, Otama's master, establishes her in this house for the very reason that it is hidden from the gaze of others. After looking over two houses into which he might move his new mistress, he reflects to himself.

> He had reasoned that he would prefer the Ike-no-hata place for *its view*, but what was the need of that when all he had to do was look out the window in the house he was now living in?[. . .] Besides, it was *not hidden enough*. It would *attract attention* . . . .
>
> When he thought about the Muenzaka house, he felt that it was somewhat gloomy, but the key point in its favor was its *out-of-the-way location* on a slope that only students seemed to stroll along at odd hours. (OG 27; emphasis added)

Suezō is concerned with the visibility of his mistress's residence, for fear that his wife might discover his infidelity. The only human contact that Suezō thinks Otama can have at the Muenzaka house is with students, whose paths are unlikely to cross with his wife's. Ironically enough, however, this factor eventually shakes his relationship with Otama in a way he least expects—for she falls in love with one of these strolling students, Okada.

Furthermore, Otama's seclusion plays a key role in the origin and development of her romance with Okada. This is how *boku* the narrator describes Otama's residence:

Among the dwellings, *the most attractive* to the people who passed belonged to a sewing teacher, and during the day young women could be *seen* through the window going about their work. If the day was pleasant and the windows were *open* when we students passed, the girls, *always talking,* raised their faces and *looked out into the street.* And then once more they would continue their *laughing and chattering.*

Next to the house was a residence whose door was always wiped clean and whose granite walk I often saw sprinkled with water in the evening. During the cold weather the sliding doors were *shut,* but even during the hot weather *the bamboo shutters were lowered.* This house always seemed conspicuously *quiet,* the more so because of *the noise* in the neighboring one. (OG 17–18; emphasis added)

The male narrator forms an impression of Otama's house through the contrast with the neighboring house: the sewing teacher's house is exposed to male gaze, Otama's is hidden; the female students' voices are audible to male passersby, Otama's voice is never heard. More important, whereas the women gathered next door look at, and apparently discuss, the male passersby, Otama's reactions to the men walking outside remains unknown and thus appears null. Thus, gaze and narration are reciprocal between the young women in the first house and the passing men, but in Otama's case such reciprocity is nonexistent—or so it appears at this moment. Otama's very invisibility and inaudibility seem to increase the male viewer's curiosity—an unintended outcome of the care Suezō took in choosing the house.

The narrative viewpoint then shifts from that of the knowing first-person narrator to that of Okada, who regularly walks outside the house, and the content of the narration shifts from experiences common to the narrator and Okada—or to any of the passing students for that matter—to Okada's private ones. Although the narration is not in Okada's own voice, his experiences are observed from his own viewpoint. On one occasion, Okada makes eye contact with Otama as she stands before the entrance to her house. His next glimpse of her is even more private and singular: "Suddenly above the plant a white face *appeared* in the background *where nothing but gray darkness had been.* Furthermore, the face *smiled at* him" (19; emphasis added).

After this second meeting of their eyes, Okada begins to wonder whether Otama is actively watching for him and thinks of him. His answer is in the positive.

From that time on, whenever Okada went out walking and passed this house, he seldom missed seeing the woman's face. *Sometimes she broke into his imagination, and there she gradually started to take liberties.* He began to wonder if she was waiting for him to pass or was simply looking outside with indifference and accidentally noticed him. [. . .] He finally concluded that perhaps the woman had recently come to *look outside* and had opened the window to wait for his passing. (19; emphasis added)

Thus, Otama, the hidden woman, is acknowledged to be observing and thinking about Okada.

However, insofar as her gaze at this point is still a "fact" perceived or surmised by Okada—to set aside for a moment the overarching presence of the male narrator—she remains spectacle, rather than spectator. In Chapter 16, however, we hear of her gaze on Okada again, this time from within the window—that is, from her own standpoint:

In Otama's house the bamboo blinds were still drawn, their unfaded green covering the window from top to bottom. Otama sat inside with nothing to do. She leaned against a post hung with fans and vacantly *looked into* the street. After three o'clock the students would pass in small groups. And she knew that whenever they came, the voices of the girls next door would rise like the sounds of so many young sparrows. And attracted by the noise, she would also *glance out*.

[. . .]

And *watching the students* in their walks along the street, she began to *speculate*: "Isn't there *a hero* out there? I'll be *rescued!*"

But when she suddenly found herself indulging in such fancies, she was startled.

It was at this point that Okada got to know her. (OG 75–77; emphasis added)

The scene on the street is now described from Otama's viewpoint, and we learn that Otama's secluded dwelling was all along "a room with a view." While male passersby have wondered about the house's invisible resident, she was looking outside, observing and evaluating them. Otama is in the advantageous position of a Peeping Tom, from which she is unseen, yet able to observe the Other.

It is interesting in this context to notice that when Okada looks out the window of his room at the Kamijō boardinghouse, he is not looking outside his world, but inside, into himself. We may recall the scene discussed above in which *boku*, made curious by Okada's odd demeanor, goes into the latter's room:

> He was sitting with his elbows on his desk and was *looking into the outside gloom* through his open window, which directly faced the Iron Gate.
>
> [...]
>
> He said all this *without looking at me*. Instead he *stared out the window*. (OG 85; emphasis added)

Here, Okada looks out the window, but, as we have seen, he does so more to collect himself and to avoid his friend's inquisitive eyes than to observe anything outside. In contrast to Otama's, his is a room without a view.

It is not just that Otama seems gifted with a wider scope of vision than does Okada. Okada's psyche also remains largely a "dark continent" yet to be explored, whereas Otama's is represented in some detail, either in her own voice or in that of the impersonal narrator. As Dennis Washburn observes:

> Otama is treated in considerably more detail, and her motivations are given some psychological depth. Her self-awareness grows throughout the story, and she changes according to her circumstances. The way in which she and Okada are treated in the narrative gives further support to reading the novel as an antiromance, for their characterizations reverse the normal type of roles they would represent. In *Gan*, the male hero is rendered passive, while the heroine not only develops a sense of herself but becomes an active plotter.[24]

In a similar vein, Koizumi Kōichirō notes:

> As has been pointed out, Okada makes his appearance in only ten chapters of the twenty-four-chapter *Gan*: in Chapters 1 to 3, a preface to the story, in Chapters 18 and 19, which concern the conquest of the snake, and in Chapters

22 to 24, the ending. We cannot afford to overlook the fact that whereas the psychological development of Otama the heroine is described in great detail, the author refrains from describing Okada's internal development.[25]

Otama is astute, and ready enough to grasp the slightest opportunity to identify the man Okada. In Chapter 16, she is quick to inform herself about Okada when her neighbor, the sewing teacher Otei, refers to him.

> In the course of their talk while Otei stood at the door, the woman said to Otama: "I believe you know Okada-san, isn't that so?"
>
> Otama had *never heard the name before*, yet it flashed through her mind that the sewing teacher had referred to the student, that she had seen Okada greeting her, and that the situation compelled her to *pretend she knew him*. After a brief hesitation that was not perceptible to the other woman, Otama readily answered: "Yes, I do."
>
> "He's handsome all right," said Otei, "and yet, I hear there's not a flaw in his conduct."
>
> "You seem to know him well," *said Otama boldly*.
>
> "Madame Kamijo tells me that none of the students at her lodging can match him." And with these words Otei returned to her house.
>
> Otama felt as though she herself had been praised and *repeated to herself*: "Kamijo! Okada!" (OG 79; emphasis added)

In the first half of this passage, Otama's mental faculties are hard at work; subsequently, her desire for knowledge of Okada emerges. The last line is most significant in that the female recites the male's name—to name the Other is, symbolically, to possess it.

In a reversal of the conventional polarity between male viewer and female object, Okada does not attempt to "view," to get to know, or to possess Otama:

> He *didn't even know her name*, and he *made no effort to learn it*. All he had to do was look at the name plate, but he couldn't bring himself to do this in her presence. At other times, when she wasn't there, he hesitated because of the neighbors and the passersby. As a result, he never looked at the characters written on the small wooden sign shadowed by the eaves. (OG 20–21; emphasis added)

It thus becomes evident that Otama's desire for Okada is stronger than Okada's for her. Similarly, Otama's gaze on Okada is much more intense than Okada's on her. When *boku* takes a walk with Okada and sees Otama waiting for Okada, *boku* notes:

> I felt she was transformed as she *fixed her eyes on Okada*. When he took off his cap, I noticed how upset he was, and I saw him unconsciously quicken his step.
>
> Having the liberty of a third party, I looked back several times and saw that she continued to *watch Okada*.
>
> He went down the slope *with his head bent* and without relaxing his hurried gait. (OG 109; emphasis added)[26]

When *boku* catches up with Okada, he tells Okada that Otama is looking at him:

> "I turned around a number of times, and *she was always watching you*. She's probably standing there right now and *looking in this direction*. It's just as it's described in the *Saden* [*Zuozhuan*]: '*His eyes received her and saw her off.*' Only in your case *it's just the reverse*." (OG 109–10; emphasis added)

Okada avoids looking at her, although aware that he is being watched by her, and moreover that his companion has noticed this one-sided gaze. In contrast, Otama's gaze is "fixed" on Okada, neither inhibited nor interrupted by the narrator's persistent observation of her.[27]

The implicit subversion in gender roles is made explicit by *boku*, who cites a sentence from the *Zuozhuan* (the *Zuo Commentary* to the *Spring and Autumn Annals*) and observes that in this case the gender roles are reversed. In this early Chinese historical commentary, a man infatuated with another man's wife sees her in the street and is unable to look away. Here another man's mistress "fix[es] her eyes upon" a man walking in the street. The sense of parody is highlighted by the narrator's use of the word *abekobe* (the reverse), suggesting an inversion in which Okada displays passivity, an attribute conventionally ascribed to "Woman." By crossing the roles of male viewer and female object in the Confucian classic, the narrative hints at a subversion of conventional attitudes.

Whereas *boku* reverses a classical text on gender relations to accord with "reality," Okada seems inclined to superimpose cultural archetypes on "real" women. The narrator summarizes Okada's views on "Woman" as follows:

> A type of woman in these romantic tales also appealed to Okada. She is the woman who makes *beauty* her sole aim in life so that, with perfect ease, she goes through an elaborate toilet even while the angel of death waits outside her door. Okada felt that a woman should be only a *beautiful object, something lovable,* a being who keeps her *beauty and loveliness* no matter what situation she is in. Okada probably picked up this sentiment unconsciously, partly under the influence of his habitual reading of old Chinese romantic love poetry and the sentimental and fatalistic prose works of the so-called wits of the Ming and Ch'ing dynasties. (OG 20; emphasis added)

In the original text of *Gan,* "these romantic tales" are a particular story—"The Legend of Xiaoqing" (*Xiaoqing zhuan*). The selection of this particular tale and its interpretation within the text of *Gan* warrant careful attention.

Both Takemori Ten'yū and Chiba Shunji point out a divergence between *boku*'s perceptions of Otama and Okada's: *boku* sees a Pan Jinlian, an archetype of the promiscuous woman (see below); Okada, a Xiaoqing, a paragon of the woman of beauty and talent who lives and dies in undeserved neglect and isolation. The critics are divided, however, over just what to make of this gap in perceptions. Chiba suggests that the "tragedy" originates in the discrepancy between the real Otama, who, like Pan Jinlian, looks out the window (to look for a better partner than her current master), and the image of Xiaoqing, one who declines to "look out," that Okada wishes to assign to Otama. Chiba modifies this identification of the real Otama with Pan Jinlian and bases his conclusion on what he terms Otama's "complex personality."[28] Takemori, on the other hand, argues that Otama's characterization should be viewed entirely as a question of narratorial intention, implying that any attempt to gain an "objective" view of her personality would be misguided.[29] I, too, problematize not Otama's personality but the ways in which *boku* and Okada read her. Okada's interpretation of "The Legend of Xiaoqing" is in fact partial. Xiaoqing is a woman of extraordinary beauty and poetic genius, who becomes a concubine of a rich man and is harassed by his principal wife. Before her premature death from a disease brought on by melancholy, she has a painter draw her portrait. Not until the third attempt is she satisfied with the way she is represented, secure in the knowledge that her name as an exemplary beauty will be immortal.

An ardent reader of Chinese fiction, Okada nonetheless seems to overlook two central attributes of Xiaoqing: her poetic talent and her self-awareness. In the text of *Gan*, there is no mention of Xiaoqing as a poet.[30] Women's talents seem a matter of no concern for Okada. He is impressed, on the other hand, that the heroine "goes through an elaborate toilet" on her deathbed and keeps up the effort to remain beautiful. Contrary to Okada's understanding, however, Xiaoqing does not make herself up as "a beautiful object" for the male gaze or desire; she does so, rather, to satisfy herself and to establish her immortal fame as a distinguished beauty. Her motive is narcissism, not subservience to the pleasure of her man. This woman is thus more self-aware than Okada seems to feel she should be. She *thinks*, when according to Okada's ideal, she is supposed to be "only a beautiful object." As for Otama, she thinks about Okada, and also about herself—her beauty, her charm, and her chances to conquer this man.

> She was a degraded woman, true, a usurer's mistress. But *she was even more beautiful than when she had been a virgin*. In addition, misfortune had taught her what she wouldn't otherwise have known: *somehow men were interested in her*. And if this were the case, Okada could not look on her with absolute disfavor. No, that was out of the question. If he had disliked her, he would not have continued to bow to her whenever they saw each other. It was because of this same interest that he had killed the snake for her some time ago. She doubted that he would have offered his assistance if the event had happened at any other house. If it had not happened at her house, he wouldn't even have turned his eyes. Moreover, since she cared for him so much, at least some of her affection, if not all of it, must have been felt by him. "Why, even the birth of a child isn't as difficult as one thinks beforehand," she assured herself. (OG 106–7; emphasis added)

This passage—which in the original is given in the first person—makes it clear that Otama is self-conscious and aware of the other's gaze upon herself. This is something that her "Other," Okada, does not seem to know, or to have any interest in knowing.

This does not mean, however, that Okada is indifferent to erotic subjects. On the contrary, he takes pleasure in reading *Jin Ping Mei*, a Chinese novel renowned for its many sexual scenes. The Chinese text is frequently mentioned in *Gan* and plays a key role in the development of the story, as Takemori and Chiba observe.[31] First, it initiates the relationship between Okada and *boku*, when both attempt to purchase a used copy of the work. Then it causes the conversation between Okada and Otama that I discuss below. In short, the plot of *Gan* cannot take a step without *Jin Ping Mei*. Given that *Gan*'s encoded author, *boku*, loves reading *Jin Ping Mei*, the number of implicit references to the Chinese text in *Gan* are not surprising. The heroines of both books—Pan Jinlian and Otama—are unhappy with the man they live with—Wu the Elder and Suezō—and hopeful of meeting better partners.

Another common element—the setting in which the heroines first espy their potential lover, the motif of the bamboo blinds—implies an analogy between Pan Jinlian and Otama.

> In Otama's house *the bamboo blinds* were still drawn, their unfaded green covering the window from top to bottom. Otama sat inside with nothing to do. She leaned against a post hung with fans and vacantly *looked into* the street. After three o'clock the students would pass in small groups. And she knew that whenever they came, the voices of the girls next door would rise like the sounds of so many young sparrows. And attracted by the noise, she would also *glance out*.
>
> [. . .]
>
> And *watching the students* in their walks along the street, she began to *speculate*: "Isn't there *a hero* out there? I'll be *rescued*!"
>
> But when she suddenly found herself indulging in such fancies, she was startled.
>
> It was at this point that Okada got to know her. (OG 75–77; emphasis added)

The parallel passage of *Jin Ping Mei* reads:

> One day in the third month, when spring was at its most beautiful, Chinlien [= Jinlian] dressed herself up alluringly and could hardly wait for Wu the

Elder's departure before taking up *her position behind the bamboo blind* that hung over the front door. She had become accustomed to standing there until her husband was expected home and then taking down *the blind* and going inside to wait for him. But this particular day was one of those occasions on which:

Something was destined to happen.

Just as she was about to take down *the blind a certain person happened to walk by.*[32] (emphasis added)

The *Jin Ping Mei* is instrumental in leading Okada to something more than the silent exchange of greetings to which he and Otama had grown accustomed: "'So I spent all morning just lying here and reading the *Kimpeibai* [*Jin Ping Mei*] you lent me. I got to the point where *I couldn't think straight*, so I went out for a walk after lunch. And something strange happened'" (OG 85; emphasis added). Had he not been reading *Jin Ping Mei*, Okada, who is renowned, as noted earlier in the narrative, for his punctuality, would have taken his stroll after supper as usual, rather than after lunch.

Instead of having Okada talk about his experiences in direct speech, the narrator paraphrases what he heard from Okada:

Okada's reading of his Chinese novel had given him *a headache*. He had gone out for some air and from habit had turned toward Muenzaka. *He felt dizzy*. In old Chinese novels, especially in the *Kimpeibai* [*Jin Ping Mei*], usually after every ten or twenty pages of innocent description, the author invariably throws in *an indecent scene* as if he were quite punctually fulfilling a promise.

"*I must have looked awfully silly* after reading that sort of book," said Okada. (OG 85–86; emphasis added)

Thus, the effect of reading *Jin Ping Mei* is described in negative terms by both Okada and the narrator. The repeated suggestion of the carnal desire that filled Okada's mind at the time colors our imagination of the way Okada might have observed Otama when he came to rescue her bird from the snake. If Okada has not consciously associated Otama with Pan Jinlian, a manipulative woman of excessive sexual desire, *boku*, the narratee of Okada's account of his encounter with Otama, draws the link at the end of Okada's story. Thus two references, the first by Okada and the second by *boku*, to *Jin Ping Mei*, frame Okada's story. This may suggest that their perceptions of the Other (Otama) are mediated by analogies drawn from their experiences of reading fictional narratives in a conventional manner. However, as soon as he succeeds in catching the snake, Okada leaves, without further conversing with Otama. In this way he manages to differentiate his roles inside and outside the "story," which seems to be a version of *Jin Ping Mei*. Okada reconfirms the status of a reader, rather than an active participant. Just as before he had habitually seen Otama within the window frame, here, he "understands" her within the framework of his favorite story while himself fleeing from its constraint. He desires to be uninvolved, to remain the outsider, except for the brief onstage act.

In contrast to the conventional associations through which the male characters seem to view her, Otama's perception of Okada is unconventional. She feels that since the incident of the snake, Okada has become a man within her reach, rather than an outsider to her world: "Otama's longing for Okada had been like that of a woman for *an expensive article* she admired from a distance, but he now turned into *an article she wanted to buy*" (OG 93; emphasis added). Interestingly, the relation between buyer and object for sale is reversed here: Otama, who has been "bought" by Suezō, is thinking of "buying" an "article" herself, namely Okada. Again, Okada could not know that such an operation was going on in Otama's mind, nor would he be pleased if he found out. Furthermore, the text makes it clear that Otama desires Okada as a companion and then as a sexual object:

> When Suezo came and talked with her over the charcoal brazier, she *imagined what it would be like if Okada were there instead*. At first, she felt she was being unfaithful, but she gradually came to feel no shame in speaking in tune with Suezo's words while *thinking of Okada* all the time. Moreover, *when she submitted to Suezo, the image of Okada was behind her closed eyes*. Sometimes *they were together in her dreams*. He was there without any troublesome arrangements to be made. But the moment she thought how happy she was, the man turned into Suezo instead of Okada. She would be startled and would awake, her nerves so strained that sometimes she cried out in a fret. (OG 97; emphasis added)

It is not only in dreams that Otama consummates her physical relationship with Okada. Implicitly yet unmistakably, the following passage suggests masturbation:

> As a safeguard against obscene thoughts, educators warn young people not to remain awake after going to bed and to get up as soon as they awaken, for in the vigor of youth kept warm in bed, an image like the flower of a poisonous plant blooming in fire is apt to be engendered. At such times *Otama's imagination was unbridled*. Her eyes would glow, and the flush would spread from her eyelids to her cheeks as though she had drunk too much sake. (OG 101; emphasis added)

As Masao Miyoshi points out when quoting the same passage—with a minor alteration to suit his taste—Otama "perfectly understands her sensual needs."[33] Since we are not informed of any specific object of her sexual desire other than Okada, we may conclude that he is in her mind as she indulges in "obscene thoughts."

This type of reversal of conventional gender roles takes place within the master/mistress relationship between Suezō and Otama as well. Suezō consistently views himself as perceptive, and Otama as naïve: "She might be *shy* in everything, in no matter what, and she might blush and fidget at the important moment" (OG 28; emphasis added). A conversation about the theater also seems to prove that Otama, though perhaps a charming spectacle, is not qualified as a spectator:

> "Who are your favorite actors, Otama-san?" Suezo said, turning to her suddenly.
>
> "I don't have any favorites," she said. She had been quietly listening to the conversation.
>
> "Oh!" interrupted her father, "she's *never been inside a theatre*!" (OG 37; emphasis added)

We are told that although not an active participant in the conversation, she has been an ardent listener. Our sense of Otama's passivity is reinforced by her father's interruption. Without her father's annotation, her speech would have been deemed incomplete. Whether or not Otama lacks the qualifications of a good speaker, as the above seems to suggest, her reply to Suezō's question, as well as her father's comment, hints that she is no spectator, whose function is to be seen by others and not to observe others in her turn.

This impression is underscored by an observation of Suezō, after Otama's move to Muenzaka. To Suezō, with his gift of "penetration," Otama appears "as transparent as fresh water in the bottom of a flat vase"—no cloudiness, no depth. Her eyes seem as if they "could not keep very great secrets." Suezō feels self-confident and comfortable with Otama, since he feels he "could clearly perceive the motion of this delicate instrument." For Suezō, Otama is not a human being to be dealt with on equal terms—she is like a mechanism to be analyzed, whose responses may be predicted (OG 48–49). Otama, however, seems to view the relationship in sharply different terms. In a passage examined above for a different purpose, she says to her father: "'He treats me as though I were an infant. I'm not surprised that his type takes that approach with me. He thinks he can go through somebody's eye and nose without being seen. But I'm not as much of a child as that'" (OG 55). Otama accomplishes several things in this statement. First, she reveals her awareness of how little regard Suezō has for her. Second, she challenges his perception of her as a child. Third, and most important, she shows that Suezō is unaware that he himself is being objectified.

The narrator's statements support Otama's observations and suggest that it is in fact Suezō who is naïve in comparison to Otama. Let us return to the transformation that Suezō experiences as he frequents Otama's house, to see this time the implication of her intellectual superiority to him: "The experience of this delight, quite a new one for him, had been giving him *unconsciously* a sort of '*culture*' [italics in original] since the start of his visits to her. After all, *a primitive beast* can be subdued by *sensitive hands*" (OG 48; emphasis added except as noted). As she uncovers Suezō's lies regarding his marital status and profession, Otama herself grows less and less honest with him. More important, she loses any sense of a guilty conscience over her dishonesty:

Whatever pain the decision might cost her, she was determined to keep her sadness to herself. And when she had made this decision, the girl, who had always depended on others, had felt for the first time her own independence.

After that, she *secretly began to watch* what she said and did, and when Suezo came, she started to serve him *self-consciously* instead of accepting him frankly and sincerely as she had previously done. She would be with him in the room, but her real self was *detached, watching the scene from the side*. And there it would deride first Suezo and then the other Otama for being under his control. When she first became aware of this condition, she was shocked. But in time she accepted it, and she said to herself: "That's the way you should feel."

Her treatment of Suezo became more cordial but her heart more remote. She came to feel that he did not deserve her gratitude for the protection he gave her, nor could she feel obligated to him for what he did. She did not even feel sorry for him because of her indifference. Conversely, in spite of the fact that she had no accomplishment she could boast of, *she couldn't help thinking*: "Ah, to be only a usurer's possession all my life." (OG 76–77; emphasis added)

The narrator goes on to relate, in explicitly critical terms, how Suezō misunderstands the change in Otama.

At first Suezo admired the maiden-like naivete of her manners. But lately they had changed, and he was even more enchanted. He saw this transformation as evidence of her understanding of love, and he was proud that she had learned what it was from him. *In spite of his insight into reality*, this was a *ridiculous misunderstanding* of his mistress' state of mind. At first she had served him faithfully, but as a result of her unhappiness and the *reflectiveness* caused by the sudden changes in her life, she had arrived at *a self-consciousness* which might almost be called impudent negligence. She had acquired that coolness of mind that most women in the world who do have it can reach only after experiences with many men. (OG 102; emphasis added)

In another exchange, the narrator makes it clear that Otama is now superior to Suezō with regard to her knowledge of self and Other:

Otama said: "*Turn around, please.*"

"Why?" he asked, lighting a cigarette.

"Because I'm washing."

"Don't worry about me. Go ahead."

"But if you sit there *staring at me*, I can't."

"My, but you're proper. How's this? All right?" And with his back toward the corridor Suezo smoked is cigarette. *"What an innocent thing she is," he thought.*

[. . .] *she had no reason to feel embarrassed at being observed.*

[. . .] she didn't notice that he had turned, but after finishing and drawing the mirror stand in front of her, *she saw his face in it*, the cigarette still in his mouth.

"Ah? So that's the kind of man you are!" she said, *continuing to comb her hair.*

A triangular patch of white skin revealing her neck and part of her back could be seen above the loosened kimono, and her soft arms, lifted high and exposed a few inches above the elbows, were *sights Suezo never tired of.*

[. . .] "[. . .] I've got to go to Chiba. If everything goes all right, I'll be able to come back tomorrow. If not, maybe the day after."

"Oh?" said Otama, wiping her comb and looking back at him. *She made herself seem sad.* (OG 102–3; emphasis added)

Otama plays the role of an "innocent" and dependent woman here, according to the code of propriety, although she is aware she has no need to "feel embarrassed at being observed." Indeed she does not try to hide from Suezō's gaze when she realizes he has been watching her—she keeps combing her hair as if nothing had happened. She knows that her arms are "sights Suezo never tires of." Furthermore, she knows Suezō will be gratified to see her look sad at the news that he will not come to visit her that night. She understands that she is expected to play the role of the lonely woman.

Although such well-developed performative skills may have come as the result of her experience as a mistress, Otama was born perceptive. When Suezō, Otama, and her father meet to finalize the "marriage" arrangement through the go-between,

she stood calmly, not at all overwhelmed, *her eyes taking in everything with curiosity.* [. . .] *His eyes probed and registered.* She was beyond anything he had imagined, and, for that, all the more beautiful.

Otama was also surprised. She had previously thought that she did not care what the merchant was like. She would sell herself to anyone, no matter what his personality. She would do anything for her father. But on *seeing Suezo's dark features, his keen but engaging eyes, and his elegant yet restrained kimono,* she felt momentarily relieved, like a person escaping from a hopeless situation. (OG 34–35; emphasis added)

It is expected that Suezō should scrutinize Otama; he has "purchased" this woman for her physical beauty and is thus "entitled" to re-examine her to see if his judgment was right. Naturally, "his eyes probed and registered." What is unusual is Otama's answering gaze. The narrator observes that she is "not at all overwhelmed," exactly because she should be "overwhelmed" in this humiliating situation, with downcast eyes and her face hidden from Suezō. Otama's eyes, however, "probe" and "register" the unfamiliar landscape, and she examines Suezō, her future master. As far as the economy of gazes is concerned, Otama is Suezō's equal; she takes it for granted that she, too, is entitled to observe him. And she likes what she sees—his face and clothes, the very things we might expect a man to look at in a woman.

Otama is a woman of masculine vision. She wants to observe, know, and possess the Other. In so doing, she subverts the patriarchal convention of male voyeurism in which Woman is compelled to remain an "unthinking beauty." Similarly, other characters in *Gan,* who would remain peripheral in conventional romances—such as Otsune, who is not even a beauty—view others and try to understand and control them. In contrast, Okada, who would have been the center of the story in a conventional romance, remains largely without vision or voice. Thus, *Gan* overturns the privileged position of intellectual males in perspective and voice, while suggesting irreducible gaps in hierarchies of gender and class.

The partly omniscient narratorship enables many characters to observe and speak (to others and/or to themselves) in *Gan.* We are made aware of the positionality of each of them, defined by gender, class, and education, by the specific diction chosen for each character on each occasion. As in *Kusamakura,* the subject of the preceding chapter, the narrator-narratee relationship is destabilized, since each party knows only so much about the other's knowledge. The encoded reader—unspecified, though expected to exist in general terms—is allowed to share the vantage point of the omniscient narrator and the viewpoint of the relatively knowledgeable *boku* narrator. This does not mean, however, the reader is led to the illusion of the "truth" as objective and tangible. On top of the positionality of the narrator and narratee of each embedded narrative, *boku* as the encoded author reminds us of his own choices of how to tell and not to tell. The context-boundedness of the narrative is thus confirmed both from inside and from outside *Gan.*

CHAPTER 5

Doing Things with Words: Acts and Effects in Tanizaki Jun'ichirō's 'Manji'

"You see, shōsetsu has a certain paradoxical relationship with what you think of as 'reality.' You might expect Miki wrote this in order to convey a message, but instead, she might perhaps have written it in order to hide something."

The Author as Narratee

ONE FEATURE OF Tanizaki Jun'ichirō's *Manji* (1931) that distinguishes it from the narratives analyzed in the preceding chapters is that its encoded author exhibits his role as the narratee of the embedded narrative more conspicuously than his role as the narrator of the primary (and, as I show below, much shorter and more fragmentary) narrative.[1] In *Kokoro*, the primary narrator's (*watakushi*) references to his own act of writing identify him as the encoded author. *Kuroi ame* has no encoded author. *Kusamakura* leaves it ambiguous whether it was "authored" by its first-person narrator. In *Gan*, the first-person narrator acts as the encoded author. Although the primary narrator in each of these narratives also listens to the speech of others, this speech does not constitute a large portion of the narrative. Rather, it is engulfed by the primary narrative.

In contrast, *Manji*'s encoded author is the narratee of a first-person narrative told by a female character, Kakiuchi Sonoko, which, although "embedded" by definition, eclipses the encoded author's narratorial voice. She tells her experiences to a narratee whom she calls "Sensei,"[2] and who in turn calls him- or herself "sakusha," or the "Author," in occasional annotations to the dominant narrative. How does this merging of the roles of encoded author and narratee affect the way the narrative is read? In terms of temporal sequence, this character was first the narratee and then the author of the text that now lies before the reader. In this sense, he or she anticipates the reader's role in receiving and interpreting the narrator's discourse. As Ken Ito puts it, the encoded author "offers opinions to shape the responses of her larger audience, the readership of the text."[3] Rather than taking the initiative in developing the story itself, the Author instructs the reader how to interpret what the narrator tells and how she tells it. The Author does not assume the narratorship, but instead mediates and criticizes the narrator. The narrator is thus distanced, objectified, and laced into a frame of the Author's choosing. The reader is invited to read the narrator's story in the same way the Author does. Although this kind of authorial guidance was present in one form or another in the other narratives analyzed here, what distinguishes the present case is that this Author's control over the reader is strictly indirect and comes only in response to the narrator. This Author never tells the reader anything about him- or herself, since this is unnecessary in his or her strictly passive role as listener. This sort of listenership itself assumes certain qualifications, but I defer discussion of these, focusing in this section on the function of this character as encoded author.

The formal diction of the annotations suggests that the encoded author has a high level of education. The gender of the Author is unspecified, although it is most likely male; the fact that earlier versions of *Manji* presented a persona easily identifiable with the historical author Tanizaki Jun'ichirō has inclined readers to such a conclusion.[4] Also, the detached tone of speech and the display of judgment unswayed by the narrator are qualities conventionally attributed to males. This is to say, the encoded author writes *like* a man. Although there is no need in terms of the final text of *Manji* to conclude that the Author, or Sensei, must be a man, I take this as a working hypothesis, even though I do not exclude altogether the possibility that the person may be a woman—a possibility that would considerably alter our perceptions of this narrative.

Both the Author and the narrator Sonoko reveal their sense that the Author is superior to Sonoko. The term *sensei* as well as the expressions of courtesy and respect surrounding it (such as "Do forgive me for bothering you again" [3];[5] "I know how busy you are *with your own writing*" [3; emphasis added];[6] and "You've always been so sweet to me I'm afraid I'm taking advantage of your kindness, and after everything you've put up with . . . I can't thank you enough" [3]) suggest the narrator's consciousness of the narratee's superiority, whether in terms of education, social status, gender, or some combination of these. This sense of hierarchy affects the tone in which the Author annotates Sonoko's narration as well. These statements, which Ito characterizes as "highly opinionated,"[7] show that the Author takes it for granted that he is entitled to pronounce judgment on her words and actions. He clearly has no intention of glorifying or mythicizing the narrator, as *watakushi* in *Kokoro* has traditionally been considered to do.

The inclination toward commentary notwithstanding, the encoded author maintains a neutral attitude toward the content of the story, to the extent that he seems to have no personal interest in the incidents. This neutrality is evidenced indirectly by the fact that Sonoko feels obliged to lay out the story from the beginning. Although Sonoko has never before had a chance to speak with Sensei about her homoerotic relationship with Tokumitsu Mitsuko, a younger, unmarried school friend, she takes it for granted that he would have learned of the affair from newspapers, since it was quite a scandal (7–8). (Sonoko was involved in a series of manipulations conducted by Mitsuko and her impotent boyfriend Watanuki, resulting in Mitsuko's involvement with Sonoko's husband, the attempted triple suicide of Sonoko, her husband, and Mitsuko, and the death of her husband and Mitsuko.) Sensei, however, would have learned of those events only as an uninvolved outsider and is thus able to remain as neutral as anyone could be.

At one point, however, the encoded author's distance from the content of the narrative is compromised. Sonoko and Mitsuko mention that he is a famous novelist, incidentally revealing one of the few biographical details given the reader. As Sonoko and Mitsuko meet privately for a second time, Sonoko tells Mitsuko about her personal life.

> Until that moment I hadn't said a word to Mitsuko about myself, but then I told her everything: how I happened to marry, and all the trouble I had over my love affair, and even about how kind you were to let me ramble on and on about my problems, in spite of your being so busy.
>
> Mitsuko was astonished to hear I knew you.
>
> "Really, you're a friend of his?" she said, and wondered if I wouldn't bring her with me to meet you someday, since she loved your novels. Whenever I saw her she asked me to take her along next time, but somehow we never got around to it. (26–27)

Why would Sonoko tell Sensei of this conversation, and why does Sensei write it down? Sonoko's and Mitsuko's comments reveal not only that he is a famous writer, but also that Sonoko is proud of her acquaintance with him. Sonoko is, intentionally or otherwise, complimenting the encoded author both for his professional success and for his personal kindness to her. Although this might be simple courtesy on her part, it might also be intended as compensation for the fact that Sensei no longer monopolizes the position of confidant. Sonoko lightly confides in Mitsuko, whom she barely knows, about her love affair, a matter so serious she had had to consult Sensei for a solution. This conveys to Sensei her sense of intimacy with Mitsuko, but could simultaneously undermine the sense of privilege Sensei had enjoyed. Sonoko may thus be trying to soothe his feelings by flattering him.

Another point worth noting is that, although Sonoko herself may not have noticed, the Author suggests the possibility that Mitsuko anticipated that Sonoko would confide in Sensei and that he would eventually write a novel about their affair. The heightened performativity of Mitsuko's later behavior may reflect a desire to be immortalized in a work of fiction. Needless to say, the "true" intentions of Sonoko or Mitsuko are not determinable, and it is not to my purpose to speculate on them. But however uncertain we may be about the characters' intentions, what is certain is that the encoded author, by choosing to record some words and actions and not others, has left open certain interpretive spaces for the reader. If the ambiguity broached above were irrelevant, this conversation between Sonoko and Mitsuko should not have been included, since it has little direct bearing on what happened inside the story.

With the sole exception of this self-reflexive moment, however, the encoded author is uninvolved in the story. His hearing and his reporting of what he has heard thus appear as objective as possible. This is not to say that he gives us a literal transcript. Rather, the text before us bears marks of rewriting by its encoded author, whom Ito describes as "both self-effacing and pushy."[8] The first characteristic is manifested in his function as narrator, as we will see in the next section, and the second, in his role as author/critic. Although we do not see the narratee as a corporeal presence, we see the Author's hand quite distinctly. Sonoko, for example, was not responsible for dividing the narrative into thirty-three sections. The pace of her narration is not evident from the text, and we cannot tell at what points she might have taken a break.[9] If she in fact told her story in thirty-three sessions, she surely would not have numbered them. This numbering, at least, is not the work of the narrator, but of the encoded author or the historical author.

The most conspicuous trace of authorial intervention is a series of notes in parentheses, most of them beginning "sakusha chū" or "Author's note." At these self-reflexive moments, the encoded author gives the reader information that the narrator did not or could not provide. An examination of these notes reveals how this written discourse interrupts and/or complements Sonoko's oral discourse. The following is the first Author's note in the text:

> *I'm sure you know who I mean.* My model—*it's all been in the newspapers anyway*—was Miss Tokumitsu Mitsuko.
>
> (*Author's note* [italics in original]: The widow Kakiuchi seemed unaffected by *her recent ordeal.* Her dress and manner were bright, even showy, just as they had been a year before. Rather than a widow, Mrs. Kakiuchi looked like the typical young married Osaka woman of good family, and she spoke in the mellifluous feminine dialect of her class and region. She was certainly no great beauty, but as she said the name "Tokumitsu Mitsuko," her face became suffused with a curious radiance.) (7–8; emphasis added except as noted)

The reader, for whom this is the first mention of Tokumitsu Mitsuko, does not at this point know what has happened to her or to Sonoko. But Sonoko presumes that her listener has some knowledge of the incident she is about to relate, as the first italicized segment shows. The reason she assumes such knowledge is shown in the second passage italicized above. At this point, the reader realizes that the incident was of journalistic interest and thus must have been something sensational. The Author's laconic reference to "her recent ordeal" reinforces the sense of the event's unusualness, as well as confirms that Sonoko's assumption of her listener's knowledge was justified. (The original phrasing, "ijōnaru keiken" [extraordinary experience], focuses less on the painful nature of the incident and more on its unusualness.) The tragic nature of the incident is hinted in passing by the Author's reference to Sonoko as "the widow Kakiuchi." Without further explanation, the reader is presented with the fact that Sonoko's husband, of whom Sonoko herself has just spoken, is deceased. What is important to note here is that narrator and narratee share a basic understanding of the events being retold, an understanding that has yet to be made available to the reader. In short, the encoded author's knowledge exceeds that of the reader.

Another aspect of the encoded author's involvement is the way he complements the narrator's statements by describing nonverbal aspects of her narrative. The visual information provided in this first note helps the reader form a more immediate sense of the narration as a performative act in a particular setting. Another example of this sort of contextual supplement occurs in a parenthetical comment near the end of the narrative: "(The widow Kakiuchi suddenly burst into tears)" (224). Since a dramatic effect seems especially desirable at the conclusion of a narrative performance, the author's note serves a useful purpose in that regard.

The next note, which again supplements the narrative with visual information, shows us the encoded author's critical response to a photograph of Mitsuko: "(*Author's note:*[. . .] Certainly she was very beautiful; there was no false modesty in the widow's remark about being a foil for her. But whether her face was in fact suitable for the benign features of the Willow Kannon was perhaps another matter)" (13–14). At an earlier point in the story, Sonoko, while trying to produce a picture of the Willow Kannon using a professional model, realizes that she has unconsciously been portraying Mitsuko. Sonoko thereafter continues to refer to Mitsuko as a Kannon in the flesh. This note shows that the encoded author agrees with Sonoko only in part—that is, he agrees with her about the contrast between Mitsuko's striking beauty and her own plain appearance, but he does not think that Mitsuko looks divine enough to represent the Willow Kannon. This suggests the distance the Author maintains from the narrator's observations, his confidence in his own judgment, and his willingness to add comments from a different viewpoint when he feels it is necessary.

The encoded author also makes his presence felt as a critic of the narrator's aesthetic judgment. When Sonoko shows him a bundle of letters that she and Mitsuko have exchanged, the Author unburdens himself of a lengthy comment, an abridged version of which I quote below:

> (*Author's note:* The letters that the widow Kakiuchi called "just a few" from their correspondence filled a silk-crepe parcel about ten inches square almost to bursting; the four corners of the cloth had been knotted together with difficulty. [. . .] I was somewhat taken aback at the sight. Doubtless no Tokyo woman would choose such garish envelopes. [. . .] Here I will only quote from several of them to illustrate the fervid emotional situation underlying this account, but it may be well to add a description of the stationery itself. In my opinion, the decorative aspect of the letters is sometimes even more revealing than their content.) (37–38)

The reader is first informed of the sheer quantity of the letters, themselves only a selection from a much larger corpus. The encoded author then candidly tells us that he does not care for the designs of the envelopes, of which the reader could have known nothing without a description from the Author. The Author's comparison of Sonoko's aesthetic taste to that of women in Tokyo implies a thorough knowledge of women's tastes in a variety of cultural milieux. More significant, however, is the Author's willingness to employ subjective terms like "garish" in an attempt to form the reader's perceptions. And given the constructed neutrality of the encoded author, the reader is likely to prove more susceptible to his judgment than to Sonoko's.

The most important fact that comes to light in this passage is that the encoded author enjoys the prerogative of selecting and rearranging bits of information provided by Sonoko. When he openly declares that the quotations presented from the two women's letters are his own selection and do not represent the entirety of the correspondence, a seam, so to speak, appears in the texture, reminding us of the authorial control that extends throughout the text. A similar instance occurs later in the narrative when the Author is about to quote a document Sonoko has shown him. The document in question records a vow she exchanged with Watanuki, Mitsuko's impotent boyfriend, that neither of them would monopolize Mitsuko's affections:

> (*Author's note:* It seems worthwhile to give the full text of the document that Mrs. Kakiuchi provided, not only to introduce its contents at this stage in her narrative but also because it will serve to indicate something of the character of the man who drafted it, Mr. Watanuki.) (124)

In contrast to the previous example, here the encoded author declares that he has not deleted anything from the document. However, his control over the text remains just as absolute, for it is his judgment that provides the rationale for presenting the document in its entirety.

Unlike the instance analyzed above in which the narrator and the encoded author shared knowledge not yet available to the reader, in the following passage the Author provides the reader with information that he himself did not know when he first read the document that Sonoko showed to him during her narration. The document in question is a letter from Mitsuko to Sonoko.

> *Ma chère soeur Mlle Jardin,*
>
> *Dearest elder sister, today, Mitsu has been in a bad temper all day long! Plucking the flowers out of the alcove, scolding poor innocent Ume (that's the name of the maid who always waits on her)—* (41)

The words within parentheses are, of course, not found in the text of the original letter. They are added by the encoded author as he quotes the letter, since the reader will probably wonder who Ume is. (It is likely, moreover, that the Author himself did not know who she was until later; see below.) The Author not only deletes but also adds information, according to his own judgment of what the reader needs to know in order to follow the story. Without the information in parentheses, the reader would have been left in doubt until the moment, several pages later, when Sonoko says: "As things stood, nothing kept me from telephoning or visiting their house every day . . . but besides her mother there was her maid, Ume, the one mentioned in the letter, and other prying eyes. It wasn't the same as being at my house" (47).

Yet another kind of Author's note, distinct from these instances of tacit concealment and foregrounded disclosure, states clearly that the Author is not prepared to disclose certain information to the reader.

After quoting from the document prepared by Watanuki, he comments on the physical appearance of two of the "letters":

> (*Author's note:*[. . .] What seemed particularly repellent were the two seeping brownish stains that looked like little flower petals impressed below the signatures; two of the same kind of stains were spread across the seams of the paper, where seals would also have been applied. The widow's own account will suffice to explain them.) (126–27)

The author does not at this point tell the reader that the stains are Watanuki's and Sonoko's blood. Instead, he leaves an ominous impression in the reader's mind by leaving the question of the precise nature of these stains unanswered. He stimulates the reader's curiosity far more effectively than he would have by explaining the stains in light of knowledge he must have acquired between seeing them for the first time and writing this text.

This delineation of the moments in which the encoded author controls the narrative contrasts with those moments in which he remains silent regarding discrepancies between the knowledge of the reader and that of the narrator. The reader first learns that Mitsuko is dead when Sonoko, rightly assuming that Sensei is aware of this fact, implies this while showing her photograph to him:

> In this picture her hairdo makes her look several years younger, though actually she was twenty-two, only a year younger than myself—if she were still alive now [in 1928], she'd be twenty-three this year. (14)

Since the encoded author provides no explanation, the reader is forced to wait to find out what caused the young woman's death. As we have seen, the Author exercises his own judgment in providing notes or withholding them, and he uses his notes either to explain or to declare that he is not ready to explain. Thus, the Author, in a variety of ways, controls the narrative as well as the range of the reader's knowledge.

Beyond the obvious formal features examined above, the polish of the narration suggests the encoded author's involvement in rewriting the narrator's account. Given the length and complexity of the story, it is surprisingly easy to follow, providing at one point or another all the information that the reader needs to know. This may lead us to wonder whether the evidence of orality one finds in the narrative may in fact have been reconstructed by the encoded author. The sporadic instances of apparently oral discourse (see below) are at odds with the remarkably artful narrative form in which Sonoko presents her extremely complicated story. All this points to a process of rewriting performed by the encoded author and then concealed behind a facade of orality in Sonoko's discourse.

In fact, Sonoko says that she herself once tried, unsuccessfully, to write her story down:

> I only wish I could put it all down on paper, like one of your novels, and ask you to read it. . . . The truth is, the other day I tried to start writing, but what happened is so complicated I didn't know where to begin. So I thought I'd just have to talk it out, and that's why I'm here. (3)

Sonoko's experience seems to confirm a gender-based division of linguistic labor: literacy for the men and orality for women. The simplistic conclusion that could be drawn from this is that women are not as good as men at thinking logically or writing coherently about complex issues. Indeed, the levels of diction employed by the encoded author and Sonoko are noticeably different: the author writes in so-called standard Japanese; Sonoko's speech is rendered in a quasi-Hanshin (Osaka) dialect. As Kōno Taeko points out, this dialect is not appropriate to Sonoko's class or upbringing.[10] This failure of verisimilitude notwithstanding, Sonoko's mock-Hanshin dialect serves to articulate the difference between the literary discourse of the Author and the oral discourse of the narrator—the former, masculine, cosmopolitan, and literate; the latter, feminine, parochial, and oral.

Female Voice, Male Hand? An Invisible Dialogue

This division of labor along gender lines proves artificial, however, when we examine this apparently monologic narrative for signs of the narratee's participation. Sensei is not only responsible for writing the text but also involved in the narration of the story. Although he remains invisible as a body, the text reveals traces of his voice. As is the case with any narrative, the particular nature of the relationship between the narrator and narratee, which is implied at several points in *Manji*, affects the way we interpret Sonoko's narration, even if Sensei's participation in it is not textually evidenced. First, she evidently feels comfortable with him as a listener, given that, as we learn, she previously consulted him about something as personal as an unconsummated love affair with another man. Sonoko, who does not talk much to her husband, has established the kind of rapport with Sensei that enables her to speak freely to him about her private life.

This does not mean, of course, that her retelling of these new experiences is transparent, which is a theoretical impossibility. But since Sonoko is our only source for the story, neither the narratee nor the reader is able to gauge the extent of her transparency against other people's testimony (the other two principals are, of course, unavailable for direct comment). As the narratee, however, Sensei does not question the accuracy of Sonoko's narration. Although he supplements Sonoko's account and notes her flattering and somewhat apologetic statement about her acquaintance with him, the narratee does not seem particularly suspicious of her self-acclaimed honesty. Instead, he seems to assume that Sonoko will try to be truthful, and not hold anything back from Sensei. Unlike *boku* in *Gan*, who readily mentions his reservations about Okada's account, the lack of a similarly critical statement here is suggestive of Sensei's trust in Sonoko. Nor does Sensei act like a detective or paparazzo as *yo* in *Kusamakura* or *boku* does, questioning what appears to be true on the surface in order to penetrate the other's personal life. His perception of Sonoko as a reliable narrator suggests not only the chemistry between the narrator and narratee but also the tightness of their collaboration in constructing a relatively consistent story to present to the reader.

The text of *Manji* consists solely of Sonoko's speech and the encoded author's notes on it. Sonoko never writes except in the letters to Mitsuko included by the Author; the Author never speaks. As Ken Ito points out, "his side of the conversation" has been "remov[ed]" "from the narrative."[11] The gender-based distribution of orality and literacy is almost absolute, enough so to strike us as artificial and odd. It is hard to believe that the narratee remained silent as Sonoko told him her story. One would expect him from time to time to have expressed agreement, disagreement, surprise, or to have asked the narrator to stop, to repeat, to fill in gaps. Such acts, however, have largely been erased from the text.

Certain clues in the text, however, reveal Sonoko's narrative as dialogic rather than purely monologic. Sonoko often utters "— haa," a word used to acknowledge and respond to a question of the listener. As Chiba Shunji points out, such utterances "introduce a dialogic nature" into the narration that would otherwise be "a monotonous soliloquy" and, further, suggest that Sonoko's narration is "skillfully directed by questions" of Sensei.[12] For example:

> According to Mitsuko, the director often called on the families of students who were well off, asking for loans like that, but had never once returned any borrowed money. If he'd used the money properly it would have been different, but he let things run down till the building was just a pigsty, a dilapidated one at that!
>
> . . . What? No, it seems he used all that money for personal expenses. (17)

The beginning of the second paragraph suggests that Sonoko was interrupted by a question from the narratee. We can guess from her answer what the question was: How did the school director use the money he borrowed from students' families, if not for the renovation of the school building, as he claimed? This question, however, has been erased and replaced with the ellipses preceding Sonoko's "What?," which is either a request that the narratee repeat his question or an interjection to give her time to think of an answer to the question.

Another example occurs in a passage in which Sonoko describes an outing with Mitsuko.

> "Mitsuko, how about gathering some bracken?" I suggested. "I know there's a lot of bracken and horsetail on the next hill." We stayed till evening, picking quantities of bracken and flowering ferns and horsetail.
>
> . . . Where were we on Mount Wakakusa? It has three peaks, you know, and we were in the hollow between the first two—you can see young herbs all over; they're especially delicious because the dead grass is burned off every spring.

> Anyway, it had begun to get dark by the time we came back over the first hill. (22)

The ellipses at the beginning of the second paragraph suggest that the narratee interrupted Sonoko's narrative with a question. The question must have been something on the order of: Where were you on Mount Wakakusa? But again, the question is recoverable only through Sonoko's reaction to it.

The effect of such erasures is to keep the narratee inaudible and to hold in abeyance any sense of dialogue. The encoded author, by suppressing his own voice, tries to maintain the monologic appearance of the narrative, while complementing it with his written comments. Sensei, instead of speaking directly in the scene of narration, silences this voice so as to control the text more fully through the act of writing. He chooses to remain absent as Sonoko's interlocutor and to become present as the encoded author of *Manji*. In effect, it is as though the narratee did not exist as a corporeal presence. He is neither seen nor heard. We do not know what he looks like, nor how he sounds. Sensei is never portrayed; he exists only as a pen or a camera (or a perceiving mind)—just as *yo* in *Kusamakura* had hoped to do. The only hitch in this project of self-erasure appears in Sonoko's reactions to his questions. These are significant in that the absence of the narratee's body from the narration is made explicit through them. Sensei's presence is highlighted as something that has been erased.

All the descriptions provided by the encoded author pertain to Sonoko, whose voice and appearance are made vividly present to the reader. The immediacy of the narrative experience shared by narrator and narratee is conveyed to the reader through her words and the Author's description of her gestures and facial expressions. Such immediacy is evident in the following scene, in which Sonoko remembers that she has a photograph of Mitsuko with her and produces it.

> Oh yes, I've brought along a photograph I'd like to show you. We had it taken of us together when we got our matching kimonos—it's the one that was in the papers and attracted so much attention. As you can see, standing side by side like this I'm just a foil for Mitsuko. (13)

With the self-address and the repeated use of "you" (which, in the original, is represented not with the second-person pronoun but with the imperative form ["goran kudasai mase"] and honorifics), Sonoko's words reconstruct a scene in which both narrator and narratee look at the photograph. Her speech generates images and invites the reader into the act. In Japanese, the scene is made even more forceful by the persistent use of pronouns indicative of the nearness of the referent: *koko* (here), *kore* ("this"; repeated three times), *konna* (like this), *kono* (this).[13] The passage demonstrates the "presentness" of the acts of narrating and listening. A similar instance occurs when Sonoko introduces another artifact before the narratee's eyes:

> As he spoke, he took from his pocket what appeared to be a pair of legal contracts.
>
> . . . Just look at this, please. It's one of the vows we signed that day. (124)

Here, on top of the ellipse, which represents the time it takes her to produce the document, and the use of "this" (*kore*—repeated twice in Japanese), Sonoko enhances the sense of performativity, probably unreflectingly, by re-enacting Watanuki's presentation of the document. Just as the reader is invited to experience the immediacy of Sonoko speaking to Sensei, both the narratee and the reader are drawn into the scene to share the moment Watanuki speaks to Sonoko. The double-layered quotation is accompanied by a double-layered physical gesture, and the text evokes a feeling of immediacy from both the recent and the remote past.

The "transcript" of Sonoko's narration bears other traces of her narrative performance. For one thing, chronological order is often not maintained. After showing Sensei the photograph of Mitsuko, Sonoko reverts in her narration to the first incident in their relationship: "Well, around that time—to go back to when we'd hardly spoken, that is—" (14). While looking at the picture along with Sensei, Sonoko breaks the train of her narrative to describe Mitsuko's physical appearance. It is at this point, as mentioned above, that the reader inadvertently learns that Mitsuko is dead by the time of narration. Sonoko's narration thus disturbs the chronological order, placing Mitsuko's death prior to her friendship with Sonoko. When Sonoko resumes narrating the story, she has to supply an explanation of where she is picking up the thread of her story; "around that time" refers not to when Mitsuko died, but to the time before Sonoko knew Mitsuko well. Written narratives frequently violate chronological order,[14] but the way that order is disturbed here (that is, by the sudden intrusion of a nonverbal artifact) and the way it is restored (by the insertion of a remark in mid-sentence) seem improvisational, accidental, and thus characteristically oral.

In the following example, Sonoko remembers *in medias res* something she should have mentioned earlier to help the narratee understand the context of the incident she is now narrating. As she relates Mitsuko's description of how the school director conspired with a councilman whose daughter was competing with Mitsuko for marriage to a desirable man, Sonoko realizes that she has not explained why the director was acting against Mitsuko: "Oh yes, and before that—this is getting to be hopelessly confused, I'm afraid—sometime before that, she said, the director had asked her father if he couldn't lend the school a thousand yen, to repair the building" (16). Because Mitsuko's father refused, the director developed a grudge against her family and sided with the councilman. With this additional information, his motive becomes clear to the narratee as well as to the reader. Sonoko's self-criticism is noteworthy. Although her talk is "confused," she is conscious of the fact and, to that extent, able to observe herself in perspective. She may appear emotional and self-absorbed at times, but she is capable of a logical self-critique.

Sonoko's critical self-awareness and underlying clearheadedness are also evident in the next quotation, from the last section of the narrative. Her narration has proceeded from the lesbian relationship between herself and Mitsuko to the love triangle involving Watanuki to the love triangle involving Sonoko's husband, who initially came onto the scene to advise Sonoko and help her out of the trouble caused by Watanuki's threat to publicize her lesbianism. All that remains to be told is already known to the narratee, as we saw above—the attempted triple suicide, which only Sonoko survived:

As for what happened later, all the newspapers carried full reports of *that* scandal, so I'm sure you've read more than enough about it. I won't try to go into everything that took place in those last days—talking on and on like this has me too excited to be coherent anyway— (222)

Although Sonoko's comment on her way of narrating—she thinks of it as long-winded and incoherent—could be taken simply as a gesture of humility, the fact that she criticizes herself is worth noting. Aware that the narratee is listening to her, she feels compelled to look back at her own narration from the listener's viewpoint. In this she is neither self-justifying nor self-absorbed, but self-critical and striving for objectivity. In fact, Sonoko's narration is not nearly as disorganized as she claims. Given the complexity of the account, it is even impressive that she is able to execute her task of recounting so articulately.[15] In this regard, Chiba Shunji maintains:

Features of the spoken language—accumulative, paralleling, and nonanalytical—are, as I have stated repeatedly, liberally included in *Manji*. It is also true, however, that [*Manji*] is remarkable for its compositional skills, which furnish the narrative with consistency and structure the plot so as to intensify the story toward the climax. It is hard to believe that the "narration" of Sonoko, who [earlier] failed to write up her own account, could have been so consistent and well structured. Naturally, the Author (Sensei) has to assume responsibility for rearranging incidents in chronological order and intentionally selecting the topic at a given moment in the process of narration. [Once again,] the Author must have been torn between Sonoko's orality and his own literacy, tormented by the dilemma and conflicts.[16]

Whereas I agree with Chiba that the encoded author has edited Sonoko's narration, I would rather argue that the polarity between "female" orality and "male" literacy is not valid, or that it has been made valid solely by the Author. If the encoded author has edited Sonoko's narration into something more readable, then it also seems true that the text of *Manji* is constructed in such a way that the orality of Sonoko's narration may be foregrounded. The written version of the narrative cannot possibly be a word-for-word transcription of what Sonoko said to Sensei. This suggests that the characteristics of "orality" observed above—the traces of dialogue, the use of certain pronouns, disturbances in the chronological order, among others—were selected for preservation, if not invented, by the encoded author. Only thus could the discourses of the Author and the narrator be distinguished so clearly from each other, and only thus could the Author maintain his privileged and yet marginal position as an outsider to the story's realm. The distinction between the two layers, however, is itself a fiction, created by the encoded author himself.

Expectations and Effects of Silence and Confessions

Although Sonoko's first-person narrative dominates *Manji*, other characters such as her husband, Mitsuko, and Watanuki, do speak within her narration. Their speech is presented either as direct quotations or as paraphrases by Sonoko. They are rather vocal, and the reader hears their voices clearly. But the absence of speech plays an equally significant role in this narrative. The recurrent motif of silence, complete or partial, as a hesitation to confess or as an active choice not to confess, directs the course of the story, along with and in contrast to the motif of confession. A speaker's decision either to keep silent about, or to confess to, something the addressee does not know suggests the nature of their relationship, as well as the speaker's intentions in making the choice and his or her expectations of the addressee's likely response.

The following passage, from the beginning of the narrative, concerns Sonoko's choice not to tell her husband of a love affair she had with another man.

> But I have to admit I never said a word to him about the other man. "It isn't healthy to hide your past mistakes from your husband," you warned me, "and since you tell me you haven't already gone too far up till now, why not make a clean breast of it?" And yet . . . I suppose even my husband may have had an inkling about what was going on, but somehow it was hard for me to confess. I told myself I'd just try not to make the same mistake over again, and I kept that love affair a secret hidden deep in my heart. So he didn't really know what we were talking about, you see; he thought you were simply giving me a lot of good advice. It's made a wonderful change in your attitude, he said. (4)

This choice of silence over confession illustrates an aspect of Sonoko's marriage. She does not feel comfortable talking with her husband about emotional matters. Although this might seem natural here, given that he is the "victim" of her infidelity, it stands in contrast to the candor with which she talks with Mitsuko later, not only of this past affair but also of her affection for Mitsuko, her jealousy of Watanuki, and other matters. This does not mean, however, that Sonoko never confides in her husband. He can be a good listener—provided he is not involved in the matter himself. He is a lawyer, and Sonoko consults him as if he were her attorney rather than her husband.

Sonoko's distance from her husband, however, does not imply a lack of trust in his decency. In fact, she appears to have no doubt that he is a trustworthy person, incapable of betrayal, voyeurism, or eavesdropping, as the following remark suggests:

> Gradually our secret notes and letters were not so secret either, and I would leave a letter from Mitsuko lying open on the desk. . . . Of course my husband was not the sort to read other people's mail on the sly, I needn't worry about that, but in the past, once I'd read a letter, I used to hurry to lock it away in a cabinet drawer. . . . (59)

Although we cannot ignore the possibility that the husband did read the letters, since we have no record of his private thoughts (unlike the case in *Kagi* [1956; trans., *The Key*, 1961],[17] a novel made up of alternating diary entries of a husband and a wife, each of whom secretly reads the other's diary), Sonoko believes that her husband did not read letters even when they were left where he could read them. Apart from the understanding that her husband respects Sonoko's privacy, her conviction suggests yet another aspect of his personality. Sonoko's confidence that her husband will not read these letters is an expression of her knowledge of his lack of interest in her private life. Indeed, the husband is not a detective or paparazzo; his passivity is so remarkable that we might even suspect connivance, if we choose to prescribe him a more active engagement in the plot. He continues to demonstrate this knack for remaining detached, both emotionally and practically, until much later in the story.[18] In fact, the long delay in his active participation as a figure of real personal interest, rather than as an advisor to Sonoko, contributes to the powerful sense of surprise we feel once he does begin to act.[19]

The husband's personality aside, Sonoko's remark that she began leaving Mitsuko's letters out in the open represents an unusual form of confession. Sonoko in effect "confesses" to an erotic correspondence with Mitsuko, but her husband's failure to "listen" makes this "confession" effectively silent. Alternatively, one might call this a confession calculated to remain silent, since Sonoko anticipated that her husband would not read the letters.

The locked cabinet drawer mentioned above reappears twice in the story and functions as a metaphor for silence. Whereas the lock serves little purpose when her husband is the potential reader of what is stored inside, it becomes vital when Sonoko fears that Mitsuko may see the concealed object. After exchanging vows with Watanuki that neither of them will monopolize Mitsuko, Sonoko stores her copy of the contract in the same place where she used to hide Mitsuko's letters: "I felt deathly afraid of him and meant to keep my promise faithfully, so I locked my copy of the oath up in the cabinet drawer. It troubled me to keep it secret from Mitsuko, but I tried not to give the least hint to her" (131). In fact, Sonoko does tell Mitsuko of the contract, without showing it to her, when Mitsuko asks if she is hiding anything. Whether or not Sonoko thinks of it this way, the lock now functions only to protect the contract from her husband's possible discovery. Sonoko does not, however, say, "it troubled me to keep it secret from my husband." Nor is there any mention of a guilty conscience when she hid Mitsuko's letters from her husband in the same drawer. In the end, it is Mitsuko, and not her husband, with whom Sonoko earnestly wants to be candid and honest.

Finally the husband does learn of the existence of the contract from an outside source—Watanuki, who uses his copy of the contract to blackmail the husband by threatening to make it public. Sonoko's husband borrows the document from Watanuki and confronts Sonoko with it:

My husband told me all this in a rush, and then demanded:

"What about it? Didn't you actually sign such a document? If you have a copy of your own, let me see it." Then he quietly waited for me to answer.

I got up without a word, opened the locked drawer, brought out the copy I had hidden there, and, still keeping my silence, placed it on the table before him. (179)

Neither Sonoko nor her husband speaks here, and their silence is repeatedly emphasized. The document itself speaks eloquently of what has happened, and the locked drawer shows how secretive Sonoko can be toward her husband.

Sonoko is not, however, the most secretive person in the story. She relies on her locked drawer to hide things, whereas others hide things in their mind. And she does not keep her secrets for long—as we will see, she rather takes pleasure in telling all. Secretiveness is most vividly embodied by Watanuki, not only in the way he withholds the truth, but also in the way that he demands confidentiality of others. In the following scene, Sonoko, who has just parted with Mitsuko, is intercepted by Watanuki, who asks for a word with her.

"Would you promise to keep our meeting secret, Sister? I can't talk unless you do."

"If I'm told to keep it to myself, you can be sure I will!" I replied sharply. "But sometimes while I'm trying not to break a promise, I find that people are making a fool of me. . . ."

"Oh, Sister. You think Mitsuko acts as she does because I've been pulling the strings, don't you? I know you have your reasons for thinking so." (131–32)

Sonoko suggests here that she is the honest one, whereas others are secretive and ready to break a promise. Sonoko has Mitsuko and Watanuki in mind here, for they appear to have deceived Sonoko in order to reconcile her with Mitsuko. However, since Sonoko is in love with Mitsuko, she is unwilling to suspect Mitsuko and attributes the deception to Watanuki, whom she views as a rival for Mitsuko's attention. Watanuki neither admits nor denies his involvement in Mitsuko's schemes to reconcile Sonoko to her. He simply sighs and tells Sonoko she has good reason to suspect him of manipulating Mitsuko. He goes on to tell Sonoko that she has far more control over Mitsuko, since Mitsuko loves Sonoko better. By portraying himself as an unfortunate man whose love is unrequited, Watanuki succeeds in convincing Sonoko that he could not possibly have manipulated Mitsuko. Furthermore, his flattery with a hint of jealousy works to disarm Sonoko and make her pity him, rather than suspect and detest him. Having successfully flattered her, Watanuki talks Sonoko into exchanging a vow making them siblings, who must share Mitsuko on equal terms. At his insistence Sonoko signs the document and drips blood on it to certify it as a binding agreement.

The next day, Mitsuko notices a cut on Sonoko's arm, and, recalling that Watanuki has a similar cut on his arm, begins to interrogate Sonoko:

> "Sister, you're hiding something from me, aren't you? Please tell me the truth about that cut." And she went on: "You're trying to deceive me, but I have a good idea what happpened. You and Eijiro [Watanuki's given name] made a private pact, without letting me know, didn't you?"
>
> Well, Mitsuko's suspicions were plainly on the right track. There was no use pretending ignorance if she saw through me like that, but although I knew I had turned white as a sheet, I wouldn't answer her.
>
> "That's right, isn't it?" she insisted. "Why won't you admit it?" (113)

Sonoko is honestly trying to keep her promise to Watanuki. Her pretense of innocence, however, is unsuccessful, not only because Mitsuko has already guessed correctly, but also because the change in Sonoko's color speaks louder than words. Paradoxically, even Sonoko's silence is expressive, as Mitsuko astutely points out: "And then: 'Since you're keeping it secret, you must think it's something I have no right to know'" (132). This is the opposite of the silenced confession we saw when Sonoko left Mitsuko's letters exposed to her husband's gaze. Whereas his gaze was blind and Sonoko's "confession" silenced, here Sonoko's silence is telling, and Mitsuko not only perceptive but shrewd enough to read the message of a blank space. As we will see, Mitsuko knows how to tell one story to conceal another, and Sonoko herself can apply this strategy to talk her husband into a false belief. With Mitsuko, however, the most Sonoko can do is to refrain from answering the question—which leaves her, under Mitsuko's gaze, utterly transparent.

Torn between the desire to keep her promise and the desire to be truthful to her lover, Sonoko tries to find a compromise:

> The longer I kept my secret, the more she would suspect me, I knew, and yet I couldn't simply blurt it out to her without consulting Watanuki.
>
> "Please wait till tomorrow," I begged her.
>
> But she asked why it had to be tomorrow, why I couldn't tell her today. If I had to get permission from someone else, she didn't even want to hear it. She certainly wouldn't cause any trouble for me if I told her in confidence. Nothing less would satisfy her.
>
> So I retorted: "You say all that, Mitsu, but aren't *you* hiding something from *me?*"
>
> "What could I be hiding?" She protested. "If that's how you feel, just ask me—I'll tell you anything you like."
>
> "Really? You're sure?"
>
> "Of course I'm sure. Maybe there's something I haven't told you about myself, but it's not because I'm trying to keep it secret." (132–33)

Mitsuko demands unconditional candor from Sonoko, proposing a closed circle in which only they matter and into which no external consideration should intrude. Needless to say, coming from Mitsuko this is a highly suspect proposition, for it is she, and not Sonoko, who has been introducing external factors such as Watanuki into their relationship. When Sonoko, thus stirred up, expresses her own suspicions, Mitsuko declares she has been hiding nothing—a claim made with much self-confidence in her own ability to devise a convincing explanation, no matter what Sonoko might accuse her of. (Indeed Mitsuko successfully does this in the subsequent exchange of questions and answers, which are examined in the next section in a different context.)

Regardless of the degree to which they practice it, the characters in *Manji* show a high regard for the virtue of candor. None of them wishes to appear to be lying or concealing something; all are quick to lay claim to total forthrightness. Hence, the plethora of "full confessions." There are many avowals of complete disclosure. Needless to say, not all these confessions are truthful—or rather, the degree of truthfulness is less an issue than the effects of the pretense of truthfulness. Full confessions are deployed in order to divert the addressee's attention from something else or to lie outright about a particular issue.

Sonoko may be unique in her ardor to confess and to convince her addressee of its candor. The first sentence of *Manji* serves as a good example: "I want you to hear my side of the story, from beginning to end" (3). She claims here as narrator of the story that she will be telling the truth as she sees it. As for her personal motives for wanting to tell Sensei what happened between her and Mitsuko "from beginning to end," she must feel that her version of the story has not been expressed—either by the police or by the journalists who reported on the unusual death of Mitsuko and Sonoko's husband. She probably feels that the public version of the story needs to be complemented by yet another version. And her choice of Sensei as an audience is appropriate, not only in terms of her rapport with him but also in terms of his fame in the world of publishing. She must have felt uncomfortable with the police or newspaper correspondents (or "detectives" and "paparazzi," to use two key words in this study), despite their likely interest in hearing her side of the story. The outcomes of their respective interviews with her (the investigation report and newspaper articles) would not have worked to her benefit—that is to say, they would not have fulfilled her wishes to represent the incident in the way she wants. Sensei is thus put in a position to make Sonoko's version of the story generally known. She seems to expect him to exert the power of his pen on a larger audience that had not heard her testify for herself.

We have seen how Sonoko felt as she strove to conceal from her husband the nature of her erotic relationship with Mitsuko. Their letters unequivocally show the two women's deep attachment to each other and—most important in this context—Mitsuko's jealousy of Sonoko's husband. Initially, however, Sonoko is candid with her husband about her friendship with Mitsuko. When her husband observes that she seems excited after her first "date" with Mitsuko, Sonoko explains how she came to meet this new friend: "'She goes to my school—the fact is, somebody started an ugly rumor about us. . . .' I had nothing to hide, so I told him everything, beginning with that silly argument I'd had with the director" (21). When there is "nothing to hide," one can tell "everything"—at least that is Sonoko's understanding at this point. Innocence generates no secrets and thus leads to complete confessions—the most simple combination of mental state and act.

Isolation and abandonment by one's friends are also motivations for confession. Such feelings of alienation and frustration lie behind Sonoko's confession to Mitsuko's maid, Ume: "Ume seemed genuinely sympathetic, and much as I disliked confiding in her, I had become so bitter, so distraught, that I wanted to tell her everything that was on my mind" (64–65). Ume, as a member of a lower class, does not, in Sonoko's perception, qualify as a confidante. Yet Sonoko tells her "everything," simply because no one else is available, and because Ume seems willing to listen to and accept her story as truth. Sonoko's husband's primary qualification is also his availability. Sonoko takes advantage of this either to vent her frustration or to seek a way out of trouble. One night, she receives a phone call from Mitsuko, who claims that her clothes have been stolen while she was taking a bath at an inn. She asks Sonoko to bring matching clothes to prevent Mitsuko's parents from finding out she was at the inn. Perplexed but concerned, Sonoko rushes to the inn, finding a convenient excuse for her husband who naturally wonders why she has to go out at night. Sonoko discovers that Mitsuko has been seeing Watanuki at this inn for a long time. Realizing that she has been used to cover up a liaison that Mitsuko's parents would not approve of, Sonoko feels betrayed and, in need of support, confesses everything to her husband. This seems similar to the case with Ume—Sonoko confesses to her husband simply because he is the only available listener: "'I'll tell you about tonight,' I said, 'but please do forgive me.' In the end, I told my husband everything" (79).[20]

This confession leaves Sonoko with a sense of gratitude to her husband that makes her temporarily faithful to him. She eventually resumes her relationship with Mitsuko, however, and enters into the conspiracy with Watanuki to share Mitsuko, all behind her husband's back. As mentioned above, her husband learns of this not from Sonoko but from Watanuki. When Sonoko produces her own copy of the contract from the drawer, he says:

"Well, you do have another copy; so this one *isn't* a fake is it?"

Even then I kept silent and only nodded. My husband couldn't tell what I was thinking and leveled a suspicious glance at me. "So all of this is true?" He asked.

"Some of it is," I admitted, "but we were lying to each other too."

As I was listening to my husband, I had made up my mind that by now there was no use trying to hide anything more; better for me to strike back at Watanuki by telling the whole story, every last detail, good or bad, whether it showed me in a favorable light or not. I'd let matters take their course—maybe it would turn out better than I feared; it might even be to my advantage. (180)

Even when Sonoko makes up her mind to tell her husband the "whole story," it is not because she wants him to trust her or because she has nothing to hide. Rather, it is because she thinks that telling him the truth may help her out of her current trouble. Her mind is focused on the pragmatic solution of problems and not on the ethical questions of trust, love, or understanding between husband and wife.

However, by this time, her husband, having learned that his wife is capable of deceiving him, has begun taking measures to protect himself:

I told him everything, from how I had been deceived by Mitsuko and Watanuki to how I had deceived *him*. For over two hours I talked on and on, spilling out everything I knew, while he only grunted in response and sighed occasionally as he listened.

"So I can believe what you've just told me?" He asked. "You're sure about Watanuki?" And then: "The fact is, I've been looking into it myself." (181)

His reaction differs from his previous response. He has done his own investigating, but demands to hear her explanation before telling her about it. He feels he needs independently verified facts to test the validity of her testimony.

Mitsuko's and Sonoko's confessions to each other are strikingly different from Sonoko's pragmatic confessions to her husband. With her husband, what is at issue are the content of the confession and the problems it raises; with Mitsuko, it is the affirmation of transparent frankness that matters. More than anything else, it is the intoxicating sense of trusting and being trusted that Sonoko seeks in confessions, whether in giving or receiving them.

When Watanuki intrudes into what had seemed her closed relationship with Mitsuko, Sonoko gradually learns that Mitsuko is capable of concealing important things from her. Madly in love, Sonoko is reluctant to suspect Mitsuko, but Watanuki's claim that Mitsuko is carrying his child is more than enough to upset her. Wondering whether Mitsuko could have been hiding such a thing from her, Sonoko finally confronts her. Whatever the truth of Mitsuko's subsequent confession, how it works as a performance and how this performance affects Sonoko are far more important in terms of the narrative. Mitsuko suggests she was too shy to tell Sonoko about her affair with Watanuki, her discovery of his impotence, his threat to publicize their relationship should she end it, and her vain efforts to escape him. "'. . . You know, sister, as close as we've been, I feel ashamed to confess all this to you, and I've been holding back, thinking it might turn you against me. I couldn't be more miserable. But today I told you everything!'" (157). Seemingly caught up in the emotions of the moment, Mitsuko now tells Sonoko "everything." This appearance of spontaneity is very effective, for Sonoko, who detests calculation and scheming—at least in others—rejoices to "discover" that her lover is so impulsive.

Mitsuko knows well that Sonoko could not possibly leave her after hearing such a passionate and unselfish confession.

> "Oh, Sister, please, please . . . you're the only one I can trust—don't let what I've said turn you against me!"
>
> "How could anything turn me against you? I'm glad you were able to come out with it. You can't imagine how happy I am to have you trust me like that!" (158)

Sonoko's reply says it all. Reassured by the quality of Mitsuko's confession, she does not question its reliability. For Sonoko, the most important thing is that Mitsuko has shown her unconditional trust by telling "everything," including shameful details. Now that Mitsuko has proved her frankness and transparency, Sonoko has no intention of leaving her. Mitsuko thus accomplishes her goal of regaining Sonoko's trust and support.

Sonoko, feeling obliged to reciprocate Mitsuko's trust, then relates the details of her pact with Watanuki.

"Now that it's come to this, I'll be honest with you," I said. "The truth is, I made a pledge as brother and sister with Eijiro [Watanuki]. We exchanged documents spelling out all the details."

And I told her everything that had happened the day before. (158)

Although she wants to keep her promise to Watanuki, Sonoko breaks it the very next day, as she is questioned by Mitsuko. She is evidently at Mitsuko's mercy—Mitsuko may even have staged her own confession in the expectation that Sonoko will explain her dealings with Watanuki in return. If this is the case, Mitsuko has demonstrated a knack for using confession, not in order to convey the truth but in order to appear frank and to procure the trust of her hearer. Sonoko is easy prey for such a strategy.

Watanuki may be using the same tactic to ascertain how much Sonoko knows about Mitsuko's "pregnancy"—and whether Sonoko knows he is impotent. Mitsuko has pretended to be pregnant and about to miscarry, and she has visited Sonoko at her home after the incident at the inn when she and Sonoko were temporarily not on speaking terms. Mitsuko's feigned predicament effectively drew Sonoko back to her. Watanuki, knowing how upset Sonoko was after the scene at the inn, asks Sonoko how she became reconciled with Mitsuko.

"How did she ever manage to get back together with you? I heard about it later, but I don't know any of the details."

So I told him all about the convulsions and hemorrhaging, to his astonishment.

"Is *that* so?" he exclaimed over and over. "I never dreamed she caused such a commotion!" (118)

One may suspect that Watanuki feigns ignorance so that Sonoko, egged on by a sense of superiority in knowing more than her rival, will tell him what she knows. Watanuki's pretense of ignorance may thus be instrumental in helping him expand his knowledge.

Narrative Versions

Three incidents in the novel circulate in conspicuously different versions: the rumor of a lesbian affair between Mitsuko and Sonoko, the loss of Mitsuko's clothes at the inn in Kasayamachi, and Mitsuko's faked pregnancy. The narrative context of each version serves to illuminate the performativity of narration. As Ken Ito admits, after his own articulate and elaborate synopsis of the novel, summarizing the plot of *Manji* is quite a daunting task.[21] This is due not only to its sheer complexity but also to the fact that the impossibility of settling on what Seymour Chatman calls the "basic story" is itself one of the main themes of the narrative.[22] The characters continually summarize their story, and their summaries are so different that the reader ends up wondering whether there is a "real" story. What become important instead are questions surrounding the act of retelling itself—how each speaker tells his or her story and why.

An honest person by nature—as she appears to be in her own narrative—Sonoko cannot at first understand why others would tell a story they know to be untrue or how their listeners could accept it as the truth. After her quarrel with the school director, who had implied that Sonoko modeled her Kannon drawing on Mitsuko, the rumor that Sonoko and Mitsuko were engaged in a lesbian relationship spread.

> But our argument in front of the students caused a sensation, and before long a nasty rumor began to spread. They said I'd made indecent advances to Mitsuko, that Mitsuko and I were altogether too close. . . . As I told you, at that time I'd hardly said a word to her, so the whole thing was nonsense, just an out-and-out lie. Of course I was aware that people were talking behind my back, though I never dreamed they were making such a fuss. But I had nothing on my conscience, so I didn't care what they said. It was all perfectly ridiculous. (12)

Mitsuko then asks her out for a chat to explain how the rumor came into being. This, the first version of the incident, is subsequently challenged by another version told by Watanuki:

Mitsuko began by saying that it was the director himself who started those malicious rumors. Of course I'd found it irritating, the way he kept coming into the classroom and embarrassing me before everyone, and I couldn't help feeling he was up to no good. But when I asked why on earth he wanted to spread a rumor like that, she said that the whole thing was aimed at *her*, that one way or another he wanted to damage her reputation. (15–16)

According to Mitsuko, her father had turned down a request by the director for funding, and the director had then agreed to cooperate with a councilman to undermine Mitsuko's reputation. This councilman's motivation, in turn, was to enable his daughter to marry a rich man, a certain Mr. M, who was himself interested in marrying Mitsuko. These, according to Mitsuko, are the motivations behind what Sonoko calls this "out-and-out lie."

Hearing this explanation, Sonoko is further perplexed: "'It's so ridiculous, isn't it, when you and I didn't really know each other until today. Making up a story like that is bad enough, but I can't imagine anybody believing it.' 'That's why you're easily taken in,' Mitsuko replied" (17). To Sonoko at this point, words are tools for representing the truth, and both speaker and hearer should behave as if bound by a sacred trust. The former should relate, and the latter accept, only what each believes to be true. Such an ideal model of communication, however, is unrealistic, not only in theoretical terms (no verbal expression can represent nonverbal or other verbal acts "truthfully," or just as they are), but also in practical terms, since unreliable narrators abound in narratives, as do narratees who, aware that they are being told untruths, choose nonetheless to keep listening. Both sides of narration are matters of intention, and willful lying and willful credulity are common. Sonoko herself grows aware of the performativity of narration through the course of the story.

Mitsuko is aware of Sonoko's simplicity and of her craving for full mutual understanding. She uses the illusion of complete transparency in order to manipulate Sonoko. Thus she says, after explaining to Sonoko at great length how the rumor about them was spread, "'I'm glad I had a chance to tell you the whole story. It's taken a weight off my mind'" (19). Mitsuko expresses relief that all the facts have been laid out and that an unfortunate incident can now be put behind them. Her "baring" of the facts, however, is later called into question by other versions, including versions supplied by Mitsuko herself. Her statement "It's taken a weight off my mind" is evidently not an expression of Mitsuko's state of mind. She must be excited and full of ideas about how to go about manipulating Sonoko next. But it is useful to Mitsuko to assert that she has just revealed the last of what had lain hidden inside of her. It seems that Mitsuko's motive in having this conversation with Sonoko is not to explain the mystery surrounding the rumors, but to gain Sonoko's confidence, to create further opportunities for the two to talk, and to draw Sonoko into a labyrinth of confessions, secrets, pretenses, betrayals, and conspiracies.

Watanuki later offers Sonoko a different explanation of how the rumor spread.

> He and Mitsuko had fallen in love and had even intended to be married. However, this spring the talk of marriage with M had come up, and they were afraid their own plans were doomed. Fortunately the rumor of a lesbian affair had the effect of breaking off M's proposal.
>
> . . . Well, that was more or less how he began. They never tried to use me, he insisted, even if it might have seemed that way at first. But gradually Mitsuko had been stirred by my own passion and had fervently returned my love, more than she ever loved him. He felt unbearably jealous; if anyone was used, it was himself. (69)

Watanuki's version does not necessarily contradict Mitsuko's version, but it develops along different lines. He does not touch upon the alleged conspiracy between the councilman and the director, focusing instead on Mitsuko's intentions with regard to him, which she had not mentioned to Sonoko. Moreover, Watanuki and Mitsuko describe the effects of the rumor on the plans for her marriage with M differently. Whereas Mitsuko does not describe herself as affected by them, Watanuki suggests that both she and he were troubled by the marriage arrangements and subsequently relieved when the rumors of lesbianism put an end to it. The two versions thus do not complement each other to form a more complete story, since the accounts of the intentions and attitudes of those involved are not consistent.

Looking back on these events as she relates them to Sensei, Sonoko considers the possibility that, regardless of the origin of the rumor and in spite of the fact that it was unfounded at the time, Mitsuko may have used it to entrap her. Although the rumor itself misrepresented the two women's relationship at that time, the way Mitsuko handled the rumor awakened Sonoko to her potential attraction to Mitsuko:

> Mitsuko herself must have realized from my behavior how I felt about her. Maybe when she passed me in the street she thought: That girl has an eye for me! She'd watch out for a chance to lead me on. Of course I was eager to strike up a conversation with her, but even though she had kept her distance, her radiant smile lured me into making an approach. [. . .] All in all, as much as I adored her, when I asked myself how I got into this relationship, I couldn't help thinking I had been affected by those rumors at school, coming just when I was feeling so dissatisfied with my husband. Mitsuko might have perceived that weakness in me and planted the suggestion before I was aware of it. In fact, even the marriage talk with the M family seemed to have been a pretext . . . .
>
> Anyway, I felt that I'd been caught in my own trap, put in the position of making all the advances. (123)

This interpretation reverses not only the positions of seducer and seduced but also relations of cause and effect. Sonoko was made to feel that she was the one who initiated the relationship. Eventually, however, she begins to suspect Mitsuko's role in manipulating her feelings. Again, this hypothesis is not in outright contradiction with either the first or the second version, but it shifts the focus to Sonoko's psyche, and to Mitsuko's manipulation of it.

Further along in the narrative, Mitsuko confesses to an even more substantial involvement with the rumor, as she explains to Sonoko how her relationship with Watanuki developed.

> She told me it was she herself who started the rumor of a lesbian affair with me, by sending anonymous postcards. She did it because he'd been insanely jealous ever since he got wind of the marriage proposal. He swore he wouldn't put up

with it and threatened to expose their relationship to the newspapers. [. . .] In short, she had purposely spread her own rumor in order to cover up the true situation.

Well, you could say she deceived me just in order to deceive other people. For her part, Mitsuko preferred to be thought of as a lesbian rather than the victim of a dubious "playboy" or a "pansy." (146–47)

Here Mitsuko claims that she herself started the rumor and admits to having willfully misled Sonoko in her earlier "confession." She thus reveals herself as both an unreliable and deceitful narrator, ready to revise her story as circumstances require.

This version, moreover, flatly contradicts Watanuki's account. Mitsuko says that she wished to end their relationship, but he prevented her; Watanuki described their love as mutual and inclining toward marriage. The motivation behind the rumor, according to Mitsuko's second account, was not to ruin her chances of marrying M, but to prevent Watanuki from carrying out his threat to make public his relationship with Mitsuko. In other words, she hoped to suppress the fact that she was involved with an impotent man by circulating the falsehood that she was a lesbian—a falsehood that, however damaging to her reputation, was preferable to the truth.

Although this version remains unverified, it goes unchallenged, and the topic disappears from the story. The only reason for finding this version more plausible than the others is that it appears last in the text. What is especially difficult to verify is Mitsuko's feelings about the continuation of her liaison with Watanuki. For her, the rumor of her lesbianism could have been intended either to protect herself from Watanuki's threat to expose their relationship or to prevent their separation. The question which, if either, of these alternatives is true is left open to speculation; this suggest that the novel is concerned not with conclusive verification but with the relative effectiveness of individual narrative performances. Each version seems plausible and ably performed in its own context, and that, it seems, is what matters in *Manji*.

The explanations of how Mitsuko came to lose her clothes at the inn in Kasayamachi are even more mystifying. Three explanations are offered, the first by Mitsuko when she telephones Sonoko at home to ask her to bring a kimono that matches the missing one:

"I've had my clothes stolen!"

"Your *clothes?* . . . What on earth were you doing?"

"I was taking a bath. It's a restaurant in the pleasure quarter, so they have a Japanese bath—"

"But why would you be in a place like that?"

"Well, actually, I've been wanting to tell you about it, Sister—anyway, you can hear all that later . . . . I'm in a terrible fix—please help me. I need that matching kimono of yours, just as soon as I can!" (60)

Mitsuko also asks Sonoko to bring a change of her husband's clothes, since there is a man in the same inn who has had his clothes stolen as well. She further request that Sonoko meet her maid Ume, whom Mitsuko has told to wait at the train station. This suggests that Mitsuko does not want Ume to intrude when she sees someone—the man whose clothes are missing. It dawns on Sonoko, who knows nothing of Watanuki at this point, that Mitsuko has been carrying on a liaison with a man. As we have seen, Sonoko has come to value a sense of mutual transparency in her relations with Mitsuko. She is thus unable to account for Mitsuko's taking a bath in a place such as she describes, nor does Mitsuko provide her at this point with a sufficient explanation—perhaps to save time, or perhaps from the fear that Sonoko might not come if she knew all of the circumstances.

Sonoko first goes to the station, where she bribes Ume and learns that Mitsuko has been dating a man without her parents' knowledge since about the time the rumors of lesbianism began spreading. On her arrival at the inn, Sonoko meets an unknown man who introduces himself as Watanuki, Mitsuko's boyfriend, and offers an explanation of how Mitsuko's clothes were stolen.

That night some people were gambling in another room at the inn, he said, and it seems there was a police raid. When Mitsuko and he heard all the commotion, they were so alarmed they fled blindly from their room, she in her underslip and he himself in his nightclothes, escaping by the roof over to the next-door house, where they hid under the floor of a laundry drying platform.

> [. . .] Then this man and woman [who had been gambling] decided to pretend they were there on a rendezvous. [. . .] But the detectives were too clever for them and arrested them on suspicion, to take them off to the police station. That's when they put on the kimonos that Mitsuko and Watanuki had left in the clothes box by their bedside. (70)

The rendezvous, as well as the relationship itself, had to be kept secret from Mitsuko's parents, and Mitsuko could not go home in someone else's clothes without arousing suspicion. The only person with an identical kimono was Sonoko. Although Sonoko cooperates with Watanuki and Mitsuko and accompanies Mitsuko home to prevent her parents from growing suspicious, Sonoko is overwhelmed by this betrayal of her trust and decides to discontinue her relationship with Mitsuko.

Mitsuko's faked pregnancy brings them back together again, however, and at Mitsuko's request, Sonoko becomes further acquainted with Watanuki. One day, Watanuki requests a secret meeting with Sonoko and tells her a different version.

> Then Watanuki said that the night their clothes were stolen in Kasayamachi, he didn't want her to call me. She should have had the nerve to borrow a kimono from one of the maids to wear home. She could have told her parents she had become involved with a certain man and it was too late to do anything about it. They could have married right away or just made up their minds to elope, and they would have had nothing to fear. How could she be so shameless as to call Sister at a time like that? Sister, who had no idea what was going on! (117)

Here, Watanuki is attempting to coax Sonoko into an agreement that will allow him to continue his relationship with Mitsuko, if not remove Sonoko from the picture entirely. He appeals to her by being solicitous of Sonoko's damaged pride, all the while suggesting that Mitsuko's affection for him has continued unabated. He hopes thus to make Sonoko more sympathetic to him, more firmly convinced of the depth of his relationship with Mitsuko, and—considering Mitsuko's alleged willingness to use Sonoko for the sake of that relationship—less fond of Mitsuko.

Watanuki's words, indeed, seem to mirror Sonoko's own thoughts on the night of the incident, when she poured out her indignation to Ume as two of them headed for the inn:

"... How on earth could she telephone me like that tonight? She must take me for a fool!"

"Really, how *could* she! But maybe she was at her wits' end."

"I don't care what trouble she was in—how could she dare to tell me she went to a restaurant with her boyfriend and they had a bath there! You can draw your own conclusions!"

"Yes, of course, but still, once she had her clothes stolen she couldn't go home naked. . . ."

"I'd have done it. Rather than make such a shameless phone call, I'd have gone home stark naked!" (65)

Watanuki's version is thus likely to be appealing to Sonoko, since it so closely matches her feelings at the time. Sonoko is not completely convinced by Watanuki, however, and never quite banishes the feeling that he may have had his own interests in mind—she does not like him in the first place and is ready to suspect him of insidious intentions.

Sonoko, however, welcomes Mitsuko's explanation, which contradicts Watanuki's, for it is less painful for her to credit. After compelling Sonoko to confess her secret agreement with Watanuki, Mitsuko tells Sonoko what really happened on the night of the incident:

The fact was, that afternoon, Mitsuko [. . .] happened to run into him. She told him she was going straight to Kasayamachi after visiting me, and he should wait for her there. Watanuki could see she was wearing one of our matching kimonos. This was his chance: If he could get that kimono away from her, she'd have to telephone me, and that would surely lead to a rift between us. While he was waiting for her at the inn, he could have bribed the employees and told them exactly what to do—Watanuki was fully capable of a scheme like that and had time to carry it out. It was much too farfetched to think that people wearing their stolen kimonos were taken down to the police station, let alone that the police never bothered to call either Mitsuko's or Watanuki's home. But Mitsuko hadn't suspected any such plot at the time and was far too upset to know what to do.

"There's only one way out," Watanuki had declared. "You've got to call Mrs. Kakiuchi and have her bring you that matching kimono."

Watanuki's account had been quite different. But Mitsuko told me she was so flustered that at first she couldn't remember which kimono she had lost. Even after he advised her to call me, she had said: "I can't ask Sister to do that."

But he kept pressing her.

"Shall we run away together, then? Or will you make that call?"

Mitsuko was desperate. She would rather die than go away with him. Utterly at a loss, she ran to the telephone. (148–49)

In this version, Mitsuko shows a sense of shame, as well as consideration for Sonoko's feelings. The Watanuki of her version seems calculating, staging the entire scene with the aid of the inn's employees. His intention is to outrage Sonoko so that she will stop seeing Mitsuko, leaving Watanuki in sole possession. Furthermore, he knew Mitsuko owned a matching kimono. And he was to await Mitsuko's arrival at the inn. Motive, means, opportunity—Mitsuko's version of events is nothing if not logical and well structured.

Mitsuko suggests that Watanuki had yet another motive:

Watanuki was so used to deceiving others that he distrusted everyone—but this time it wasn't just nastiness; he had reason to be suspicious. Since he knew about my relations with Mitsuko, he thought I must know about his relations with her, and I had never shown any jealousy over it simply because I felt safe, because I'd been told he wasn't a real man. Otherwise wouldn't I have exposed them? That was why he had me called to the Kasayamachi inn: so I would see that he often went to such places with Mitsuko and could hardly be a man of doubtful sexuality. (151)

Mitsuko also points out flaws in Watanuki's account. As Watanuki had told Sonoko, he was worried that the police might identify Mitsuko as the kimono's owner, because her train pass was with it (71). In that case, the police should at least have contacted her, to report that her train pass had been found with the criminals. The police might also have discovered that the kimono did not belong to the arrested woman, and if they did, they could have been expected to search for the real owner. The lack of official inquiries would seem to suggest that the police were not involved at all—that the whole commotion was faked. Mitsuko tells Sonoko that when she confronted Watanuki with this possibility, Watanuki "seemed stung by her question and shrugged it off with an embarrassed grin" (154). Watanuki's apparent inability to answer this question would seem to confirm Mitsuko's suspicions.

As with the incident of the rumor, the "whole truth" in this matter is not revealed. Each version sounds plausible enough, although Watanuki's is not without gaps. The participants' motives and reactions to unexpected incidents are accounted for in different ways, but each interpretation makes sense insofar as we accept the framework in which it is presented. Again, it seems that it is contextual effectiveness, rather than ultimate verification, that is at stake.

The most conspicuously divergent accounts surround Mitsuko's alleged pregnancy. In an attempt to effect a reconciliation with Sonoko, Mitsuko invents a story on a greater scale than the incidents that had estranged them. Mitsuko first has a man telephone Sonoko, claiming that he works for a hospital. On Mitsuko's instructions, he tells her that a Mrs. Nakagawa's pregnancy has been complicated by her unsuccessful attempt at abortion; she had attempted to follow the instructions in an English book on the subject that Sonoko had previously lent Mitsuko. Sonoko takes this report seriously and feels compelled to meet Mitsuko despite their estrangement. Sonoko's husband, informed of this state of affairs by telephone, gives his approval to the meeting. Mitsuko then arrives at her house and "confesses" that it is not "Mrs. Nakagawa" but she who is in trouble. The confessions are false, as Sonoko soon sees, but she does not tell Mitsuko that she has found her out:

> But as soon as she began making all the fuss about it "coming out," I realized that everything she was doing today was only an act. . . . To tell the truth, that had begun to dawn on me gradually, but I had played along, and Mitsuko herself saw I was pretending to be deceived and kept up her own playacting all the more boldly. After that both of us were simply trying to maintain mutual deception.
>
> . . . I'm sure you understand very well what was going on. The fact is, I had deliberately walked into the trap that Mitsuko set up before my very eyes. (95)

This passage shows how far Sonoko has come from her original beliefs about the function of communication. Aware that Mitsuko is "making up" the story that she is in danger of miscarrying, Sonoko consciously decides to pretend to be deceived and to collaborate with Mitsuko in order to keep the act going. At this point neither of them is trying to represent or seek the truth. Both accept narration as an activity which, if well-performed, may be intoxicating.

When her husband comes home, Sonoko tells him that she must visit Mrs. Nakagawa in the hospital the following day—an excuse to meet with Mitsuko. The next day she stages a false confession when her husband says he has discovered that no one by the name of Mrs. Nakagawa is registered in the hospital: "I was startled but quickly thought of an excuse" (102). Sonoko tells her husband that she had been deceived by Mitsuko, who used the name Mrs. Nakagawa when in fact it was she herself who had been pregnant and that Mitsuko had confessed to the truth only when, the two having met to visit Mrs. Nakagawa together, her pain became intolerable. This story is, indeed, partly true: Sonoko did discover that Mitsuko's story about the pregnancy was fake. But she has cunningly shifted the time of her discovery, as well as its exact nature: "That's how I poured my story out to him, making up one thing after another and weaving in what happened the day before wherever it would fit" (104). Thus her story is neither entirely false nor composed entirely of falsehoods. Such "weaving" of truth and falsehood is much more skillful than Sonoko's earlier choice of either complete confession or total silence.

Since she now wishes to be able to see Mitsuko constantly, Sonoko has to deceive her husband into believing that Mitsuko is still pregnant and needs to be watched.

> We'd have to say that Mitsuko was still pregnant—the medicine she took didn't work, and the doctor refused to give her an abortion—and that as her stomach got bigger and bigger, she finally confessed to her mother and it was arranged for her to be taken in by her father's mistress until the baby was born. His mistress was living at the Izutsu inn in Kasayamachi, we'd say. (110–11)

Taking her lead from a lie that Mitsuko has told her parents—that

Sonoko's husband's office has a branch in Kasayamachi—Sonoko makes up this explanation herself. She enlists the employees at the inn to help her in hiding the truth from her husband, in the event he should suddenly appear there. Mitsuko likes Sonoko's plan and is amused by the thought of the role she would play in the event of such a visit:

> At this Mitsuko burst out laughing. "I'll have to stuff padding around my stomach before I come to your house!" she said. But that's what we decided to be on the safe side.
>
> My husband was completely taken in. "So Mitsuko's really pregnant, is she?" he asked, looking quite sympathetic. (111)

Sonoko, however, begins to wonder if she is the one who has been "taken in" by Mitsuko when she hears from Watanuki that Mitsuko really is pregnant:

> According to Watanuki, she was already in her third month and had been to see a doctor. In that case, she would have been pregnant at the time she made that scene about hemorrhaging, though at around three months only a doctor could have told her what her condition was—and I had even heard her say from her own lips: "I don't think I could be having a baby." There's no question that she was putting on an act that day, but if what Watanuki said was true, she still might have been trying to conceal her pregnancy from me. (115)

If Sonoko accepts Watanuki's account and incorporates it into what she already knows, then Mitsuko pretended to pretend to be pregnant in order to convince Sonoko that she was not. In other words, Mitsuko "confesses" to being pregnant in such a way as to be suspected of fabrication and thus conceals her real pregnancy.

As Watanuki repeatedly tells Sonoko, Mitsuko now has no choice but to marry him, and Sonoko begins to be persuaded by his version of events:

> "All the more so in her present condition—where else could she go?"
>
> . . . Yes, from what he was telling me, Mitsuko must have been pregnant after all! I listened with amazement as he went on.
>
> "She says her father is positively furious and would never let her marry anyone who isn't worth at least a million yen, certainly not a penniless, no-account

fellow. If she has a baby, they'll send it out for adoption. That's ridiculous! Most of all, there's the poor baby—it's inhuman, isn't it? What do you think, Sister?" (114)

The concrete details Watanuki supplies, such as Mitsuko's father's stipulations, make his account sound more plausible to Sonoko. Nonetheless, she tells Watanuki that she cannot believe him:

> I couldn't believe she was pregnant, I told him, and he replied that Mitsuko was determined not to get married, but once her pregnancy was obvious to everyone she'd be forced to, no matter what.
>
> "I'm sure she's going to hide it as long as she can," he said. (116)

When Watanuki is able to offer explanations for all of Sonoko's objections, she begins to wonder if Mitsuko has deceived her: "Above all, why would she keep her pregnancy secret from me? To be so cold hearted, after making me worry so much—surely that meant she had nothing but contempt for me. Or could it be that he had revealed her secret out of a wish to drive us apart?" (123–24). Whether or not Watanuki's version represents the truth, his intention must have been to alienate Sonoko from Mitsuko. He seems to have achieved this goal to some extent, for Sonoko feels slighted by Mitsuko's apparent deception. The last sentence, however, suggests that Sonoko is aware of Watanuki's motivations and shows her increased sophistication in reading narratives in context.

Nonetheless, Sonoko takes it as a fact that Mitsuko is pregnant by Watanuki, or, at any rate, takes it as a working hypothesis in dealing with Watanuki, as is evident when she bargains with Watanuki over the contract to share Mitsuko equally: "'Since Mitsu has to carry the baby long enough to be married, I suppose it can't be helped. But I want you to promise you won't have any more children'" (127). Sonoko, however, does wonder if Mitsuko is really pregnant, probably because she hopes that this is not the case and is reluctant to accept the hypothesis as a fact. Sonoko is an unwilling audience for Watanuki. Eventually Sonoko confronts Mitsuko directly with her suspicions:

> "Well, how about the day you came to my house in so much pain? Were you really pregnant?"

"Oh, that time," she said, her face reddening with embarrassment. "But I was putting on an act. I just wanted to see you . . . ."

"That's not what I'm asking. I'd like to know whether you were *pregnant*."

"Well, I wasn't."

"And you still aren't, even now?"

"Of course I'm not. Why are you being so suspicious?"

"I can't tell you why, but I have my reasons."

"Oh, Sister!" Suddenly Mitsuko looked as if she understood. "Sister, I'm sure Eijiro told you I was pregnant, didn't he? That must be it! But the truth is, he isn't *capable* of fathering a child—" (133)

Sonoko, significantly, asks not if Mitsuko was putting on an act, but if she was pregnant in reality. Moreover, she tries to prevent Mitsuko from drifting away from the question of the fact itself to that of her possible motivation. Questioned about the facts regarding her feigned pregnancy, Mitsuko reveals a new "fact" to support her position, a fact that sheds an entirely new light on the relations among the three. If Watanuki is truly impotent, there can be no room for speculating on Mitsuko's pregnancy (assuming that she has no other heterosexual relationship). The original question thus drops from the story, even as it becomes evident in the course of events that Mitsuko is not pregnant.

This revelation, along with Mitsuko's subsequent confessions that she has not loved Watanuki for a long time, end his intrusion as Sonoko's rival. Instead, he takes up the role of potential informer, capable of blackmailing the two women or Sonoko's husband. His leverage is no longer Sonoko's jealousy but a material object—the contract she signed. Furthermore, the implication that Mitsuko remains technically a virgin becomes significant, both for Sonoko, who feels her status as Mitsuko's lover is unchallenged, as well as for Mitsuko and Sonoko's husband. In short, the revelation that Watanuki is impotent, originally offered by Mitsuko as a substitute for a direct answer to Sonoko's question about her pregnancy, becomes a driving force that takes the story into a completely different direction.

From the Pleasure of Deception to the Agony of Honesty

It does not take Sonoko long to master the art of narrating to deceive others. Her victim is her husband, whom she places in a lower rank in the hierarchy of narrative sophistication. As he becomes less approving of her friendship with Mitsuko and begins to make comments, and as Sonoko realizes how attached she is to Mitsuko—and how indifferent to her husband—she begins actively deceiving him:

> To tell the truth, I'd gone through so much, all unknown to him, that I myself had become quite worldly and more than a little clever at concealing what I was up to. He was blind to that and kept on treating me like a child. At first I could hardly bear his condescending manner, but when I got annoyed he made fun of me even more, until finally I thought: All right, if I seem childish to you, I'll encourage it, I'll pull the wool over your eyes! I can put on a show of being a horribly spoiled little girl, and fret and coax whenever I want to get my own way. So just go ahead, if it pleases you to consider me a child, I said to myself, but aren't *you* the gullible one? Getting around a man like you is the easiest thing in the world!
>
> Mocking him became more and more enjoyable, and I amazed myself by my own skill at playacting. After even a few words from him I would burst into tears or begin shouting angrily . . . .
>
> I'm sure you know this better than I, since you're a novelist, but our state of mind does seem to change completely, depending on circumstances, doesn't it? (46)

Sonoko has grown proficient at narrating as a means not of naïve self-expression but of adopting a role so that her husband may mistake it for her true identity. She takes advantage of her husband's credulity, just as her schoolmates had taken advantage of hers.

Just as she has become a canny narrator, she becomes a prudent narratee. Upon Mitsuko's request, Sonoko agrees to meet and reconcile with Watanuki. When Watanuki and Mitsuko argue in her presence, Sonoko thinks to herself: "Possibly they had planned this silly quarrel to flatter me, but I kept silent, thinking it would be foolish to join in" (109). As Sonoko has learned, speech is a verbal act, and the question of its truth or falsehood is by definition irrelevant. Naïve as she may have been in the beginning, Sonoko has been influenced by Mitsuko in her understanding of how to narrate and how to listen.

Mitsuko, in turn, claims to have learned these techniques from Watanuki. When he realizes that Mitsuko and Sonoko have reconciled, he tries out of jealousy to learn from Mitsuko how it happened. Having failed to achieve the goal by sharply interrogating Mitsuko, Watanuki resorts to another technique:

> A few days later he brought the subject up again, this time with a touch of flattery.
>
> "Mrs. Kakiuchi must have been good and angry—I wonder how you managed to get around her," he said. "That's something I'd like you to teach me!" And: "You're remarkably clever, for such a sweet-looking girl . . . . The women in the pleasure quarter are no match for you!"
>
> After this rather backhanded praise, she decided she might as well give in and tell him the whole story of tricking me into a reconciliation.
>
> "Where did you learn to perform that little farce?"
>
> "I learned it from *you*, of course!"
>
> "Don't be absurd! I imagine you've played that kind of hoax on *me*."
>
> "There you are, being suspicious again. I've never done a thing like that before." (154–55)

As an unreliable and manipulative narrator himself, Watanuki cannot help suspecting others of deceiving him in turn. The acts of deception and suspicion operate mutually and incessantly, and the hierarchical relationship between the victim and the victimizer is continually reversed and counter-reversed.

The torturing and yet mesmerizing reciprocity of deception and suspicion finally involves even Sonoko's husband, who is quintessentially detached and logical. After achieving a full understanding of the nature of the triangle involving Sonoko, Mitsuko, and Watanuki, he tries to be more responsible in controlling Sonoko. She rather likes to be with Mitsuko and with her alone, and the two finally decide to commit double suicide while the husband is away. The attempt fails and ushers in another phase of the tragedy: while Sonoko is still unconscious from the drug overdose, Mitsuko, who has recovered consciousness, becomes physically involved with the husband who is taking care of Sonoko. The latter then falls madly in love with Mitsuko, now forming another triangle. Sonoko fears that her husband and Mitsuko might want to marry and that she will be divorced. Still, she trusts her husband, who promises to maintain the three-way relationship, even though she cannot trust Mitsuko.

Sonoko's husband then tries to maintain propriety by preventing Watanuki from making public the relationship between Mitsuko and Sonoko, so that he and Sonoko can continue seeing Mitsuko in the guise of a married couple befriending an unmarried woman. When he convinces Mitsuko's parents that Mitsuko's friendship with Sonoko is healthy and vows to take responsibility for the two, Sonoko is surprised at how deceitful he can be: "To think that love would make a man talk like that, a man who hadn't even known *how* to lie!" (208). Both Sonoko and her husband take advantage of the fact that they are married in order to make the public believe that neither of them is sexually involved with Mitsuko.

Since Mitsuko's parents accept the husband's explanation—and since Watanuki apparently remains silent at this point—the three should have been able to live in harmony. However, Sonoko and her husband begin to be tortured by doubts as to which of them Mitsuko loves more: "All this was going as smoothly as could be, but my own home life was more tense and suspicious than ever, worse than when Watanuki was involved. Day by day our torment deepened" (209). The reason for their torment is the doubt each feels concerning their agreement to share Mitsuko's affections equally—a dispensation that had previously been enshrined in the contract between Watanuki and Sonoko. This causes more trouble and stress than relief: "Of course we had agreed not to keep any secrets from each other, so she had to let him know" (210). There are two reasons for the agony that Sonoko and her husband experience. First, although love triangles have played a major role in the development of the story, no substantial conversation has involved more than two characters. If any of the conversation between Mitsuko and Sonoko, Sonoko and her husband, Ume and Sonoko, Watanuki and Sonoko, Mitsuko and Watanuki, or Watanuki and Sonoko's husband had occurred in the presence of an informed third party, the narrator would have been shown to be lying, and the narratee deprived, perhaps, of the pleasure of being deceived, or of being trusted. The performance of narration, which unfolds between the narrator's motive and the narratee's expectations, cannot take place in the presence of an independent witness. Even when three characters are together, one remains silent and does not contradict the other two. For example, when Sonoko's husband comes home early and finds Sonoko and Mitsuko together, Mitsuko does not speak. Also, Sonoko keeps silent as Mitsuko and Watanuki quarrel. The perfect transparency that Sonoko, Mitsuko, and Sonoko's husband promise one another is a completely new state for them, for three is a number not for secrecy but for communality. The second cause of their pain is that, ironically enough, candor is more painful than secrecy. When there is no room to hide anything, narrator and narratee cannot feel complacently at home with each other. Instead, they suffer from unobstructed sight and unsilenced narration. Omniscience does not guarantee happiness. It is soberingly cruel, whereas secrecy intoxicates with its cycles of illusion, deception, and suspicion.

The threesome does not last long. For one thing, the triangle is not based on equality. Mitsuko is at the center, desired by the other two, as in the case of the previous triangle. This time, however, Mitsuko takes every precaution to prevent the other two from conspiring behind her back as Watanuki and Sonoko did. She administers sleeping pills to the married couple so that they may not sleep together in her absence. This causes the spouses to suspect that each is taking advantage of the period of unconsciousness to sleep with Mitsuko. Having witnessed so many instances of deception, they cannot help being suspicious even when there is no evidence. Eventually the three agree to commit suicide together, by drugging themselves. And as the lone survivor, Sonoko still suspects her husband and Mitsuko of a conspiracy to commit double suicide and thus exclude her.

Manji ends, appropriately enough, without providing a definite answer to any question, and without resolving this story in search of a conclusion. Rather than leading us to the exit, the narrative leaves us wandering in a labyrinth where there is no final truth, only endless retellings. Words are not to describe—or "constate" as Austin puts it—but to perform, or to "do things." It is neither what they represent nor whether they represent truth, but how effectively they influence the participants in the narrative act—narrator and narratee—that matters. How words do things depends on the relationship between the narrator and narratee. This is not only true with regard to the "oral" narration constructed inside *Manji*. The encoded reader, unspecified here, is led through the "oral" narration, which is "written" by the encoded author in a particular way—apparently with an effect in mind: namely, the construction of "orality" and "literacy" as contrasts. But they are contrastive only when we perceive them to be so—just as the "feminine" and "masculine," respectively representing "oral" and "written" discourse within the text, are performed and perceived sets of attributes.[23] Indeed, *Manji* is performative on multiple layers—as a narrative, and as a text, and for its engenderedness.

CONCLUSION

Literature/Criticism as a Speech Act

IN THE INTRODUCTION I called the present text a narrative and, as such, a performance. Similarly, the Conclusion is another act of narration. What Barbara Herrnstein Smith points out in regard to a novel and its plot summaries seems applicable to the summary of this critical study:

> Each of these summaries would simplify the narrative at a different level of abstraction, and each of them would preserve, omit, link, isolate, and foreground different features of the summarizing. It is evident, moreover, that each of these summaries would, in effect, be another version of the novel: an abridged and simplified version, to be sure, but, in that respect, like the one-volume version of *Clarissa* constructed for busy or impatient readers or like the abridged and simplified *Gulliver's Travels* constructed for the amusement of children. My point here is that what narratologists refer to as the basic stories or deep-plot structures of narratives are often not abstract, disembodied, or subsumed entities but quite manifest, material, and particular retellings—and thus versions—of those narratives, constructed, as all versions are, by someone in particular, on some occasion, for some purpose, and in accord with some relevant set of principles.[1]

What follows, then, should not be taken as an abstract, basic story but as a particular retelling, written in order to foreground some of the features of the narratives discussed—the features I promised to explore in the Introduction—and to create a sense of a framework.

My intended and manifested goal in this study was to examine the intentions, skills, and accomplishments of the narrator, as well as the narratee's expectations of the narration, the narratee's skills as a listener, and the effects the narration might have on the narratee. Four of the narratives I analyzed are examples of first-person narrations, and their encoded authors even resemble the historical authors. What prevents us from reading any of these narratives as *shi-shōsetsu* is the framework in which each narrative emerges. The monopolizing of voice by the encoded author or omniscient narrator and of viewpoint by the encoded author or protagonist, as well as the illusory identification of the historical author with the encoded author, the omniscient narrator, and/or the protagonist, is broken in each of the narratives. And this is true, we saw, even in *Kuroi ame*, which appears to share these features of *shi-shōsetsu*. Each text instead confirms not only its multivalence and/or heterogeneity of viewpoint but also the narrator's awareness of either or both features. Hence, we, too, are made aware of the particular set of conditions that format the particular way in which writing, narrating, listening, and reading take place—that is to say, we become aware of the contextuality of narration.

We also saw that the narratees, as well as the narrators, are active participants in the narrative acts, no less responsible for the particular narrative performances than the narrators. The theoretical articulations of Mary Louise Pratt, Barbara Herrnstein Smith, and Ross Chambers discussed in the Introduction are confirmed in these works in practical and explicitly textual ways. The narratees of the primary narratives are not specified, but those of the embedded narratives—*watakushi* in *Kokoro* (for example, as he reads Sensei's testament), Shigematsu in *Kuroi ame* (as he reads Yasuko's diary), *yo* in *Kusamakura* (as he interviews local people in Nakoi), *boku* in *Gan* (as he listens to Okada), and Sensei in *Manji* (as he annotates Sonoko's account)—do not remain passive receptacles of the narrators' accounts. Nor do they intend to. They are determined not simply to make sense of what they hear but also to shape how they hear. Thus, *watakushi* interprets Sensei's behavior in the past in light of what he chooses to believe in the narrative present; Shigematsu reads, copies, and edits Yasuko's text even as he speculates upon her silence; *yo* voraciously seeks out gossip and practices voyeurism; *boku* cannot help informing the audience and talking to himself of what he had known, or what he has subsequently learned, that contradicts Okada's version of narrative; and in *Manji* Sensei's extensive explanations of Sonoko's narrative offer guidance for the reader of his writing. Stalker (*Kokoro*), compiler (*Kuroi ame*), "detective" or anthropologist (*Kusamakura*), "third-party" or paparazzo (*Gan*), and novelist (*Manji*)—these are roles that the narratees assume at times, if not always consistently.

Such active participation in the narrative performance cannot but affect the narrators. Sensei is compelled by his insistence on the privilege of companionship to choose *watakushi* as his last and perhaps only confidant. Yasuko, who originally is ready to share with Shigematsu her own diary, becomes taciturn and secretive, choosing not to explain anything important in her life to him. Nami and others exchange information about *yo* behind his back, including the fact that he has been probing into Nami's privacy, and deploy the information to challenge his authority. Okada, though apparently not fully aware of *boku*'s curiosity and superior knowledge, equals *boku* in terms of holding back information. Sonoko, on the contrary, seems to count on the fact that Sensei is a professional novelist who, presumably, can represent her complex account; she even produces visual props to help him further elaborate his account.

Threats, the desire to violate others' privacy, distrust, disdain, fear, retaliation, secrets, theatrical self-exposure, self-silencing—such are the attitudes of significant narrators and narratees as they participate in narrative acts. Yet such negatively construed terms of relationship do not signal the void of narration. Quite the contrary, narration is prompted by the very desire to conquer or erode the other party—hence, the complexity and ambiguity of the narrator-narratee relationship. The narrator can be knowing, condescending, patronizing, overpowering, or even harassing, but so can the narratee. Neither of them is autonomous of the other, or of the relationship with the other—the relationship, which is, in turn, ever changing in the course of narrative performance, as words, uttered and heard, written and read, do things to the relationship. Or rather, relationships are defined through speech acts, even as speech acts are directed by the relationships among the participants. Chambers's pun-like mention of the verb with the double meaning—"to *relate*"—is indeed profoundly suggestive of the fact that speech does things to people.

To read one's own writing on a narrative as a narrative—a self-reflexive act, enacted in this Conclusion—is not an untrodden path in literary criticism. The recent development of Japanese scholarship suggests an increasing self-consciousness on the part of critics, as well as a growing perception of narrative (which includes critical narrative) as a speech act. Hasumi Shigehiko, in his reflections on the classic concept of "poetic language"—discussed by the Russian formalists and Roland Barthes,[2] among others—reminds the reader of performativity of criticism, although perhaps as a side effect:

> What human beings can write is nothing more or less than language. Nor is what human beings can read anything but language. No one writes or reads literature. It is simply that one comes across, or does not come across, language as circumstance. "Poetic language" is not a closure of any privileged area somewhere *inside* language as circumstance. If such a thing [as "poetic language"] existed, there would be no borderline between everyday language and "poetic language." Something that deserves to be called "poetic language" is not something that exists, but an *incident*, a happening that vertically pierces the environment [of language], which would never leave a scar on language. It is not to be owned, but to be experienced. To encounter it, one has to be a reader. I maintain the above not because I wish to promote criticism vis-à-vis creative writing, but because it is the very *act of reading* that can be firmly related to the entire area of the human activity that is most distinct from the "myth" called literature.[3]

Unmaking the notion of literature as a constative, intrinsic, and sustaining entity distinct from, or opposed to, what is not literature, in a manner similar to Terry Eagleton's classic article "What Is Literature?,"[4] Hasumi suggests that the act of reading is the only way to make a given writing into literature, that literature happens in the moment of the act (rather than existing for a duration of time), and that readers make literature "happen"—hence, it is a "human activity."

A similar awareness of the mission and effect of criticism seems to be shared by other critics, as is evident from the titles of their works. A book by Komori Yōichi is entitled *Dekigoto to shite no yomu koto* (Reading as an incident; 1995). The title suggests, explicitly, his consciousness of critical reading as something that "happens." Another example of scholarly work on the literary speech act is *Dekigoto to shite no bungaku* (Literature as an incident; 1995) by Kobayashi Yasuo (1950–), a scholar of French literature, philosophy, and phenomenology and a translator of Jean-François Lyotard.

A book that Kobayashi edited and published recently is more blatantly entitled *Bungaku no gengo kōi ron* (Literary speech act; 1997). This is an anthology of critical essays on speech acts in prose narratives by Ōe Kenzaburō, Kawabata Yasunari, James Joyce, Fyodor Dostoyevsky, Marcel Proust, André Breton, Margurite Duras, Charlotte Brontë, and others (thus neutralizing the national boundaries of literature). Although lacking an introduction that would define the theoretical framework of the book, it becomes evident that the individual chapters draw upon J. L. Austin and, perhaps more significantly, Shoshana Felman, who was inspired by Austin. As such, this book and my own *Kōi to shite no shōsetsu* (1996) complement each other, offering French and Anglo-American literary speech act theories, respectively. I point this out not to explore it—exploration of the remarkably French-oriented Japanese literary criticism of today deserves another book-length study, but not one for me to write—but to call attention to a statement made by Kobayashi in the postscript to this volume, which, despite the different origins of critical inspiration, earns my genuine agreement:

> A literary text is not "texture of significance" but "a site of acts" in which a variety of acts—acts of characters, acts of the writer, acts of the narrator—intermingle with each other. We, too, enter the "site" as the subjects of the act of criticism. If there is anything in particular that motivated the editing of this volume of anthology, it should be nothing but the awareness of such an act that is consistent throughout this anthology.[5]

Renouncing structuralism, Kobayashi defines criticism as an act, and literature as an incident, suggesting that we should remain aware of our own act of reading as we are engaged in it.

My acts of reading, and retellings of these narratives, have, if I have achieved my stated goals, made these texts into performances. I let them become performances, or narrative acts. In turn, I become someone else—and so do you. Such is the effect of narrative as an act. I, the narrator, and you, the narratee, participate in the act by playing these roles, within our own qualifications (or lack thereof). The result is that we are affected by the performance. Where do we go from here? To silence, yes, but not silence as a state (of death), or as an annihilation of language, but as a choice (hence, another action) of the absence of words, in order to think, or do things again, with words that are unheard.

Reference Matter

Notes

For complete author names, titles, and publication data on works cited here by short forms, see the Works Cited, pp. 255–63.

Introduction

1. See Ian Reid, "Beyond Narratology?" in idem, *Narrative Exchanges*, 1–19, which is a concise survey of challenges to, and attempts to go beyond, narratology, made by Barbara Herrnstein Smith and Ross Chambers, whom I discuss below, and the counter-responses of narratologists such as Slomith Rimmon-Kenan. See also Seymour Chatman, "What Can We Learn from Contextualist Narratology?"

2. J. L. Austin, "Preliminary Isolation of the Performative," in idem, *How To Do Things with Words*, 4–7.

3. See, e.g., Jacques Derrida, "Signature Event Context."

4. Mary Louise Pratt, "The Literary Speech Situation," in idem, *Toward a Speech Act Theory of Literary Discourse*, 114.

5. For a brief survey of usage of each term, see "implied author" and "implied reader" in Gerald Prince, ed., *A Dictionary of Narratology*, 42–43.

6. Barbara Herrnstein Smith, "Narrative Theories, Narrative Versions," 221–22.

7. Ross Chambers, *Story and Situation: Narrative Seduction and the Power of Fiction*, 3–4.

8. See Gerald Prince, "Introduction to the Study of the Narratee."

9. See, e.g., Susan R. Suleiman and Inge Crosman, eds., *The Reader in the Text: Essays on Audience and Interpretation.*

10. Prince, "Introduction to the Study of the Narratee," 227.

11. See Booth, *The Rhetoric of Fiction*; and Wolfgang Iser, *The Implied Reader: Patterns of Communication in Prose Fiction from Bunyan to Beckett.* Prince ("Introduction to the Study of the Narratee," 216) defined the "virtual reader" as "a certain type of reader" whose "function" "each author" "develops in his [*sic*] narrative," and "whom he bestows with certain qualities, faculties, and inclina-

tions according to his opinion of men in general (or in particular) and according to the obligations he feels should be respected." Following Prince, I have coined the term "virtual writer" to refer to the writer to whom actual readers attribute the narrative and whom they make responsible for value judgments, characterization, and emplotment.

12. Susan R. Suleiman, "Introduction," 14.

13. Susan Sniader Lanser, "Toward a Feminist Narratology." The republication of this article in the Hoffman and Murphy volume suggests that its significance is acknowledged in both feminist and narrative studies.

14. See Robyn R. Warhol, *Gendered Interventions: Narrative Discourse in the Victorian Novel*, esp. Part I, "Proposing a Model: Feminism and Narratology," 3–44.

15. Sally Robinson, *Engendering the Subject: Gender and Self-Representation in Contemporary Women's Fiction*, 198*n*23.

16. Roland Barthes's reflections on the *prétérit* ("the preterite" in trans.) and the third person as crucial factors in the *roman* ("the novel" in trans.) in "Writing and the Novel" (*Writing Degree Zero*, 29–40) have inspired many Japanese critics writing on the *shōsetsu* and the *genbun itchi* style, such as Hasumi Shigehiko or Karatani Kōjin. However, they do not always credit Barthes explicitly—a practice that may owe as much to the mode of Barthes as it does to the customs of Japanese critical discourse.

17. Karatani Kōjin examined the use of the *-ta* ending in the *genbun itchi* style, in place of *-keri* in the classical language, as the eraser of position markers in several articles such as "Sōseki to 'bun.'" Suga Hidemi touches upon the necessity of examining *-de aru* as a more crucial sign of the style in *Nihon kindai bungaku no <tanjō>: genbun itchi undō to nashionarizumu*.

18. Hasumi Shigehiko, "Monogatari = shomotsu = bungaku," in idem, *Shōsetsu ron = hihyō ron*, 323. Hasumi has made similar observations elsewhere as well. In a remark that is not specifically about *shōsetsu*, but about *bungaku* (literature), he points out more explicitly the universality of the transitive function of language: "Everything can become the 'something,' or the subject [of a book], and everyone can become the subject of the acts of writing and reading" (ibid., 328–29). Although Hasumi's focus is on the "transitive function" of the verbs *kaku* (to write) and *yomu* (to read), the easy access to language guaranteed everyone and the perception of language as a tool to express something else seem to me particularly relevant to *shōsetsu* as a product of humanism and democracy.

19. Roland Barthes, "To Write: An Intransitive Verb?" (1966), in idem, *The Rustle of Language*, 11–21.

20. Suga Hidemi and Watanabe Naomi, *Soredemo sakka ni naritai hito no tame no bukku gaido*, 38.

21. See Tomi Suzuki, *Narrating the Self: Fictions of Japanese Modernity*, 10.

22. Linda Hutcheon, *Narcissistic Narrative: The Metafictional Paradox.*

23. See Karatani Kōjin, "The Extinction of Genres," 175–84.

24. Here I am thinking of the two features commonly found in the novel, explicated by E. M. Forster in *Aspects of the Novel.*

Chapter 1

1. Komori Yōichi, "'Kokoro' o seisei suru 'hāto.'" Komori later published a revised version entitled "*Kokoro* ni okeru hanten suru 'shuki': kūhaku to imi no seisei"; this is the version cited below.

2. See James A. Fujii, "Death, Empire, and the Search for History in Natsume Sōseki's *Kokoro.*"

3. This, of couse, is not to say that *kokubungaku* scholars had had no prior exposure to structuralist narrative studies or to narratology. Nor was it the case that classical Japanese literature had never been studied in this light; indeed, many scholars, including such *Genji* scholars as Takahashi Tōru and Mitani Kuniaki, not only knew of the methodology but also had applied it. For a survey of narrative studies in and outside Japan, see Tomiyama Takao et al., "Zadankai: Kindai bungaku ni okeru 'katari.'"

In the United States, Ken Ito has rightly evaluated Komori's accomplishments in the context of structuralist narrative studies, represented by Genette, Chatman, and Prince, in his "Writing Time in Sōseki's *Kokoro.*"

4. See, e.g, Nakamura Miharu, "Kore wa *Kokoro* de wa nai: naratorojii no kanata e." The title, literally "This is not *Kokoro,*" is evidently meant to echo, along with Michel Foucault and others, René Magritte's *This Is Not a Pipe.*

5. For a list of all the high school *kokugo* textbooks in use in 1993, see Miyakawa Takeo, "Saiwa sareta *Kokoro,*" 193–201.

6. In light of Komori's intent to challenge the authoritative reading of *Kokoro*, it is worth noting that the *Chikuma bunko* paperback edition of *Kokoro* (which appeared in December 1985) included a slightly revised version of Komori's article as the "Kaisetsu" (an interpretive essay customarily attached to novels in Japan and intended to guide the reading). The *Chikuma bunko* thus in

effect "authorized" the Komori version, in its turn, as a prescription of the "correct" way of reading the novel. Indeed, this edition, whose circulation far outnumbers that of academic journals, especially new ones like the *Seijō kokubungaku*, had a strong impact on readers' attitudes.

7. Patricia Merivale, "Silences: Soseki Natsume's *Kokoro* and Canadian Elegiac Romance."

8. Ibid., 127.

9. Ibid., 128.

10. Ibid., 128.

11. Ibid., 131–32.

12. Ibid., 133.

13. Ibid., 134.

14. For more on hierarchy in the site of communication—or the impossibility of equally mutual communication—see, e.g., Oshino Takeshi, "'Shizu' ni koe wa arunoka: *Kokoro* ni okeru yokuatsu no kōzō."

15. Ōoka Shōhei, "Seijō dayori III."

16. Ibid., 170.

17. Ibid., 171.

18. Oshino Takeshi, "*Kokoro* ronsō no yukue."

19. See Ōkawa Kōichi, "'Zen'aku no Higan sugimade' to shite no *Kokoro*," 75. Ōkawa's article is a report on a conference at which Komori orally presented his ideas.

20. Oshino, "*Kokoro* ronsō no yukue," 14. The statement by Tanaka Minoru originally appeared in "*Kokoro* to iu kakehashi," 4. The article by Tanaka critically assesses Komori's initial article.

21. Komori Yōichi, "*Kokoro* no yukue," 59.

22. Natsume Kinnosuke (Sōseki), *Kokoro: A Novel by Natsume Soseki*, trans. Edwin McClellan, 121 (hereafter cited as McClellan).

23. The other quotation from the testament, which is inserted in Part 2 as it catches *watakushi*'s eye, "By the time this letter reaches you, I shall probably have left this world—I shall in all likelihood be dead" (McClellan, 122), does, however, reappear in Part 3, with no alteration (McClellan, 247).

24. Miyoshi Yukio, "Tenbō: Kokubungaku—kindai gendai."

25. Ibid., 45.

26. Ibid.

27. Quoted, without script, in Miyoshi Yukio, "<Sensei> wa kokyu ka," 190.

28. Komori, "*Kokoro* ni okeru hanten suru 'shuki,'" 437.

29. Komori, "*Kokoro* no yukue."

30. Komori, "*Kokoro* ni okeru hanten suru 'shuki,'" 417.

31. Natsume Kinnosuke, *Kokoro: Sensei no isho*, 3. The 1994 Iwanami shoten edition that I use here is based largely on Sōseki's manuscript (1914) and thus takes the original title of the novel.

32. McClellan, 1. I suspect that McClellan's elimination of the last sentence of the first paragraph is one reason why Merivale, in her structuralist reading of *Kokoro*, declared: "But can such an epilogue do even more than fill the gap to show the narrator discovering himself, freeing himself from his obsession with the dead hero, and setting out [. . .] on a new, adult, independent path? No such possibility seems to inhere in the text" (132). Merivale draws an intensive series of analogies between *watakushi* and Sensei, moving within the text from *watakushi*'s narrative to Sensei's, and she would, one assumes, have noted the connection that Komori makes between the two instances in which initials are problematized.

33. Komori, "*Kokoro* ni okeru hanten suru 'shuki,'" 418.

34. Ibid., 419–20. The quotation from *Kokoro* is drawn from McClellan, 1.

35. Ōkawa 76.

36. As I discuss below, the Komori of 1994 thinks that *watakushi* tries to convince himself that he is not responsible for Sensei's death by writing Parts I and II—and perhaps by editing Part III—in such a way that it appears that he did not affect Sensei's mood negatively.

37. Miyoshi Yuko, "Watoson wa haishinsha ka: *Kokoro* saisetsu," 9.

38. Ibid., 10.

39. Ishihara Chiaki and Komori Yōichi, "<Taidan> Sōseki *Kokoro* no genkō o yomu."

40. Merivale, 128.

41. McClellan, 6.

42. McClellan, 7–8.

43. Komori, "<Watakushi> to iu <tasha>-sei: *Kokoro* o meguru ōtoku-riteikku," 20.

44. McClellan, 8.

Chapter 2

1. See, e.g., Terayoko Takeo, "*Kuroi ame* chūkai."

2. All English-language quotations from *Kuroi ame* are taken from Ibuse Masuji, *Black Rain*, trans. John Bester.

3. John Treat ("Ibuse, *Black Rain*, and the Present Day," 208) sees this change of the title instead as making "poetic sense," in that the second title represents two common elements in Ibuse's *ouevre*—the significant color of black and the motif of water.

The title is not the only thing that has been altered, however. Nor did all the editorial changes take place during the process of serialization in *Shinchō*. Terayoko ("*Kuroi ame* chūkai") has outlined the major revisions and stages in the making of *Kuroi ame*: Ibuse's collection of memoirs of *hibakushas*, and his selection and incorporation of excerpts from some of them into his text; collation of the original version in *Shinchō* and later versions; possible reasons for revisions, both textual and circumstantial; and Ibuse's responses to readers' response, positive and negative, publicized and imagined. In addition to what Terayoko lists as major revisions (which are all in the "Journal of the Bombing"), Yasuko's wartime diary has been considerably shortened in the later versions, and omits the original reference to *War and Peace*. This could be accounted for either by the shift of focus from Yasuko's marriage arrangements to the atomic bomb, which I discuss here, or by the intention to silence her further in the narrative. See Ibuse Masuji, *Mei no kekkon* (February 1965): 257–58.

4. "This was *four years and nine months after the end of the war*, when Yasuko had the chance of a match which seemed, if the truth be told, almost too good for her" (15; emphasis added).

5. As an example of the ways "irresponsible talk" was controlled, Shigeko (65–66) recounts an experience of an acquaintance, Mrs. Miyaji, who was questioned by the authorities and admonished for "misconduct": she had told a passenger in a train that the government should not have revised a poem by Miyazawa Kenji, since it was cited in a school textbook, to reflect current social conditions.

6. Incidentally, the parenthetical mention of Shibata's book marks a schism in the narrative. According to *Kuroi ame*, the book was published (as *Genbaku no jissō* by a publisher called Bunkasha; see Terayoko, 363) on "the tenth anniversary of the bomb," that is, in 1955, which is many years after the story time of the primary narrative (i.e., 1950). In other words, Shigematsu could not have known of Shibata's book at the time he rewrites his journal. The only way to account for this is to assume the intrusion of either the omniscient narrator, the implied author, or the historical author Ibuse Masuji, who wrote *Kuroi ame* in 1965 to 1966.

7. Ibuse Masuji, *Kuroi ame*, 130–31.

8. Treat (228) characterizes Shigematsu's copying as "typical of Ibuse and his heroes," since he deals with other works by Ibuse in addition to *Kuroi ame*.

9. Incidentally, it is common in *Kuroi ame* that the ending of a chapter and the beginning of the next chapter duplicate the same information. The narrative was first serialized in the monthly periodical *Shinchō*, and the author must have felt he needed to remind the audience where the story had left off. The monthly installments, in most cases, became chapters, without much redrawing of boundaries, when the narrative was published as a book.

10. This relative lack of privacy seems to be a constant state; consider the following example: "A former pupil of the school—an army man with the forces in northern China—had written Yasuko a rather fulsome letter of thanks for a gift parcel, and had followed it up with five or six poems, all written by himself. Shigematsu still remembered how, when Yasuko had showed them to his wife, Shigeko had blushed inappropriately for someone of her age, and had said, 'Yasuko, these must be what they call "*love poems*"'"(10–11). The content of the letter is more passionate than someone like Shigeko can take lightly. Yasuko, however, did not keep the letter to herself, but seems to have voluntarily shown it to Shigeko. Yasuko apparently felt no need to keep her personal life secret from Shigeko or Shigematsu.

11. I thank Masako Sugihara for the notion that Yasuko's silence is a strategy; this idea has helped me considerably in analyzing Yasuko's narrative (or absence thereof).

12. Adrienne Rich, "Disloyal to Civilization," in idem, *On Lies, Secrets, and Silence*, 308.

13. The square brackets mark passages that I have modified or added. The original is as follows; I have added italics and brackets to correspond to the ones in translation given in the text:

> *Boku wa [asu no] asa ga hayai node*, kyakujin ni shitsurei shite tonari no sanjō-ma de nedoko ni tsuita. Kyakujin no hanashi-goe ni yoru to [. . .].
>
> [*Ijō wa sakuban no kiroku de aru.*]
>
> *Kyō wa asa hayaku oki*, ofukuro ni kotodukeru tegami o kakikaketaga, bankan komogomo kite dōnimo kakenakatta. (Ibuse, *Kuroi ame*, 186)

14. This is one of the few examples in which the chapter break does not coincide with the divisions of the monthly installments. The transition from the "Journal of the Bombing" to the narrative present occurred within the

fourth installment when the novel was serialized, and thus may not have struck readers as forcefully as it does in the book form.

15. Treat, 238.

Chapter 3

1. Despite the well-conceived English title, *The Three-Cornered World*, that Alan Turney has given the work, many seem to prefer the more literal "Grass Pillow" or "Pillow of Grass." To avoid confusion, I use *Kusamakura*.

2. See Dorrit Cohn, *Transparent Minds: Narrative Modes for Presenting Consciousness in Fiction*.

3. Gérard Genette, *Narrative Discourse: An Essay in Method*, 227–31.

4. Ōtsu Chisako, "Hadōsuru setsuna: *Kusamakura* ron," 46. This is one of the most frequently cited articles on *Kusamakura* and is included in both Ishihara Chiaki, ed., *Natsume Sōseki: Hanten suru tekusuto, Nihon bungaku kenkyū shiryō shinshū*, vol. 14, 67–81; and Kataoka Yutaka and Komori Yōichi, eds., *Botchan. Kusamakura, Sōseki sakuhin ron shūsei*, vol. 2, 269–82. Both of these multivolume series are published by prestigious academic publishers in the field of *kokubungaku*.

5. Unless otherwise noted, all English-language quotations of *Kusamakura* are taken from Natsume Kinnosuke (Sōseki), *The Three-Cornered World*, trans. Alan Turney.

6. Ōtsu, 46.

7. Ibid., 47.

8. It is worth noting here, for the sake of a later argument, that the narrator defines his neutral observer as a poet, rather than a playwright or a novelist. He thus privileges the genre of poetry as representing the ideal state of mind detached from human emotions and affairs.

9. Imanishi Junkichi and Izuhara Takatoshi, eds., "Chūkai: *Kusamakura*," 471.

10. See Roman Jakobson, "Two Aspects of Language and Two Types of Aphasic Disturbances."

11. Stephen Owen, ed. and trans., *An Anthology of Chinese Literature: Beginnings to 1911*, 386.

12. Genette (29–30) enumerates terms used by Plato, Henry James, and Tzvetan Todorov for "perfect imitation" and "pure narrative": "mimesis" (Plato), "showing" (James), and "representation" (Todorov) for the former, and "diegesis," "telling," and "narration" for the latter.

13. Leslie Pincus, "Transgressing the Frames of Fiction," *Japan Quarterly*, 440.

14. Natsume Sōseki, "Yo ga *Kusamakura*," 544.

15. Karatani Kōjin, "Sōseki to janru," 198–99.

16. Maeda Ai, "Seikimatsu to tōgenkyō: *Kusamakura* o megutte," 261.

17. Ibid., 261–62.

18. Sōseki gave a self-justifying and yet patronizing overview on the objects of *shaseibun*: "In narrating human affairs, the attitude of the writer of *shaseibun* is not like that of a nobleman surveying the lowly. It is not that of the wise man regarding fools. Nor is it that of a man regarding a woman or a woman regarding a man. The writer of *shaseibun*, that is to say, is an adult looking at children. It [the attitude] is that of a parent toward a child" ("Shaseibun"; translation [modified] from Karatani, "Extinction of Genres," 180–81).

19. Trinh T. Minh-ha, "Gossip and Science: A Conversation on What I Love According to Truth," in idem, *Woman, Native, Other: Writing Postcoloniality and Feminism*, 67–68.

20. In connection with this passage, Kamei Hideo ("*Kusamakura* no sutorатejii," 68) criticizes the totalization of sensibility by the mass media, and the accompanying annihilation of local oral traditions.

21. Natsume Sōseki, *Kusamakura*, 39.

22. See Miyazaki Takahiro, "Tantei."

23. Trinh, 68.

24. Natsume, *Kusamakura*, 159.

25. See Ōno Susumu, "Joshi ha to ga no kinō ni tsuite," 91.

26. Trinh, 68.

27. Turney gives a footnote on *sensei*, the term of address used by Nami here: "Sensei literally means teacher, but may be used as a term of respect to anybody." Although this is quite right, one might also add that *sensei* can also be used when the addressor is teasing the addressee, mocking the addressee while on the surface paying respect to him/her. And this is the case here when Nami addresses *yo*. The term *sensei* is thus appropriate, mirroring—and revealing as pretentious—the narrator's own use of the first-person pronoun *yo* and thus in accordance with the inversion of the hierarchies of knowledge and gaze that takes place here.

28. Seki Reiko, "'Yosooi' no *sekushuariti*: *Kusamakura* no Nami no hyōshō o megutte."

29. Ōtsu, 52.

30. Judith Butler, "Identity, Sex, and the Metaphysics of Substance," in idem, *Gender Trouble: Feminism and the Subversion of Identity*, 25.

31. Pincus, 442. The translations from *Kusamakura* in Pincus's text are her own. For the original of the passage cited here, see Natsume, *Kusamakura*, 171.

32. Ōtsu, 59. The quotations from *Kusamakura* are from Turney, 184.

33. Maeda, *Bungaku tekusuto nyūmon*, 66. I have translated the terms *naihō sareta sakusha* and *naihō sareta dokusha* as the "implied author" and the "implied reader" respectively, retranslating the critical terms introduced into Japanese academic discourse.

34. Karatani, "*Kusamakura*," 272–73.

35. Maeda, "Seikimatsu to tōgenkyō," 263.

36. Natsume, "Yo ga *Kusamakura*," 545.

Chapter 4

I owe part of the main title, as well as its implications of subversion of gender relationships, to Jeffner Allen and Iris Marion Young, eds., *The Thinking Muse: Feminism and Modern French Philosophy*.

1. There are two English translations of *Gan* to date: *The Wild Geese*, trans. Ochiai Kingo and Sanford Goldstein; and *The Wild Goose*, trans. Burton Watson. All English-language quotations from *Gan* are cited from one of these two translations (cited as OG and W, respectively). Since both of these fine translations prioritize readability over literal accuracy and completeness of information, I cite whichever best reflects the particular point I am making.

2. Stephen Snyder, "Ōgai and the Problem of Fiction: *Gan* and Its Antecedents." For Genette's views on "order" and "voice," see *Narrative Discourse*, 33–85 and 212–62, respectively.

3. Takemori Ten'yū, "*Gan* ni tsuite."

4. Ibid., 33–35.

5. Unlike *yo*, as a term of self-reference, *boku* does not sound pompous. It rather sounds as though the narrator is claiming to be youthful, and thus the pronoun is suited to the shifting between present and past that takes place in the narrative.

6. Tanaka Minoru, "<Kyokō no naka no aidenteitei>: *Gan*," 12. Quotations drawn from OG 13.

7. See, e.g., Koganei Kimiko, *Ōgai no omoide*, which explains that the Moris moved from Mukōjima to Kita Senju, although it does not specify the date of the move.

8. Kishida Yoshiko, "*Gan* gūkan," 183.

9. Masao Miyoshi, "The Imported Life. Mori Ōgai: The Wild Goose," 50n.

10. Mori Ōgai, *Gan*, 68.

11. In fact, the time between the events and the act of recording them would have allowed a certain scope for moving up and down the social ladder, as Takemori Ten'yū suggests, and thus the possibility of *boku*'s getting to know Suezō's wife or Otama's father is not entirely to be discounted. The characters of *Gan* live in the same area, and encounters could have happened naturally at any time, without any air of dramatic coincidence. Otama's father comes across Fukuchi Ōchi in a theatre, for example. Perhaps more relevant to the theme of the story—Suezō's "retaliation" against the university students for whom he worked by lending them money and keeping a mistress whom they find attractive—is the one-time appearance of an amateur street performer whom Suezō pays and then sniffs at as he meets Otama and her father at Matsugen (OG 36–37).

12. Mori, 12, 13, 14.

13. Ibid., 34, 35.

14. Ibid., 34.

15. Ibid., 36.

16. Ibid., 20.

17. Note that the moneylender's name is transcribed without representing the long vowel—as "Suezo" rather than "Suezō" in this translation—a practice I respect when quoting from the text.

18. Snyder, 368.

19. Ibid., 18.

20. Mori, 61.

21. It is understandable that *boku* may simply be drawing on the well-known lines from a poem by Su Shi, for the sake of rhetoric:

> I would like to compare
> West Lake to the Lady West
> Light makeup and heavy powder
> both are becoming.

("Drinking on the Lake: At First It Was Clear, Later It Rained, second of two," trans. Michael Fuller, in idem, *The Road to East Slope: The Development of Su Shi's Poetic Voice*, 167).

22. Snyder, 369.

23. Takemori, 601.

24. Dennis Washburn, "The Individual in History: The Narrative Voice of Mori Ōgai," 188.

25. Koizumi Kōichirō, "Gan," 120.

26. Incidentally, Watson's translation is misleading in that it says that Otama is looking at both *boku* and Okada, which is not the case here:

> As though in a trance, Otama fixed her eyes on Okada. He raised his cap in a flustered greeting and then unconsciously quickened his pace.
>
> With the unreserve of a third party, I turned several times to look back. She watched *us* for a long time.
>
> Okada, his eyes glued to the ground, continued his hurried pace to the bottom of the hill. (W 148; emphasis added)

27. Snyder reads this passage as proof of the transformation of the protagonist: "But in the latter part of the novel, the boku narrator seems intent on finding fault with Okada. The hero, who has been described as healthy, handsome, and innocent, if slightly dense, begins to seem somewhat priggish and cold in the narrator's eyes" (368).

28. Chiba Shunji, "'Mado no onna' kō: *Gan* o megutte," 35.

29. Takemori, 594.

30. I thank Patrick Hanan for pointing out the significance of Okada's failure to mention Xiaoqing's poetry, which is a significant departure from the conventional Chinese reception of the mythical figure. For more information on readers' responses to Xiaoqing, see Ellen Widmer, "Xiaoqing's Literary Legacy and the Place of the Woman Writer in Late Imperial China"; and Dorothy Ko, *Teachers of the Inner Chambers: Women and Culture in Seventeenth-Century China*, 91–112.

31. Takemori, 593; Chiba, "'Mado no onna' kō," 28. Takemori points out that the characters' relationships in *Jin Ping Mei* are visible to *boku* and Okada, if not explicitly explained to the reader.

32. Hsiao-hsiao-sheng, *The Plum in the Golden Vase, or, Chin P'ing Mei*, 1: 48.

33. Miyoshi, 50.

Chapter 5

1. Chiba Shunji ("Shōwa shonen-dai no Tanizaki bungaku ni okeru <kikigaki>-teki yōso ni tsuite," 9–10) distinguishes *Manji* from other narratives of

Tanizaki such as *Chijin no ai* (1924–25; trans. as *Naomi*, 1985) in that *Manji* presents a narratee inside the text, whereas *Chijin no ai* has only a narrator who speaks to an unspecified audience. The apparatus that Chiba calls "kikigaki" ("dictation of oral narrative," or "interview report") is, nonetheless, different from that found in classical Japanese literature. Chiba argues rightly that *kikigaki* in modern *shōsetsu* is a "pretense at *kikigaki*," for "*shōsetsu* is an action to sever the self from the tradition of oral transmission, depending on inscribed characters (or books) in the isolated and closed room in the first place."

2. The noun *sensei*, used as a substitute second-person pronoun for a senior person, is not preserved in Howard Hibbett's translation, *The Quicksand*. Instead, descriptions of the nature of the relationship between Sonoko and Sensei are added to compensate for the explanation that would otherwise have been needed for an English-speaking audience. (Edwin McClellan [1] footnotes *sensei* in his translation of *Kokoro*, maintaining the original word in the main text.) Compare the following passages from translation and the original:

> I told her everything [. . .]. Even about how kind *you* were to let me ramble on and on about my problems, *in spite of your being so busy* [emphasis added]. (26)
>
> Watashi, [. . .] sore ni tsuite *Sensei* ni iroiro shinpai shite itadaita koto made, sono toki sukkuri iute shimai mashita. (Tanizaki Jun'ichirō, *Manji*, 415; emphasis added)

The replacement of the culturally encoded word *sensei* with a gesture of courtesy and gratitude made by the speaker Sonoko functions well in place of annotation.

3. Ken K. Ito, *Visions of Desire: Tanizaki's Fictional Worlds*, 124.

4. *Manji* was first serialized in the journal *Kaizō*, intermittently from March 1928 to April 1930, and then was published as a book by Kaizōsha in 1931. It was subsequently included in a variety of editions of the *Works of Tanizaki Jun'ichirō*. The serialization was in 22 installments; the final six installments covered 2 to 4 chapters each. The number of the chapters in the first book-length edition is 36, three more than in the *zenshū* version. As Kōno Taeko (*Tanizaki bungaku to kōtei no yokubō*, 46) explains, Chapters 12 and 13 in the original were eliminated, and the last two chapters were merged into one. In the beginning of the fourteenth chapter of the serialized version, the Author adds a note:

> (The Author's Note: The last two installments have turned out to be erroneous due to the misunderstandings on the part of the Author. I intend to

> revise the manuscript when it is published as a monograph later, but to make the long story short, [. . .]. Please be advised you should read the following in this new understanding.) (*Kaizō*, April 1929, 84)

This statement seems to suggest an authorial gesture, similar to the one made by *boku* in *Gan*, since the Author mentions not only his act of writing but also his intention of publishing his writing, as the historical author Tanizaki did. I thank Howard Hibbett for information on the earlier versions, which are considerably different from the final version in terms of the positioning of the implied author / narratee vis-à-vis the historical author.

On the other hand, the earlier version or, to put it more precisely, the change in diction conspicuous in the first edition (which Kōno [7–26] discusses extensively) does undermine the compositional authority of Tanizaki Jun'ichirō. It is known that he had two women from the Kansai region "translate" Sonoko's account into a Kansai dialect, which he did not feel competent enough to do himself. Hence, one could say that *Manji* is a multiauthor work. That Tanizaki is not the sole historical author is also true to varying degrees in the cases of later narratives, since he dictated the narrative to secretaries, who did the actual writing.

5. All English-language quotations are taken from Tanizaki Jun'ichirō, *The Quicksand*, trans. Howard Hibbett.

6. The italicized portion is an addition to the original, presumably to satisfy English readers' urge to know the identity of the addressee. Thanks to the addition, the occupation of the narratee becomes known to the reader much earlier in the translation than it does in the original.

7. Ito, *Visions of Desire*, 123.

8. Ibid.

9. It is true that the following statement toward the end of the narrative seems to suggest she has been talking nonstop all along: "talking on and on like this has me too excited to be coherent anyway—" (222). It is hard to believe, however, that Sonoko's narration is completed all at once. Sonoko says earlier in the narrative that it took her two hours to narrate a particular incident with Watanuki for her husband ("For over two hours I talked on and on, spilling out everything I knew, while he only grunted in response and sighed occasionally as he listened" [181]). Thus it seems unlikely that she could have finished the session with Sensei in one sitting.

10. Kōno, 12–26.

11. Ito, *Visions of Desire*, 123.

12. Chiba Shunji, "Katarite no koe: *Manji* no <katari>," 258.

13. Tanizaki, 404.

14. Structuralists have explored the discrepancy between the order in which events (hypothetically) take place and that in which they are narrated. See Genette, 33–85, for terms such as "analepsis" and "prolepsis," which correspond, respectively, to "flashback" and "flashforward" in Chatman's terminology (*Story and Discourse*, 64).

15. I thank Hisaaki Wake for pointing out that Sonoko's account is, in fact, extremely logical, given the complexity of the story. This observation, made in a seminar session on *Manji* in Spring 1996, helped me become aware of the constructedness of "orality" of Sonoko's narrative.

16. Chiba Shunji, "Katarite no koe: *Manji* no <katari>," 259–60.

17. One could also speculate that a document left lying open is less likely to provoke curiosity than one suspected to be hidden with special care, which is the case in *Kagi*.

18. In the original version in *Kaizō*, however, the husband confesses to Sonoko that he had read letters without her knowing or permission:

> "I have seen the letters in that drawer while you were out [to visit Mitsuko in Kasayamachi]." "What? Did you just say you had opened my drawer without asking for my permission? You have deceived me!!" [. . .] "I admit I was wrong. I would apologize to you as profusely as you would want me to if I had upset you. But I just wanted to know the truth—what had been really happening." (*Kaizō*, Feb. 1929, 34)

Although this version might effectively foreshadow the later change in his personality, as Kōno Taeko suggests, it nonetheless contradicts the fact that Sonoko had stopped hiding the letters from her husband.

19. Saeki Shōichi (*Monogatari geijutsu ron: Tanizaki, Akutagawa, Mishima*), agreeing here with Kōno Taeko, notes that the transformation of Sonoko's husband is too sudden and roughly narrated to be convincing.

20. This is altered from the initial *Kaizō* edition (see note 4 to this chapter). The current version is more in keeping with the passive character of the husband, as well as with Sonoko's impulse to confess "everything" to passive persons.

21. Ito, *Visions of Desire*, 127.

22. See Chatman, "What Novels Can Do That Films Can't (and Vice Versa); and also Smith.

23. Butler. 25.

Conclusion

1. Smith, 213–14.

2. Barthes, "Is There Any Poetic Writing?" in idem, *Writing Degree Zero*, 41–52.

3. Hasumi Shigehiko, "Kyokō no jiba" (The magnetic field of fiction), in idem, *Shōsetsu ron = Hihyō ron*, 320.

4. Terry Eagleton, *Literary Theory: An Introduction*, 1–16.

5. Kobayashi Yasuo, "Atogaki" (Postscript), in idem and Ishimitsu Yasuo, eds., *Bungaku no gengo kōi ron*, 243.

Works Cited

Allen, Jeffner, and Iris Marion Young, eds. *The Thinking Muse: Feminism and Modern French Philosophy*. Bloomington: Indiana University Press, 1989.

Austin, J. L. *How to Do Things with Words*. 1962. Rev. ed. Cambridge: Harvard University Press, 1975.

Barthes, Roland. *The Pleasure of the Text*. 1973. Trans. Richard Miller. New York: Hill and Wang, 1975.

———. *The Rustle of Language*. 1984. Trans. Richard Howard. 1986. Berkeley: University of California Press, 1989.

———. *Writing Degree Zero*. 1953. Trans. Annette Lavers and Colin Smith. 1967. New York: Noonday Press, 1968, with the preface by Susan Sontag.

Booth, Wayne C. *The Rhetoric of Fiction*. 1961. Rev. ed. Chicago: University of Chicago Press, 1983.

Butler, Judith. *Gender Trouble: Feminism and the Subversion of Identity*. London: Routledge, 1990.

Chambers, Ross. *Story and Situation: Narrative Seduction and the Power of Fiction*. Minneapolis: University of Minnesota Press, 1984.

Chatman, Seymour. *Story and Discourse: Narrative Structure in Fiction and Film*. Ithaca, N.Y.: Cornell University Press, 1978.

———. "What Can We Learn from Contextualist Narratology?" *Poetics Today* 11 (1990): 309–28.

———. "What Novels Can Do That Films Can't (and Vice Versa)." In W. J. T. Mitchell, ed., *On Narrative*, 117–36. Chicago: University of Chicago Press, 1981.

Chiba Shunji. "Kataribe no koe: *Manji* no <katari>." In idem, *Tanizaki Jun'ichirō: kitsune to mazohizumu*, rev. ed., 239–64. Tokyo: Ozawa shoten, 1994.

———. "'Mado no onna' kō: *Gan* o megutte." *Mori Ōgai kenkyū* 2 (May 1988): 26–47.

———. "Shōwa shonen-dai no Tanizaki bungaku ni okeru <kikigaki>-teki yōso ni tsuite." *Nihon bungaku* 29, no. 6 (June 1980): 9–16.

Cohn, Dorrit. *Transparent Minds: Narrative Modes for Presenting Consciousness in Fiction*. Princeton: Princeton University Press, 1978.

Derrida, Jaccques. "Signature Event Context." 1977. Trans. Samuel Weber and Jeffrey Melman. In Gerald Graff, ed., *Limited Inc.*, 1–23. Evanston: Northwestern University Press, 1988.

Eagleton, Terry. *Literary Theory: An Introduction*. London: Basil Blackwell, 1983.

Felman, Shoshana. *The Literary Speech Act: Don Juan with J. L. Austin, or Seduction in Two Languages*. 1980. Trans. Catherine Porter. Ithaca, N.Y.: Cornell University Press, 1983.

Forster, E. M. *Aspects of the Novel*. 1927. Middlesex, Eng.: Penguin, 1976.

Fowler, Edward. *The Rhetoric of Confession: Shishōsetsu in Early Twentieth-Century Japanese Fiction*. Berkeley: University of California Press, 1988.

Fujii, James A. "Death, Empire, and the Search for History in Natsume Sōseki's *Kokoro*." In idem, *Complicit Fictions: The Subject in the Modern Japanese Prose Narratives*, 126–50. Berkeley: University of California Press, 1993.

———. "*Kokoro* ni okeru shi, teikoku, soshite rekishi no tankyū." Trans. Tōda Masaru. *Bungaku*, Autumn 1992, 50–65.

Fuller, Michael. *The Road to East Slope: The Development of Su Shi's Poetic Voice*. Stanford: Stanford University Press, 1990.

Genette, Gérard. *Narrative Discourse: An Essay in Method*. Trans. Jane E. Lewin. Ithaca, N.Y.: Cornell University Press, 1980.

Hasumi Shigehiko. *Monogatari hihan josetsu*. 1982, 1984. Tokyo: Chūō kōronsha, 1985.

———. *Shōsetsu kara tōku hanarete*. 1987–88. Rev. ed. Tokyo: Nihon bungeisha, 1989.

———. *Shōsetsu ron = Hihyō ron*. Tokyo: Seidosha, 1982.

Hata Kōhei. *"Kokoro" no kodoku to ai. Umi no hon* 2 (September 1986).

———. "Sensei wa *kokyu* de wa nai." *Chikuma*, no. 188 (December 1986): 24–27.

Hijiya-Kirschnereit, Irmela. *Rituals of Self-Revelation: Shishōsetsu as Literary Genre and Socio-cultural Phenomenon*. Cambridge: Harvard University, Council on East Asian Studies, 1996.

Hirakawa Sukehiro. "Hirakawa Sukehiro ga yomu: *Kusamakura*." *Kumamoto nichinichi shinbun*, Sept. 15, 1996.

Hsiao-hsiao-sheng. *The Plum in the Golden Vase, or, Chin P'ing Mei*. Vol. 1. Trans. David Tod Roy. Princeton: Princeton University Press, 1993.

Hutcheon, Linda. *Narcissistic Narrative: The Metafictional Paradox*. London: Methuen, 1984.

Ibuse Masuji. *Black Rain*. Trans. John Bester. New York: Kodansha International, 1969.

———. *Kuroi ame*. Published in 14 installments. *Shinchō*, Aug. 1965–Sept. 1966. Reprinted in *Ibuse Masuji zenshū*. Tokyo: Chikuma shobō, 1975. 13: 3–298.

———. *Mei no kekkon*. Published in 7 installments. *Shinchō*, Jan. 1965–July 1965.

Imanishi Junkichi and Izuhara Takatoshi, eds. "Chūkai: *Kusamakura*." In Natsume Sōseki, *Sōseki zenshū*, 3: 461–506. Tokyo: Iwanami shoten, 1967.

Iser, Wolfgang. *The Implied Reader: Patterns of Communication in Prose Fiction from Bunyan to Beckett*. Baltimore: Johns Hopkins Press, 1974.

Ishihara Chiaki. "Hanten suru kansei: *An'ya kōro* ron." *Nihon kindai bungaku* 39 (May 1988): 27–37.

———. "Seido to shite no 'kenkyū buntai.'" *Nihon kindai bungaku* 37 (Oct. 1987): 114–18.

Ishihara Chiaki, ed. *Natsume Sōseki: Hanten suru tekusuto*. Nihon bungaku kenkyū shiryō shinshū, 14. Tokyo: Yūshōdō, 1990.

Ishihara Chiaki and Komori Yōichi. "<Taidan> Sōseki *Kokoro* no genkō o yomu." *Bungaku* 3, no. 4 (Autumn 1992): 2–12.

Ito, Ken K. *Visions of Desire: Tanizaki's Fictional Worlds*. Stanford: Stanford University Press, 1991.

———. "Writing Time in Sōseki's *Kokoro*." In Dennis Washburn and Alan Tansman, eds., *Studies in Modern Japanese Literature: Essays and Translations in Honor of Edwin McClellan*, 3–21. Ann Arbor: University of Michigan, Center for Japanese Studies, 1997.

Jakobson, Roman. "Two Aspects of Language and Two Types of Aphasic Disturbances." In idem and Morris Halle, eds., *Fundamentals of Language*, 53–82. The Hague: Mouton, 1956.

Kamata, Tadashi, ed. *Shunjū sashi den, 1*. Shinshaku kanbun taikei, 30. Tokyo: Meiji shoin, 1971.

Kamei Hideo. "*Kusamakura* no sutoratejii." *Kokubungaku kaishaku to kyōzai no kenkyū* 39, no. 1 (Jan. 1994): 65–71.

Karatani Kōjin. "The Extinction of Genres." 1991. Trans. Brett DeBary. In idem, *Origins of Modern Japanese Literature*, 175–84. Durham, N.C.: Duke University Press, 1993.

———. "*Kusamakura*." 1981. Reprinted in idem, *Sōseki ron shūsei*, 270–76. Tokyo: Daisan bunmei sha, 1992.

———. "Sōseki to 'bun.'" 1990. Reprinted in idem, *Sōseki ron shūsei*, 233–60. Tokyo: Daisan bunmei sha, 1992.

———. "Sōseki to janru." 1990. Reprinted in idem, *Sōseki ron shūsei*, 197–232. Tokyo: Daisan bunmei sha, 1992.

Kataoka Yutaka and Komori Yōichi, eds. *Botchan. Kusamakura*. Sōseki sakuhin ron shūsei, 2. Tokyo: Ōfūsha, 1990.

Kishida Yoshiko. "*Gan* gūkan." 1946. In Yoshida Seiichi, ed., *Mori Ōgai kenkyū*, 182–94. Tokyo: Chikuma shobō, 1960.

Ko, Dorothy. *Teachers of the Inner Chambers: Women and Culture in Seventeenth-Century China*. Stanford: Stanford University Press, 1994.

Kobayashi Yasuo and Ishimitsu Yasuo, eds. *Bungaku no gengo kōi ron*. Tokyo: Miraisha, 1997.

———. *Dekyoto to shite no bungaku*. Tokyo: Sakuhinsha, 1995.

Koganei Kimiko. *Ōgai no omoide*. Tokyo: Yagi shoten, 1956.

Koizumi Kōichirō. "Gan." 1980. In idem, *Mori Ōgai ron jisshō to hihyō*, 107–29. Tokyo: Meiji shoin, 1981.

Komori Yōichi. *Dekigoto to shite no yomukoto*. Tokyo: University of Tokyo Press, 1996.

———. "*Kokoro* ni okeru hanten suru 'shuki': kūhaku to imi no seisei." In idem, *Kōzō to shite no katari*, 415–37. Tokyo: Shin'yōsha, 1988. (Rev. version of "*Kokoro* o seisei suru 'hāto.'")

———. "*Kokoro* no yukue." *Seijō kokubungaku* 3 (Mar. 1987): 55–61.

———. "*Kokoro* o seisei suru 'hāto.'" *Seijō kokubungaku* 1 (Mar. 1985): 41–59. Rev. version printed in idem, *Buntai to shite no monogatari*, 293–317. Chikuma shobō, 1988.

———. "'Watashi' to iu <tasha>-sei: *Kokoro* o meguru ōtokuriteikku." *Bungaku* 3, no. 4 (Autumn 1992): 13–27.

Komori Yōichi, Nakamura Miharu, and Miyakawa Takeo, eds. *Sōryoku tōron Sōseki no "Kokoro."* Tokyo: Kanrin shobō, 1994.

Kōno Taeko. *Tanizaki bungaku to kōtei no yokubō*. Bungei shunjūsha, 1976.

Lanser, Susan Sniader. *Fictions of Authority: Women Writers and Narrative Voice*. Ithaca, N.Y.: Cornell University Press, 1992.

———. *The Narrative Act: Point of View in Fiction*. Princeton: Princeton University Press, 1981.

———. "Sexing the Narrative: Propriety, Desire, and the Engendering of Narratology." *Narrative* 3, no. 1 (Jan. 1995): 85–94.

———. "Toward a Feminist Narratology." 1986. Reprinted in Robyn R. Warhol and Diane Price Herndl, eds., *Feminisms: An Anthology of Literary Theory and Criticism*, 610–29. New Brunswick, N.J.: Rutgers University Press, 1991.

Also reprinted in Michael J. Hoffman and Patrick D. Murphy, eds., *Essentials of the Theory of Fiction*, 453–72. Durham, N.C.: Duke University Press, 1996.

Legge, James. *The Chinese Classics*, vol. 5, *The Ch'un Ts'ew, with the Tso Chuen*. Oxford: Oxford University Press, 1871(?).

Maeda Ai. *Bungaku tekusuto nyūmon*. 1988. Reprinted in *Maeda Ai chosaku shū*, 6: 57–189. Tokyo: Chikuma shobō, 1990.

———. "Ōgai no Chūgoku bungaku shumi." 1965. Reprinted in *Maeda Ai chosaku shū*, 2: 74–87. Tokyo: Chikuma shobō, 1989.

———. "Seikimatsu to tōgenkyō: *Kusamakura* o megutte." 1985. Reprinted in *Maeda Ai chosaku shū*, 6: 261–74. Tokyo: Chikuma shobō, 1990. Also reprinted in Kataoka Yutaka and Komori Yōichi, *Botchan. Kusamakura*, 260–68. *Sōseki sakuhin ron shūsei*, 2. Tokyo: Ōfūsha, 1990.

McCullough, Helen Craig. *Ōkagami, The Great Mirror: Fujiwara Michinaga (966–1027) and His Times*. Princeton: Princeton University Press, 1980. Reprinted—Ann Arbor: University of Michigan, Center for Japanese Studies, 1991.

McLaren, Anne E., trans. and introd. *The Chinese Femme Fatale: Stories from the Ming Period*. The University of Sydney East Asian Series, 8. Australia: Wild Peony, 1994.

McMahon, Keith. *Misers, Shrews, and Polygamists: Sexuality and Male-Female Relations in Eighteenth-Century Chinese Fiction*. Durham, N.C.: Duke University Press, 1995.

Merivale, Patricia. "Silences: Soseki Natsume's *Kokoro* and Canadian Elegiac Romance." In Kinya Tsuruta and Theodore Goosen, eds., *Nature and Identity in Canadian and Japanese Literature*, 127–41. Toronto: University of Toronto and York University Joint Centre for Asia Pacific Studies, 1988.

Mezei, Kathy. "Introduction: Contextualizing Feminist Narratology." In idem, *Ambiguous Discourse: Feminist Narratology and British Women Writers*, 1–20. Chapel Hill: University of North Carolina Press, 1996.

Mimura Aya. Review of Sakaki Atsuko, *Kōi to shite no shōsetsu: naratorojii o koete*. *Hikaku bungaku kenkyū* 69 (Dec. 1996): 149–51.

Miyakawa Takeo. "Saiwa sareta *Kokoro*." In Komori Yōichi et al., eds., *Sōryoku tōron Sōseki no "Kokoro,"* 179–201. Tokyo: Kanrin shobō, 1994.

Miyazaki Takahiro. "Tantei." In Miyoshi Yukio, ed., *Natsume Sōseki jiten*. *Bessatsu Kokubungaku*, no. 39 (1990): 182–83.

Miyoshi, Masao. "The Imported Life. Mori Ōgai: *The Wild Goose.*" In idem, *Accomplices of Silence*, 38–54. Berkeley: University of California Press, 1974.

Miyoshi Yukio. "<Sensei> wa kokyu ka." *Kaien* 5, no. 11 (Nov. 1986): 190–91.

———. "Tenbō: Kokubungaku—kindai gendai." In Kokuritsu kokugo kenkyūjo, ed., *Kokugo nenkan*, 44–45. Tokyo: Shūei shuppan, 1986.

———. "Watoson wa haishinsha ka: *Kokoro* saisetsu." *Bungaku* 56, no. 5 (May 1988): 7–21.

Mori Ōgai. *Gan*. Published in 11 installments. *Subaru*, Sept. 1911–May 1913. Reprinted in *Mori Ōgai zenshū*, 8: 489–603. Tokyo: Iwanami shoten, 1972.

———. *The Wild Geese*. Trans. Ochiai Kingo and Sanford Goldstein. Rutland, Vt.: Tuttle, 1959.

———. *The Wild Goose*. Trans. Burton Watson. Michigan Monograph Series in Japanese Studies, no. 14. Ann Arbor: University of Michigan Center for Japanese Studies, 1995.

Nakamura Miharu. "Kore wa *Kokoro* de wa nai: naratorojii no kanata e." In Komori Yōichi et al., eds., *Sōryoku tōron Sōseki no "Kokoro,"* 40–53. Tokyo Kanrin shobō, 1994.

Natsume Kinnosuke (Natsume Sōseki). *Kokoro: Sensei no isho*. 1914. Reprinted in *Sōseki zenshū*, vol. 9. Tokyo: Iwanami shoten, 1994.

———. *Kokoro: A Novel by Natsume Soseki*. Trans. Edwin McClellan. Washington, D.C.: Regnery Gateway, 1957.

———. *Kusamakura*. 1906. Reprinted in *Sōseki zenshū*, 3: 1–171. Tokyo: Iwanami shoten, 1994.

———. "Sakumotsu no hihyō." 1907. In *Sōseki zenshū* [new ed.]. 16: 38–47. Tokyo: Iwanami shoten, 1995.

———. "Shaseibun." *Sōseki zenshū* [new ed.], 16: 48–56. Tokyo: Iwanami shoten, 1995.

———. *The Three-Cornered World*. Trans. Alan Turney. London: Peter Owen, 1965.

———. "Yo ga *Kusamakura*." 1906. In *Sōseki zenshū*, 16: 543–45. Tokyo: Iwanami shoten, 1967.

Ōkawa Kōichi. "'Zen'aku no Higan sugimade' to shite no *Kokoro*." *Seijō kokubungaku* 2 (Mar. 1986): 69–77.

Ong, Walter J. *Orality and Literacy: The Technologizing of the Word*. 1982. London: Routledge, 1989.

Ōno Susumu, "Joshi ha to ga no kinō ni tsuite." 1975. Reprinted in idem, *Bunpō to goi*, 85–113. Tokyo: Iwanami shoten, 1987.

Ōoka Shōhei. "Seijō dayori III: 8." *Bungakukai*, Oct. 1985, 170–71.

Oshino Takeshi. "*Kokoro* ronsō no yukue." In Komori Yōichi et al., eds., *Sōryoku tōron Sōseki no "Kokoroī,"* 12–39. Tokyo Kanrin shobō, 1994.

———. "'Shizu' ni koe wa arunoka: *Kokoro* ni okeru yokuatsu no kōzō." *Bungaku* 3, no. 4 (Autumn 1992): 41–49.

Ōtsu Chisako. "Hadōsuru setsuna: *Kusamakura* ron." *Seijō kokubungaku*, no. 4 (Mar. 1988): 46–59.

Owen, Stephen, ed. and trans. *An Anthology of Chinese Literature: Beginnings to 1911*. New York: Norton, 1996.

Pincus, Leslie. "Transgressing the Frames of Fiction." *Japan Quarterly* 37, no. 4 (Oct.–Dec. 1990): 433–49.

Pratt, Mary Louise. *Toward a Speech Act Theory of Literary Discourse*. Bloomington: Indiana University Press, 1977.

Prince, Gerald. "Introduction to the Study of the Narratee." 1973. Reprinted in Michael J. Hoffman and Patrick D. Murphy, eds., *Essentials of the Theory of Fiction*, 213–33. Durham, N.C.: Duke University Press, 1996.

———. "On Narratology: Criteria, Corpus, Context." 1990. Rev. version published in *Narrative* 3, no. 1 (Jan. 1995): 73–84.

Prince, Gerald, ed. *A Dictionary of Narratology*. Lincoln: University of Nebraska Press, 1987.

Reid, Ian. *Narrative Exchanges*. London: Routledge, 1992.

Rich, Adrienne. *On Lies, Secrets, and Silience*. New York: Norton, 1979.

Robinson, Sally. *Engendering the Subject: Gender and Self-Representation in Contemporary Women's Fiction*. Albany: State University of New York Press, 1991.

Saeki Shōichi. *Monogatari geijutsu ron: Tanizaki, Akutagawa, Mishima*. 1974–79. Tokyo: Kōdansha, 1979.

Saitō Minako. "Watch bungei: 'shōsetsu' o kobamu setsujitsusa ni kinchōkan." *Asahi shinbun*, July 25, 1996.

Sakaki Atsuko. *Kōi to shite no shōsetsu: naratorojii o koete*. Tokyo: Shin'yōsha, 1996.

Seki Reiko. "'Yosooi' no sekushuariti: *Kusamakura* no nami no hyōshō o megutte." *Sōseki kenkyū*, no. 3 (1994): 122.

Snyder, Stephen. "Ōgai and the Problem of Fiction: *Gan* and Its Antecedents." *Monumenta Nipponica* 49, no. 3 (Autumn 1994): 353–73.

Smith, Barbara Herrnstein. 1980. "Narrative Theories, Narrative Versions." In W. J. T. Mitchell, ed., *On Narrative*, 209–32. Chicago: University of Chicago Press, 1981.

Suga Hidemi. *Nihon kindai bungaku no <tanjō>: genbun itchi undō to nashionari-zumu*. Tokyo: Ōta shuppan, 1995.

Suga Hidemi and Watanabe Naomi. *Soredemo sakka ni naritai hito no tame no bukku gaido*. Tokyo: Ōta shuppan, 1993.

Suleiman, Susan R. "Introduction." In idem and Inge Crosman, eds., *The Reader in the Text: Essays on Audience and Interpretation*, 3–45. Princeton: Princeton University Press, 1980.

Suleiman, Susan R., and Inge Crosman, eds., *The Reader in the Text: Essays on Audience and Interpretation*. Princeton: Princeton University Press, 1980.

Suzuki, Tomi. *Narrating the Self: Fictions of Japanese Modernity*. Stanford: Stanford University Press, 1996.

Takayama Hiroshi. "Book Garden: Migotona monogatari kōi ron koto hajime—Sakaki Atsuko *Kōi to shite no shōsetsu: naratorojii o koete*." *Subaru*, Oct. 1996, 129.

Takemori Ten'yū. "*Gan* ni tsuite." 1982–83. Reprinted in idem, *Ōgai sono mon'yō*, 575–629. Tokyo: Ozawa shoten, 1984.

Tanaka Minoru. "*Kokoro* to iu kakehashi." *Nihon bungaku* 35, no. 12 (Dec. 1986): 1–13.

———. "<Kyokō no naka no aidenteitei>: *Gan*." *Nihon bungaku* 35, no. 10 (Oct. 1986): 12–22.

Tanizaki Jun'ichirō. *Manji*. Published in 22 installments. *Kaizō*, Mar. 1928–Apr. 1930. Published as a book in a rev. ed., 1931. Reprinted in *Tanizaki Jun'ichirō zenshū*, 11: 393–569. Tokyo: Chūō kōronsha, 1967.

———. *The Quicksand*. Trans. Howard Hibbett. New York: Knopf, 1993.

Terayoko Takeo. "*Kuroi ame* chūkai." 1972, 1983. Reprinted in Isogai Hideo, ed., *Ibuse Masuji kenkyū*, 343–79. Hiroshima: Keisuisha, 1984.

Tomiyama Takao, Fujii Sadakazu, Torii Kunio, and Komori Yōichi. "Zadankai: Kindai bungaku ni okeru 'katari.'" *Kokubungaku kaishaku to kanshō* 56, no. 4 (Apr. 1991): 14–38.

Treat, John Whittier. "Ibuse, *Black Rain*, and the Present Day." In idem, *Pools of Water, Pillars of Fire: The Literature of Ibuse Masuji*, 199–257. Seattle: University of Washington Press, 1988.

Trinh T. Minh-ha. *Woman, Native, Other: Writing Postcoloniality and Feminism*. Bloomington: Indiana University Press, 1989.

Warhol, Robyn R. *Gendered Interventions: Narrative Discourse in the Victorian Novel*. New Brunswick, N.J.: Rutgers University Press, 1989.

Washburn, Dennis C. "The Individual in History: The Narrative Voice of Mori Ōgai." In idem, *The Dilemma of the Modern in Japanese Fiction*, 180–94. New Haven: Yale University Press, 1995.

Watanabe Naomi. "Mendan bungei jihyō '96." *Bungei* 35, no. 4 (Winter 1996): 436–47.

Watanabe Sumiko. "Ōgai no josei kan: 'Hannichi,' 'Honke bunke,' 'Yasui fujin' and 'Haran' o shiza to shite." *Utako* 2 (1994): 33–54.

Widmer, Ellen. "Xiaoqing's Literary Legacy and the Place of the Woman Writer in Late Imperial China." *Late Imperial China* 13, no. 1 (June 1992): 111–55.

"Xiaoqing chuan." In Zhang Chao, ed., *Yuchu xinshi*. Beijing: Shinhua shudian, 1954.

Yoshikawa Yasuhisa. "20-seiki no shōsetsu o yomu tame ni wa: kōzōshugi-teki na naratorojii bunseki to gengo kōi ron. Sakaki Atsuko *Kōi to shite no shōsetsu: naratorojii o koete* o megutte." *Nihon tosho shinbun*, Dec. 21, 1996.

Index

HARVARD EAST ASIAN MONOGRAPHS

(out-of-print)*

*1. Liang Fang-chung, *The Single-Whip Method of Taxation in China*
*2. Harold C. Hinton, *The Grain Tribute System of China, 1845–1911*
3. Ellsworth C. Carlson, *The Kaiping Mines, 1877–1912*
*4. Chao Kuo-chün, *Agrarian Policies of Mainland China: A Documentary Study, 1949–1956*
*5. Edgar Snow, *Random Notes on Red China, 1936–1945*
*6. Edwin George Beal, Jr., *The Origin of Likin, 1835–1864*
7. Chao Kuo-chün, *Economic Planning and Organization in Mainland China: A Documentary Study, 1949–1957*
*8. John K. Fairbank, *Ching Documents: An Introductory Syllabus*
*9. Helen Yin and Yi-chang Yin, *Economic Statistics of Mainland China, 1949–1957*
*10. Wolfgang Franke, *The Reform and Abolition of the Traditional Chinese Examination System*
11. Albert Feuerwerker and S. Cheng, *Chinese Communist Studies of Modern Chinese History*
12. C. John Stanley, *Late Ching Finance: Hu Kuang-yung as an Innovator*
13. S. M. Meng, *The Tsungli Yamen: Its Organization and Functions*
*14. Ssu-yü Teng, *Historiography of the Taiping Rebellion*
15. Chun-Jo Liu, *Controversies in Modern Chinese Intellectual History: An Analytic Bibliography of Periodical Articles, Mainly of the May Fourth and Post–May Fourth Era*
*16. Edward J. M. Rhoads, *The Chinese Red Army, 1927–1963: An Annotated Bibliography*
17. Andrew J. Nathan, *A History of the China International Famine Relief Commission*
*18. Frank H. H. King (ed.) and Prescott Clarke, *A Research Guide to China-Coast Newspapers, 1822–1911*
19. Ellis Joffe, *Party and Army: Professionalism and Political Control in the Chinese Officer Corps, 1949–1964*
*20. Toshio G. Tsukahira, *Feudal Control in Tokugawa Japan: The Sankin Kōtai System*
21. Kwang-Ching Liu, ed., *American Missionaries in China: Papers from Harvard Seminars*
22. George Moseley, *A Sino-Soviet Cultural Frontier: The Ili Kazakh Autonomous Chou*

23. Carl F. Nathan, *Plague Prevention and Politics in Manchuria, 1910–1931*
*24. Adrian Arthur Bennett, *John Fryer: The Introduction of Western Science and Technology into Nineteenth-Century China*
25. Donald J. Friedman, *The Road from Isolation: The Campaign of the American Committee for Non-Participation in Japanese Aggression, 1938–1941*
26. Edward LeFevour, *Western Enterprise in Late Ching China: A Selective Survey of Jardine, Matheson and Company's Operations, 1842–1895*
27. Charles Neuhauser, *Third World Politics: China and the Afro-Asian People's Solidarity Organization, 1957–1967*
28. Kungtu C. Sun, assisted by Ralph W. Huenemann, *The Economic Development of Manchuria in the First Half of the Twentieth Century*
*29. Shahid Javed Burki, *A Study of Chinese Communes, 1965*
30. John Carter Vincent, *The Extraterritorial System in China: Final Phase*
31. Madeleine Chi, *China Diplomacy, 1914–1918*
*32. Clifton Jackson Phillips, *Protestant America and the Pagan World: The First Half Century of the American Board of Commissioners for Foreign Missions, 1810–1860*
33. James Pusey, *Wu Han: Attacking the Present through the Past*
34. Ying-wan Cheng, *Postal Communication in China and Its Modernization, 1860–1896*
35. Tuvia Blumenthal, *Saving in Postwar Japan*
36. Peter Frost, *The Bakumatsu Currency Crisis*
37. Stephen C. Lockwood, *Augustine Heard and Company, 1858–1862*
38. Robert R. Campbell, *James Duncan Campbell: A Memoir by His Son*
39. Jerome Alan Cohen, ed., *The Dynamics of China's Foreign Relations*
40. V. V. Vishnyakova-Akimova, *Two Years in Revolutionary China, 1925–1927*, tr. Steven L. Levine
*41. Meron Medzini, *French Policy in Japan during the Closing Years of the Tokugawa Regime*
42. Ezra Vogel, Margie Sargent, Vivienne B. Shue, Thomas Jay Mathews, and Deborah S. Davis, *The Cultural Revolution in the Provinces*
*43. Sidney A. Forsythe, *An American Missionary Community in China, 1895–1905*
*44. Benjamin I. Schwartz, ed., *Reflections on the May Fourth Movement.: A Symposium*
*45. Ching Young Choe, *The Rule of the Taewŏngun, 1864–1873: Restoration in Yi Korea*
46. W. P. J. Hall, *A Bibliographical Guide to Japanese Research on the Chinese Economy, 1958–1970*
47. Jack J. Gerson, *Horatio Nelson Lay and Sino-British Relations, 1854–1864*
48. Paul Richard Bohr, *Famine and the Missionary: Timothy Richard as Relief Administrator and Advocate of National Reform*
49. Endymion Wilkinson, *The History of Imperial China: A Research Guide*
50. Britten Dean, *China and Great Britain: The Diplomacy of Commercial Relations, 1860–1864*
51. Ellsworth C. Carlson, *The Foochow Missionaries, 1847–1880*
52. Yeh-chien Wang, *An Estimate of the Land-Tax Collection in China, 1753 and 1908*
53. Richard M. Pfeffer, *Understanding Business Contracts in China, 1949–1963*

54. Han-sheng Chuan and Richard Kraus, *Mid-Ching Rice Markets and Trade: An Essay in Price History*
55. Ranbir Vohra, *Lao She and the Chinese Revolution*
56. Liang-lin Hsiao, *China's Foreign Trade Statistics, 1864–1949*
*57. Lee-hsia Hsu Ting, *Government Control of the Press in Modern China, 1900–1949*
58. Edward W. Wagner, *The Literati Purges: Political Conflict in Early Yi Korea*
*59. Joungwon A. Kim, *Divided Korea: The Politics of Development, 1945–1972*
*60. Noriko Kamachi, John K. Fairbank, and Chūzō Ichiko, *Japanese Studies of Modern China Since 1953: A Bibliographical Guide to Historical and Social-Science Research on the Nineteenth and Twentieth Centuries, Supplementary Volume for 1953–1969*
61. Donald A. Gibbs and Yun-chen Li, *A Bibliography of Studies and Translations of Modern Chinese Literature, 1918–1942*
62. Robert H. Silin, *Leadership and Values: The Organization of Large-Scale Taiwanese Enterprises*
63. David Pong, *A Critical Guide to the Kwangtung Provincial Archives Deposited at the Public Record Office of London*
*64. Fred W. Drake, *China Charts the World: Hsu Chi-yü and His Geography of 1848*
*65. William A. Brown and Urgrunge Onon, translators and annotators, *History of the Mongolian People's Republic*
66. Edward L. Farmer, *Early Ming Government: The Evolution of Dual Capitals*
*67. Ralph C. Croizier, *Koxinga and Chinese Nationalism: History, Myth, and the Hero*
*68. William J. Tyler, tr., *The Psychological World of Natsume Sōseki*, by Doi Takeo
69. Eric Widmer, *The Russian Ecclesiastical Mission in Peking during the Eighteenth Century*
*70. Charlton M. Lewis, *Prologue to the Chinese Revolution: The Transformation of Ideas and Institutions in Hunan Province, 1891–1907*
71. Preston Torbert, *The Ching Imperial Household Department: A Study of Its Organization and Principal Functions, 1662–1796*
72. Paul A. Cohen and John E. Schrecker, eds., *Reform in Nineteenth-Century China*
73. Jon Sigurdson, *Rural Industrialism in China*
74. Kang Chao, *The Development of Cotton Textile Production in China*
75. Valentin Rabe, *The Home Base of American China Missions, 1880–1920*
*76. Sarasin Viraphol, *Tribute and Profit: Sino-Siamese Trade, 1652–1853*
77. Ch'i-ch'ing Hsiao, *The Military Establishment of the Yuan Dynasty*
78. Meishi Tsai, *Contemporary Chinese Novels and Short Stories, 1949–1974: An Annotated Bibliography*
*79. Wellington K. K. Chan, *Merchants, Mandarins and Modern Enterprise in Late Ching China*
80. Endymion Wilkinson, *Landlord and Labor in Late Imperial China: Case Studies from Shandong by Jing Su and Luo Lun*
*81. Barry Keenan, *The Dewey Experiment in China: Educational Reform and Political Power in the Early Republic*

HARVARD EAST ASIAN MONOGRAPHS

*82. George A. Hayden, *Crime and Punishment in Medieval Chinese Drama: Three Judge Pao Plays*

*83. Sang-Chul Suh, *Growth and Structural Changes in the Korean Economy, 1910–1940*

84. J. W. Dower, *Empire and Aftermath: Yoshida Shigeru and the Japanese Experience, 1878–1954*

85. Martin Collcutt, *Five Mountains: The Rinzai Zen Monastic Institution in Medieval Japan*

86. Kwang Suk Kim and Michael Roemer, *Growth and Structural Transformation*

87. Anne O. Krueger, *The Developmental Role of the Foreign Sector and Aid*

*88. Edwin S. Mills and Byung-Nak Song, *Urbanization and Urban Problems*

89. Sung Hwan Ban, Pal Yong Moon, and Dwight H. Perkins, *Rural Development*

*90. Noel F. McGinn, Donald R. Snodgrass, Yung Bong Kim, Shin-Bok Kim, and Quee-Young Kim, *Education and Development in Korea*

91. Leroy P. Jones and Il SaKong, *Government, Business, and Entrepreneurship in Economic Development: The Korean Case*

92. Edward S. Mason, Dwight H. Perkins, Kwang Suk Kim, David C. Cole, Mahn Je Kim et al., *The Economic and Social Modernization of the Republic of Korea*

93. Robert Repetto, Tai Hwan Kwon, Son-Ung Kim, Dae Young Kim, John E. Sloboda, and Peter J. Donaldson, *Economic Development, Population Policy, and Demographic Transition in the Republic of Korea*

94. Parks M. Coble, Jr., *The Shanghai Capitalists and the Nationalist Government, 1927–1937*

95. Noriko Kamachi, *Reform in China: Huang Tsun-hsien and the Japanese Model*

96. Richard Wich, *Sino-Soviet Crisis Politics: A Study of Political Change and Communication*

97. Lillian M. Li, *China's Silk Trade: Traditional Industry in the Modern World, 1842–1937*

98. R. David Arkush, *Fei Xiaotong and Sociology in Revolutionary China*

*99. Kenneth Alan Grossberg, *Japan's Renaissance: The Politics of the Muromachi Bakufu*

100. James Reeve Pusey, *China and Charles Darwin*

101. Hoyt Cleveland Tillman, *Utilitarian Confucianism: Chen Liang's Challenge to Chu Hsi*

102. Thomas A. Stanley, *Ōsugi Sakae, Anarchist in Taishō Japan: The Creativity of the Ego*

103. Jonathan K. Ocko, *Bureaucratic Reform in Provincial China: Ting Jih-ch'ang in Restoration Kiangsu, 1867–1870*

104. James Reed, *The Missionary Mind and American East Asia Policy, 1911–1915*

105. Neil L. Waters, *Japan's Local Pragmatists: The Transition from Bakumatsu to Meiji in the Kawasaki Region*

106. David C. Cole and Yung Chul Park, *Financial Development in Korea, 1945–1978*

107. Roy Bahl, Chuk Kyo Kim, and Chong Kee Park, *Public Finances during the Korean Modernization Process*

108. William D. Wray, *Mitsubishi and the N.Y.K, 1870–1914: Business Strategy in the Japanese Shipping Industry*

109. Ralph William Huenemann, *The Dragon and the Iron Horse: The Economics of Railroads in China, 1876–1937*

110. Benjamin A. Elman, *From Philosophy to Philology: Intellectual and Social Aspects of Change in Late Imperial China*
111. Jane Kate Leonard, *Wei Yüan and China's Rediscovery of the Maritime World*
112. Luke S. K. Kwong, *A Mosaic of the Hundred Days:. Personalities, Politics, and Ideas of 1898*
113. John E. Wills, Jr., *Embassies and Illusions: Dutch and Portuguese Envoys to K'ang-hsi, 1666–1687*
114. Joshua A. Fogel, *Politics and Sinology: The Case of Naitō Konan (1866–1934)*
*115. Jeffrey C. Kinkley, ed., *After Mao: Chinese Literature and Society, 1978–1981*
116. C. Andrew Gerstle, *Circles of Fantasy: Convention in the Plays of Chikamatsu*
117. Andrew Gordon, *The Evolution of Labor Relations in Japan: Heavy Industry, 1853–1955*
*118. Daniel K. Gardner, *Chu Hsi and the "Ta Hsueh": Neo-Confucian Reflection on the Confucian Canon*
119. Christine Guth Kanda, *Shinzō: Hachiman Imagery and Its Development*
*120. Robert Borgen, *Sugawara no Michizane and the Early Heian Court*
121. Chang-tai Hung, *Going to the People: Chinese Intellectual and Folk Literature, 1918–1937*
*122. Michael A. Cusumano, *The Japanese Automobile Industry: Technology and Management at Nissan and Toyota*
123. Richard von Glahn, *The Country of Streams and Grottoes: Expansion, Settlement, and the Civilizing of the Sichuan Frontier in Song Times*
124. Steven D. Carter, *The Road to Komatsubara: A Classical Reading of the Renga Hyakuin*
125. Katherine F. Bruner, John K. Fairbank, and Richard T. Smith, *Entering China's Service: Robert Hart's Journals, 1854–1863*
126. Bob Tadashi Wakabayashi, *Anti-Foreignism and Western Learning in Early-Modern Japan: The "New Theses" of 1825*
127. Atsuko Hirai, *Individualism and Socialism: The Life and Thought of Kawai Eijirō (1891–1944)*
128. Ellen Widmer, *The Margins of Utopia: "Shui-hu hou-chuan" and the Literature of Ming Loyalism*
129. R. Kent Guy, *The Emperor's Four Treasuries: Scholars and the State in the Late Chien-lung Era*
130. Peter C. Perdue, *Exhausting the Earth: State and Peasant in Hunan, 1500–1850*
131. Susan Chan Egan, *A Latterday Confucian: Reminiscences of William Hung (1893–1980)*
132. James T. C. Liu, *China Turning Inward: Intellectual-Political Changes in the Early Twelfth Century*
133. Paul A. Cohen, *Between Tradition and Modernity: Wang T'ao and Reform in Late Ching China*
134. Kate Wildman Nakai, *Shogunal Politics: Arai Hakuseki and the Premises of Tokugawa Rule*
135. Parks M. Coble, *Facing Japan: Chinese Politics and Japanese Imperialism, 1931–1937*
136. Jon L. Saari, *Legacies of Childhood: Growing Up Chinese in a Time of Crisis, 1890–1920*
137. Susan Downing Videen, *Tales of Heichū*
138. Heinz Morioka and Miyoko Sasaki, *Rakugo: The Popular Narrative Art of Japan*

139. Joshua A. Fogel, *Nakae Ushikichi in China: The Mourning of Spirit*
140. Alexander Barton Woodside, *Vietnam and the Chinese Model.: A Comparative Study of Vietnamese and Chinese Government in the First Half of the Nineteenth Century*
141. George Elision, *Deus Destroyed: The Image of Christianity in Early Modern Japan*
142. William D. Wray, ed., *Managing Industrial Enterprise: Cases from Japan's Prewar Experience*
143. T'ung-tsu Ch'ü, *Local Government in China under the Ching*
144. Marie Anchordoguy, *Computers, Inc.: Japan's Challenge to IBM*
145. Barbara Molony, *Technology and Investment: The Prewar Japanese Chemical Industry*
146. Mary Elizabeth Berry, *Hideyoshi*
147. Laura E. Hein, *Fueling Growth: The Energy Revolution and Economic Policy in Postwar Japan*
148. Wen-hsin Yeh, *The Alienated Academy: Culture and Politics in Republican China, 1919–1937*
149. Dru C. Gladney, *Muslim Chinese: Ethnic Nationalism in the People's Republic*
150. Merle Goldman and Paul A. Cohen, eds., *Ideas Across Cultures: Essays on Chinese Thought in Honor of Benjamin L Schwartz*
151. James Polachek, *The Inner Opium War*
152. Gail Lee Bernstein, *Japanese Marxist: A Portrait of Kawakami Hajime, 1879–1946*
153. Lloyd E. Eastman, *The Abortive Revolution: China under Nationalist Rule, 1927–1937*
154. Mark Mason, *American Multinationals and Japan: The Political Economy of Japanese Capital Controls, 1899–1980*
155. Richard J. Smith, John K. Fairbank, and Katherine F. Bruner, *Robert Hart and China's Early Modernization: His Journals, 1863–1866*
156. George J. Tanabe, Jr., *Myōe the Dreamkeeper: Fantasy and Knowledge in Kamakura Buddhism*
157. William Wayne Farris, *Heavenly Warriors: The Evolution of Japan's Military, 500–1300*
158. Yu-ming Shaw, *An American Missionary in China: John Leighton Stuart and Chinese-American Relations*
159. James B. Palais, *Politics and Policy in Traditional Korea*
160. Douglas Reynolds, *China, 1898–1912: The Xinzheng Revolution and Japan*
161. Roger Thompson, *China's Local Councils in the Age of Constitutional Reform*
162. William Johnston, *The Modern Epidemic: History of Tuberculosis in Japan*
163. Constantine Nomikos Vaporis, *Breaking Barriers: Travel and the State in Early Modern Japan*
164. Irmela Hijiya-Kirschnereit, *Rituals of Self-Revelation: Shishōsetsu as Literary Genre and Socio-Cultural Phenomenon*
165. James C. Baxter, *The Meiji Unification through the Lens of Ishikawa Prefecture*
166. Thomas R. H. Havens, *Architects of Affluence: The Tsutsumi Family and the Seibu-Saison Enterprises in Twentieth-Century Japan*
167. Anthony Hood Chambers, *The Secret Window: Ideal Worlds in Tanizaki's Fiction*
168. Steven J. Ericson, *The Sound of the Whistle: Railroads and the State in Meiji Japan*

HARVARD EAST ASIAN MONOGRAPHS

169. Andrew Edmund Goble, *Kenmu: Go-Daigo's Revolution*
170. Denise Potrzeba Lett, *In Pursuit of Status: The Making of South Korea's "New" Urban Middle Class*
171. Mimi Hall Yiengpruksawan, *Hiraizumi: Buddhist Art and Regional Politics in Twelfth-Century Japan*
172. Charles Shiro Inouye, *The Similitude of Blossoms: A Critical Biography of Izumi Kyōka (1873–1939), Japanese Novelist and Playwright*
173. Aviad E. Raz, *Riding the Black Ship: Japan and Tokyo Disneyland*
174. Deborah J. Milly, *Poverty of the Japanese State: Knowledge and the Pursuit of Accommodations*
175. See Heng Teow, *Japan's Cultural Policy Toward China, 1918–1931: A Comparative Perspective*
176. Michael A. Fuller, *An Introduction to Literary Chinese*
177. Frederick R. Dickinson, *War and National Redefinition: Japan in the Great War, 1914–1919*
178. John Solt, *Shredding the Tapestry of Meaning: The Poetry and Poetics of Kitasono Katue (1902–1978)*
179. Edward Pratt, *Japan's Protoindustrial Elite: The Economic Foundations of the Gōnō*
180. Atsuko Sakaki, *Recontextualizing Texts: Modern Japanese Fiction as Speech Act*
181. Soon Won Park, *Colonial Modernity and Its Legacy: Korean Workers in Japanese Factories*